THE BEST OF DECADES

The Best of Decades

IRELAND IN
THE NINETEEN SIXTIES

Fergal Tobin

GILL AND MACMILLAN

Published in Ireland by
Gill and Macmillan Ltd
Goldenbridge
Dublin 8
with associated companies in
Auckland, Dallas, Delhi, Hong Kong,
Johannesburg, Lagos, London, Manzini,
Melbourne, Nairobi, New York, Singapore,
Tokyo, Washington
© Fergal Tobin 1984
0 7171 1342 6
Print origination in Ireland by
Keywrite Ltd, Dublin.
Printed in Hong Kong.

For Catherine

Contents

The author and publisher are grateful to the following sources for permission to reproduce illustrations. The letter t or b after a page reference indicates the top or bottom of the page in the event of there being more than one picture on that page. G.A. Duncan (pp. 11, 17t, 35, 42, 43, 69, 82, 92, 93, 101, 106t, 122b, 134, 144b, 150b, 160, 164b, 173, 177). The *Irish Times* (pp. 144t, 151, 192, 202t, 214b). Colman Doyle (pp. 16, 25). Radio Telefis Éireann (pp. 62, 63, 214t). Harland and Wolff Ltd (p. 29). BBC Hulton Picture Library (pp. 87, 225). Shannon Free Airport Development Company (p. 106b). Festival of Kerry (p. 112). Popperfoto Limited (pp. 122t, 155, 203, 220t, 221). Camera Press Limited/Colman Doyle (p. 220b). Charles Fennell (p. 128). Northern Ireland Tourist Board (p. 129b). Lensmen Limited (p. 139). John Donat (p. 165b).

Preface

IT is perhaps best to begin by saying what this book is not. It is not a history, for the 1960s are too recent to allow a history to be written. The sources for such a book are still not available to scholars, and the process of making them available will not be complete until the turn of the century. This book is, rather, a selective chronicle of public events, a somewhat nostalgic recollection of what is still remembered as the pivotal decade of change in modern Ireland.

Since it makes no particular claim to scholarship, the book deals with those years which are commonly, if incorrectly, thought of as constituting the 1960s. For most people, the sixties encompass the years from 1960 to 1969; for people who are scrupulously careful about such matters, the decade properly begins in 1961 and ends in 1970. I have thought it best, in a book like this, to follow popular usage.

I wish to thank the many people who have discussed the events and issues of the 1960s with me. I am particularly grateful to the staffs of the National Library of Ireland, the Library of Trinity College, Dublin, and the Dublin Corporation Library in Pearse Street. Michael Duncan provided invaluable help with illustrations from his astonishing collection.

D Rennison bore the burden of about half the typing with her usual efficiency and good humour. The other half was borne by my mother, who, in the process, continued to wage that war on her son's slack grammar and syntax which she has been waging for as long as I can remember. For this, as for so much else, my debt to her can never be repaid.

I am grateful to Brian Farrell, who read the book in typescript and made many valuable suggestions. My particular thanks are due to my editor and friend, Colm Croker, for giving me the benefit of his peerless skills: it is impossible to pay adequate tribute to one who is such a master of his craft.

Surely no fate is worse than to live with someone who is writing a book. For over two years now, my wife Catherine has endured the bad temper, the sullen introversion, and occasional fits of mad enthusiasm without which, it seems, no book ever gets written. More to the point, she made sure that I worked when I wanted to idle, and was my first and best critic. This book is dedicated to her.

F.T.   Dublin

Chapter One

INTRODUCTION

No one knew she was beautiful

Meehawl MacMurrachu had good reason to be perplexed. He was the father of one child only, and she was the most beautiful girl in the whole world. The pity of it was that no one at all knew she was beautiful, and she did not even know it herself. At times when she bathed in the eddy of a mountain stream and saw her reflection looking up from the placid water she thought that she looked very nice, and then a great sadness would come upon her, for what is the use of looking nice if there is nobody to see one's beauty?

JAMES STEPHENS

Ireland, forsooth, 'a nation once again!'
If Ireland was a nation, tell me when?
For since the civil modern world began,
What's Irish history? Walks the child a man?

WILLIAM ALLINGHAM

NEARLY fifteen years have elapsed since the 1960s passed into history, and the decade now occupies a position half way between the end of the Second World War and our own time. All over the western world, it is remembered as one of those curiously individualised decades whose essential quality has been captured in an adjective: the naughty nineties; the roaring twenties; the swinging sixties. The sixties swung all right. It was a time of rude energy, a contempt for tradition, in which the material fruits of post-war sacrifices and reconstruction could be enjoyed. Like all such times, it threw up a generation that believed itself to have discovered the world anew and to have cracked codes that had eluded its elders.

Ireland is a very peripheral part of the western world, whose enthusiasms it has not always been in the habit of sharing. The principal strain in its political history — the nationalist struggle to break free of dominance by Britain — has perforce caused it to regard the outside world with suspicion, because the outside world has usually been imported through the medium of the English language, English fashions, English scholarship and English architecture. Nationalism, in its resistance to anglicisation, set its face against the wider world. It turned to what still survived of a Gaelic world sunk in neglect and defeat, and from it fashioned a new nationalist ideology, glorifying the Irish language, traditional Gaelic music, dress and dance, and

1

a romantic ideal type of Irishman: the Western smallholder, uncorrupted by modern materialism and representing what was believed to be an immemorial Irish way of life. That this Gaelic world still existed at all was almost entirely a product of its remoteness. It survived in the barren fastnesses of the West of Ireland, ignored by the rest of Europe.

The Gaelic cultural renaissance was born in the 1890s and entered upon its inheritance in the 1920s, with the foundation of the Irish Free State. The naughty nineties and the roaring twenties! The country was in no state for frivolity in either decade. The nineties opened with the fall of Parnell, an event that seemed to paralyse Irish nationalism for a generation. It was the post-Parnell world that Joyce captured so ruthlessly, an Ireland of frustrated hopes, shabby, unkempt, 'the centre of paralysis'. The twenties were ushered in by the War of Independence and the Civil War, which left the country exhausted, its energies consumed in arms. Thereafter it turned in on itself, no longer a single state — for the Protestant North had managed to keep itself outside the Gaelic arcadia. Of the South, meanwhile, Sacheverell Sitwell wrote in 1936:

Its shapes and contours make of it a paradise that is unhappy. And so it must forever remain, far away from the stream of life and with the sadness of all things that are a little remote from reality.[1]

'And so it must forever remain ...' The Second World War came and went. The Free State, now named Éire and soon to be additionally designated the Republic of Ireland, asserted its independence from Britain by remaining neutral. With uncharacteristic understatement, the years 1939-45 were simply referred to as 'the Emergency'. Independence was confirmed, but at the price of the country removing itself one degree further from the pressing concerns of the modern world. Nor did the Republic experience the effects of the post-war economic revival: the 1950s saw a dismal combination of economic recession and heavy emigration. Not until 1958 was there any sign of a new economic order, when the government launched the First Programme for Economic Expansion.

Significant changes were occurring in Northern Ireland, however. The 1947 Education Act had thrown open second-level schooling to all children, regardless of means or creed; the great social reforms of the Attlee government of 1945-51 were applied in Northern Ireland as in all other parts of the UK; the economy was expanding — roads and public housing were being built on a hitherto unthought-of scale and to a very high standard of excellence. The two parts of Ireland were moving further apart. Leaders of Protestant opinion in the North rejoiced in this, but not in the means of its accomplishment, for some of them, at least, deplored the idea of lavishing public money on Catholics and Protestants alike. Catholics, in their eyes, were the enemy within. Sure enough, from 1956 onwards, a pathetically feeble IRA campaign had been in progress along the border of Northern Ireland with the object of securing a united Ireland. But it was being easily contained and was to peter out in 1962. For all the material changes emanating from Britain, mental attitudes within Northern Ireland remained set in their ancient moulds. In 1960 Lord Brookeborough was entering upon his seventeenth year as Prime Minister, and the political hegemony of his stern, monolithic Unionist Party seemed unbreakable.

An emigrant returning to the Republic of Ireland in the late fifties after thirty years abroad would have had few recognition problems. The country had no television station, although the few homes on the east coast which could afford TV sets picked up programmes from the British stations. Shopping was still the homely experience it had always been, for there were no supermarkets or shopping centres. If he could afford to buy a car — which most people who had remained in Ireland could not — the state would not oblige him to undergo any test of his driving proficiency. The ferocious literary and film censorship was as vigilant as it had been when he left. Those most conservative of Irish institutions, the churches, were very much as they had been in 1930, enjoying their last few years of complacent peace before ecumenism and post-Conciliar theology burst upon them. Late marriages, large families and high rates of emigration were as common as ever. A nasty Anglo-American phenomenon, 'rock 'n' roll', had made a tentative appearance (principally in those areas where the British TV programmes could be picked up), but there was no native pop music industry: few Irish bands, no Irish Top Twenty. Industry was still protected by tariff barriers erected in the 1930s, and agriculture had seen few changes since the turn of the century. Ireland was still a great country in which to be thirsty, but a bad one in which to be hungry — there were hardly any restaurants of quality. Secondary education all the way to Leaving Certificate was still a minority privilege, based largely on the ability to pay school fees, for there was no state-financed assistance to poorer families, and only a few public scholarships available. The physical appearance of the nation's cities and towns was unchanged — in Dublin only the new bus station, opened in 1953, made any concessions to modernity. The IRA, as we have noted, was still prosecuting the good old cause in the good old way and getting nowhere. Tourism remained underdeveloped, and foreign holidays were a very great luxury. All in all, the progress from the Irish Free State of the late twenties to the Republic of the late fifties had involved the moving of very little national furniture.

The man who had wrought the great constitutional change would not, it seems, have had it otherwise. In 1959 Eamon de Valera became President of Ireland, having finally retired from active politics. Our emigrant's years abroad were the years of de Valera's power. He started as a constitutional radical and gave short shrift to those features of Anglo-Irish relations which were not to his liking. Eventually he replaced the Free State constitution with one closer to his own heart. And Mr de Valera's heart — into which Mr de Valera had once announced that he looked whenever he wanted to know what the Irish people were thinking — was full of admiration for the romantic, rural Ireland of the Gaelic image-makers. In a celebrated radio broadcast on St Patrick's Day 1943 (appropriately in the middle of the European war, or 'Emergency') he set forth his social vision of Ireland for the middle of the twentieth century:

That Ireland which we dreamed of would be the home of a people who valued material wealth only as the basis of right living, of a people who were satisfied with frugal comfort and devoted their leisure to the things of the spirit — a land whose countryside would be bright with cosy homesteads, whose fields and villages would be joyous with the sounds of industry, with the romping of sturdy children, the contests of athletic youths and the laughter of comely maidens, whose firesides would be forums for the wisdom of serene old age. It would, in a word, be the home of a people living the life that God desires that man should live.[2]

It was a touching, idealistic and wholly fantastic piece of nonsense. But it did not seem like nonsense to a majority of Irishmen in 1943, or in 1950, or in 1955. In those years it enshrined a national ideal in which it was still possible for people to believe. It was the conventional wisdom.

By 1970 it was no longer so, and even de Valera's own political party, Fianna Fáil, did not take it seriously. It was, indeed, quite common for Mr de Valera's speech to be quoted in jest, as an example of hyperbolic fantasy, which is roughly how it has been regarded ever since.

What happened in Ireland between 1960 and 1970 to effect this change of attitude?

Prosperity was the key to everything. Irish living standards rose by a half in the 1960s and gave the country the material and psychological basis for national recovery. It was an unprecedented surge of affluence, made all the more remarkable by the appalling slump of the fifties, which had threatened the country with social and economic destruction.

The old Sinn Féin ideal foundered in the 1950s. Between 1949 and 1956 the Republic's national income rose by only one-fifth of the rate for Western Europe overall. Between 1955 and 1957 Ireland was the only country in the western world where the total volume of goods and services consumed actually fell. Between 1955 and 1958 two out of every five workers in the building industry lost their jobs. Unemployment reached a record 78,000 in 1957, and 54,000 others emigrated, again a record; in all, over 400,000 Irish men and women emigrated between 1951 and 1961, an enormous haemorrhage for such a sparsely populated country. At the start of the 1960s the population of the twenty-six counties was smaller, after forty years of independence, than it had been in the days of British rule in Ireland.

What was wrong with Ireland? In the midst of a worldwide boom in capitalist countries, Ireland was on the verge of national destitution. Three things characterised the Irish economy: a reliance on native capital for the generation of wealth; the employment of that capital behind a protective wall of tariffs and quotas; and the concentration on social rather than productive objectives in the public investment programme.

It was the challenging and the overturning of these precepts which enabled the Irish economy to expand in the 1960s by attaching itself to the boom in world trade. The legislation which prevented the employment of large amounts of foreign capital was amended in 1957 and abolished altogether five years later. The consequent influx of foreign investment was decisive: over 350 such manufacturing enterprises were established between 1960 and 1969.[3]

The dismantling of protection ran parallel to the attraction of foreign capital. The moves towards free trade were verbal until 1961, when they were formalised by the decision to apply for membership of the European Economic Community. De Gaulle's 'non' to Britain's application in January 1963 appeared at the time to be no more than a temporary setback, and national planning continued to operate on the assumption that Ireland would be a member of the Community before 1970. The Anglo-Irish Free Trade Area Agreement of 1965 was the practical culmination of this process. It was the most eloquent testimony possible to the fact that the old economics, first enunciated by Arthur Griffith in *The Resurrection of Hungary* in 1904 and embraced in some form by all Irish governments, particularly from the 1930s onwards, had at last been abandoned.

The question of public investment was the one on which most attention was lavished at the start of the recovery period. In 1960 a United Nations body, the Economic Commission for Europe, dismissed the traditional view that Ireland was short of capital. It noted that the proportion of national income invested by Ireland was much the same as in other European countries, but that our return on that investment was almost unbelievably bad.

A similar concern lay behind the thinking of T. K. Whitaker, the secretary of the Department of Finance. He emphasised the supreme importance of ensuring that public expenditure be concentrated on productive rather than socially useful projects. His essay, *Economic Development*, which, almost uniquely for a civil servant, he was allowed to publish under his own name, is rightly thought of as the intellectual fountainhead of the economic recovery. It formed the basis of the First Programme for Economic Expansion, published in the same year, 1958. The First Programme was a new departure, the first attempt in the history of the state to give a systematic public direction to economic development. In the view of one distinguished Irish historian, it was little more than 'the intelligent application to the local Irish situation of doctrines that had been current among economists elsewhere for years',[4] but it was none the less a watershed in the history of modern Ireland.

The First Programme for Economic Expansion aimed, through a radical redirection in public investment from social objectives, such as the construction of houses and hospitals, to productive ones, such as new industry, tourism and agricultural research, to achieve a growth rate of 2 per cent per annum in the Irish economy for five years. Beyond this modest target, however — which was doubled by the actual achievement, as events turned out — lay a desire to chart a definite course out of the fog of despair and gloom that enveloped the Republic of Ireland in the mid-fifties. The emergence of a rational solution to the terrible crisis, and the realisation that Ireland was not fated simply to self-destruction, had a profound effect on public confidence.

The early 1960s duly witnessed a steady influx of foreign-controlled industry, combined with a growing public acceptance of the inevitability of free trade. Capital grants, tax concessions and an increase in the resources of the Industrial Credit Corporation combined to attract and stimulate industry in Ireland. Inevitably the new industries found difficulties. The absence of an industrial tradition in Ireland meant that there was not always a readily available supply of quality labour; lower wage costs were frequently offset by the need for companies to invest in the retraining of staff. In general, though, the first few years of the new dispensation were a roaring success. For instance, from mid-1959 to mid-1960 alone, the volume of national output rose by 8 per cent and the value of the country's exports rose by nearly 35 per cent.

The great success of the First Programme emboldened the planners' resolve for the Second. It proposed an annual rate of growth equal to that achieved in the First, 4 per cent, to cover the operative years, 1964-70. In general, industry was asked merely to maintain the momentum of the early sixties, but the planners also banked on an expansion in agriculture, to be effected by the anticipated early entry to the EEC. This, of course, never materialised, and before the Second Programme was half way through its allotted span its targets were regarded as no longer attainable.

The general expansion of the economy continued, however, if not in the groove predicted in the Second Programme. In addition, the habit of planning had led to the establishment of a series of somewhat corporatist bodies, in which the major social and economic partners were involved in a consultative way in the determination of policy. The Committee on Industrial Organisation, the National Employer/Labour Conference and the National Industrial and Economic Council are the best known. The latter, founded in 1963, was intended to provide a direct input into national planning. It brought the leadership of the trade union movement into the corridors of power in Ireland for the first time, which proved a mixed blessing for the unions, but was typical of Seán Lemass's pragmatic and managerial style of government.

The middle years of the decade, 1965 and 1966, witnessed another slowing down in world growth, which in turn affected Ireland. It proved to be no more than a temporary setback. The Irish economy resumed its healthy pattern of growth in 1967 and maintained it for the rest of the decade. The planners' hopes were not fulfilled, however. The Second Programme was first amended and then abandoned, to be superseded by the Third Programme. But by the end of the decade it too was off the rails, and economic planning was formally put aside in the early seventies. The Programmes for Economic Expansion had proved to be inaccurate. The First exceeded its targets by a long way, the Second and Third fell hopelessly short, all of which raised questions about the value of planning *per se*. This is not the place to pursue that point, but it is worth reiterating the vital *psychological* impact of the First Programme on a demoralised country.

In the most crucial area of all, the performance of the Irish economy in the 1960s did not fully satisfy the optimists. Total employment did not rise. But industrial employment increased sufficiently to absorb the flight from the land and thus stop emigration. To all who remembered the fifties, this fact more than any other marked the sixties out as the best of decades. Employment, security, and the prospect of reasonable material comfort in Ireland for all her population: that was a revolutionary set of expectations for a country that had known little other than abject failure in the material world since the Great Famine.

History does not fall neatly into decades, nor do historical transformations occur clearly and completely. But no one in Ireland in 1970, looking back on the decade that had just ended, could doubt that the country had seen unprecedented changes. The isolation and introspection of generations did not finally disappear — in some degree they never can — but the blinds were let up, the windows were thrown open, the doors were unlocked; and good, bad or indifferent, the modern world came in among us at last.

All those features of modern life which the returned emigrant of the late fifties found absent in the Republic of Ireland were present by 1970. Some were a consequence of stirrings that had begun before 1 January 1960, and others were not to blossom completely until the seventies. But the popular perception of the sixties as the decisive decade of change is none the less accurate.

The vigour and optimism of the period threatened briefly to break those frozen Northern moulds as well. But the inability to accept radical change was to tumble Northern Ireland into anarchy and violence before the end of the 1960s and ensure that, in one corner of the island at least, ancient antagonisms and hatreds would continue to flourish.

It was an ironic conclusion to a decade which raised expectations that can now be so easily dismissed as absurd and inflated. But that was the mood of the time — buoyant, cocky, optimistic. The naughty nineties and the roaring twenties had bypassed Ireland. The swinging sixties, for better or worse, did not.

Chapter Two

1960

Good times coming

It is often said, by the heedless, that we are a conservative species, impervious to new ideas. I have not found it so. I am often appalled at the avidity and credulity with which new ideas are snatched at and adopted without a scrap of sound evidence. People will believe anything that amuses them, gratifies them, or promises them some sort of profit.
BERNARD SHAW

The worship of the dead is not
A worship that our hearts allow,
Though every famous shade were wrought
With woven thorns above the brow.
We fling our answer back in scorn:
'We are less children of this clime
Than of some nation yet unborn
Or empire in the womb of time.
We hold the Ireland in the heart
More than the land our eyes have seen,
And love the goal for which we start
More than the tale of what has been.'
GEORGE RUSSELL (AE)

NINETEEN sixty slipped in quietly. The bad weather which had lasted through the second half of December 1959 persisted to the end, and it rained heavily on New Year's Eve. In the area south of Athlone families had been cut off by flood waters since Christmas. Dubliners trudged through the rain to enjoy traditional entertainments: at the Gaiety, Jimmy O'Dea and Maureen Potter in *Aladdin*; at the Olympia, Cecil Sheridan in *Humpty Dumpty*; at the Royal, Jack Cruise in *Christmas Chimes*. Provincial patrons of the panto were being catered for by CIE, who were running special trains for them, with combined train and theatre tickets available at selected centres throughout the country.

Cinema was as traditional in its concerns as the theatre. On New Year's Day it was announced that the Film Appeals Board had upheld the censor's decision to cut two scenes from the Boulting Brothers' comedy, *I'm All Right, Jack*. The offending scenes were set in a nudist colony. The Boultings, having already protested at the 'notorious' Irish film censorship, now proposed to 'have no truck' with it and refused to allow the censored version to be distributed. Things then took an absurd twist, for the Boultings announced a few days later that they were going to ask Pope John XXIII to adjudicate on the film's propriety! They pointed out that the British Catholic press had praised it: why, the *Catholic Herald* had even nominated it film of the year. They ventured the opinion that the decision 'indicates that the Appeals Board does not know its own mind'. One would have imagined that their true grievance proceeded from the fact that the Board knew its mind only too well; but this hardly mattered to the Brothers, who added the rider that in their view the Board's mind was not worth knowing. It is not recorded if the Pope gave his opinion of *I'm All Right, Jack*, but eventually it did open in Dublin, in November, still minus the offending scenes.

The seemingly immutable film censorship was, however, part of an Ireland already under threat. As the country recovered from the economic crisis of the mid-1950s, with its appalling levels of unemployment and emigration, there was a real sense that, at last, a corner had been turned. The new economic policies of Seán Lemass and T. K. Whitaker were working, and for the first time since independence the prospect existed of a sustained improvement in the material prosperity of Irish people in Ireland.

More typical of that mood was another story in the newspapers on New Year's Day 1960. Shannon Free Airport's new industrial complex, which was to become a symbol of the country's changed fortunes, expected to provide 500 to 600 new jobs in the coming year in factories then under construction. The duty-free shop at Shannon was Ireland's biggest dollar-earner, and while fewer passengers had used Shannon in 1959 — the first full year of transatlantic jets, which were able to overfly it — freight volume was up by a quarter and showing every sign of maintaining its advance. Even the drop in the number of passengers was caused in part by the most heartening possible development: fewer Irish people were emigrating.

It would be hard to exaggerate the sense of buoyancy about the future. Garret FitzGerald, then an economic columnist with the *Irish Times*, summed it up with uncharacteristic brevity in a headline to an article in July 1960: 'Good Times Coming'. For the man in the street, changed times meant more money in his pocket, and more to spend it on. Sales of private cars, a particularly sensitive indicator of prosperity, ran at an astonishing 32,000 in 1960, up 40 per cent on 1959 and more than 53 per cent on the previous record year, 1955. There were plenty of new models to choose from too, like the Ford Anglia with the funny sloped back window, costing £535 ex works.

The most dramatic indicator of economic recovery came on 22 October 1960. Figures released on that date showed that the number of those unemployed had fallen to 40,600, a full 20 per cent less than the figure only one year earlier.

T.K. Whitaker, an unlikely revolutionary. Yet revolution is not too strong a word to describe the changes that occurred largely as a result of his thinking when he was secretary of the Department of Finance. He was the principal influence behind the First Programme for Economic Expansion which helped to lift Irish society off its knees.

It was not hard to see where the jobs were coming from, for there was good news on every hand. Bord na Móna's annual report for 1959-60 showed profits, production and sales revenue at an all-time high; at the peak of the season 6,962 people had been employed. Full-time employment for another hundred was announced in October when Erskine Childers, the Minister for Transport and Power, opened a new briquette factory at Derrinlough, Co. Offaly. There had been a big increase in home demand for peat briquettes, and Bord na Móna was not looking just to satisfy that, but beyond it to the prospect of developing export sales to the United Kingdom. Nor was it the only public enterprise — or semi-state body, to use the coy official phrase — with ambitious plans. In April the Irish Sugar Company, which also had a record-breaking year in 1960, announced that the world's first accelerated freeze-drying plant for the processing of vegetables was to be opened at Mallow, Co. Cork, at a cost of £200,000; most of the production would be for export. The new process allowed food to be preserved for longer periods. In addition to this development, the company expected to open a pilot cannery in Carlow for processing fruit and vegetables by conventional means. Between 130 and 150 additional staff would be employed at both plants in the initial stages. The UK was once again seen as the main market.

At the end of July Gouldings, the fertiliser company, announced the opening of two sulphuric acid plants, one each in Dublin and Cork. Aer Lingus passenger traffic was up by 25 per cent in the second quarter of the year, indicating a boom in the tourist industry. Verlome Dockyard, Cork, was officially opened in October. Just before Christmas a £4 million chemical plant was announced for New Ross, Co. Wexford.

Firmer economic links were being forged with the outside world. In addition to joining the newly formed Organisation for Economic Co-operation and Development, Ireland also joined the International Development Association — an affiliate of the World Bank — and indicated a desire to join the General Agreement of Tariffs and Trade, subject to the maintenance of existing trade relations with the United Kingdom. GATT aimed at the reduction, and later the abolition, of tariffs between the member nations. This was an unambiguous declaration of the government's future intentions. The Taoiseach, Seán Lemass, underlined them further in a speech to the national convention of Junior Chambers of Commerce at Shannon in June. Western Europe, he said, was marching strongly into a free trade future, and 'it is clear that this country must be prepared to move in that direction also'. We could not stop the European movement, even if we wanted to; we could not have high protective tariffs on the home market while expecting other countries to open up their markets freely to us.

This speech touched on the three related themes that lay at the heart of the 'new' economics associated with Lemass's name: free trade; a vigorous export-orientated manufacturing base; and the need to involve ourselves in the European movement. Advocates of change in Irish society tended to rally around these causes over the next few years, while conservatives viewed them with suspicion.

Turning towards the outside world involved more than Ireland's formal participation in international bodies. In the short run it meant the attraction of foreign industries to Ireland with a package of inducements centred on the absence of any taxation on profits in the first twenty years of production. To facilitate this it was necessary to amend the Control of Manufactures Acts (1932-34), which had specified that a controlling interest in all new Irish industries must be held by Irish nationals. The acts had been cornerstones of the whole protection system, and the legislation amending them in 1957 opened the door for foreign capital in Ireland. From 1958 foreign industrialists were encouraged to set up in Ireland, and by 1960 the process was well advanced.

The scale of foreign investment at this time and its critical role in the provision of jobs can be seen at a glance in figures given by the government in the Dáil in mid-1960. In 1959 fifteen new industries had started and there were a further twenty in the pipeline. The total investment came to £22.5 million and involved 6,500 jobs; even discounting the huge Whitegate Oil Refinery, the other thirty-four projects stood to produce an average of 180 new jobs each. The overwhelming proportion of the capital employed was foreign, an observation which still held true if one again discounted Whitegate. The creation of jobs on the scale required in order to secure both full employment and an end to emigration could only be achieved by attracting foreign capital. The magnitude of the risk capital required for the task was such that it was, in the words of one Irish businessman, 'as far beyond the capacity of the Irish economy as an ocean-going yacht is beyond the capacity of the average Irish family'.[1]

The foundation of the Economic Research Institute (expanded to become the Economic and Social Research Institute in 1965) in July 1960 led for the first time to proper scientific research into the structure and nature of the Irish economy. The principal functions of the ERI were research and education in economics and the social sciences, especially with reference to Ireland. It was typical of many autonomous, non-civil-service advisory bodies established in the Lemass years, for it drew together the disparate elements of Irish economic life in a single umbrella organisation.

In political terms, the outstanding economic achievement of 1960 was the new Anglo-Irish trade pact signed in London on 13 April. It updated the famous pact of 1938 which had ended the Economic War. In the subsequent

Dáil debate Lemass admitted quite openly that the Irish negotiators had pressed hard for a full Anglo-Irish free trade area, but that the British had been blunt in their rejection. No advantages which Ireland could offer them could overcome the practical difficulties which would arise for them with their other trading partners. Nevertheless, the 1960 trade pact was a staging-post on the road to the eventual Anglo-Irish Free Trade Area Agreement of 1965. It emphasised Lemass's concern to regulate affairs with what was still our biggest trading customer before committing himself to any further involvement with the larger free trade blocs.

When the end-of-year Dáil adjournment debate came round, the Taoiseach luxuriated in a recital of favourable economic figures. Exports were up by £20 million; national income had increased by 4 per cent; there was every prospect of seventy new factories opening in 1961 with an employment potential between them of up to 7,000 jobs. This was heady stuff for any leader of an Irish government to offer in a review of the passing year, especially with the memory of recent wretched years so fresh in the national mind.

Not everyone was enraptured by the new Ireland. Shortly before Lemass's adjournment debate speech Seán MacBride of Clann na Poblachta spoke in the Four Courts in Dublin on the theme 'Forty-Four Years After Pearse'. He declared himself shocked by a failure to grasp opportunities:

None of our political leaders has been prepared to give a bold imaginative lead that would evoke a generous and enthusiastic response from the people.... The extent to which we have to persuade foreigners to bring their capital here is a yardstick of the failure of our banking system and our government to promote investment in Ireland. We have over £500 million invested in Great Britain. The bulk of this money is controlled by the banks and the government.

He added that in a proper economic plan the government would ensure that half of this money would be gradually reinvested here for development purposes. His point about the banks was well made, as they themselves were to recognise before the decade was out, but the opportunity for any realistic proposal based primarily on the employment of native capital had disappeared in the débâcle of 1956.

The views of Mr MacBride, by 1960 firmly established as a man of the past, were unlikely to cause government ministers any loss of sleep. More serious was the hostility in the remarks of John Conroy, general president of the Irish Transport and General Workers' Union, at the union's annual conference in June. In an oblique reference to Lemass's fondness for gambling — James Dillon never tired of referring to 'this gambler's government' — Mr Conroy offered the view that there were now more gambling-houses than

14

churches in Dublin; he also condemned the later opening hours permitted by the recently enacted Intoxicating Liquor Act, perhaps in deference to his colleagues in the barmen's union who had been opposed to the measure. He then went on:

If you are unlucky enough to be employed ... in the lower wage bracket and have no bargaining strength, you get no justice in Ireland.... I would like to ask the Taoiseach and the low wage advocates why they think a few shillings a week extra to the working man is so injurious to our economy.... Extra millions of pounds have been paid out this year to many thousands of people in the higher-income group, to dividend-drawers, commission agents, profit-takers, gamblers and others. Much of this unearned and unneeded higher income would be spent in pleasure trips abroad and on luxury imports.... There is not a pip-squeak from one of our influential citizens, our economists or other experts, about this wastage of millions of pounds. All their concentrated criticism is reserved entirely for the condemnation of the conceding of a few shillings increase in wages to the lower-paid manual and white-collar worker.

It was a rather hysterical speech, with generalised accusations flung in every direction, but it made one thing very clear. Trade unionists were cynical and suspicious of developments which they assumed to be for the benefit of the middle class and in which they themselves expected to have little share. They had no confidence in the ability of a rising tide to lift all boats. Union leaders like Conroy, who had been schooled in the lean years when gains were hard won and bitterly defended, were defensive and conservative men. They had spent their lives prising what they could from the native capitalist class — not the sort of experience likely to develop an expansive or liberal cast of mind. They still felt remote and alienated from the important centres of Irish life: outsiders.

In this view they echoed faithfully the sentiments of their membership at large. When Lemass succeeded, in 1964, in fulfilling a long-standing ambition by securing a national wage agreement which symbolised the final admission of the trade union leadership to the inside of Irish political life, that leadership soon found itself distanced from its own rank and file, whose suspicious and fractious attitude to the agreement caused some traumatic upheavals in the trade union movement, not least in the ITGWU itself.

The Bishop of Cork, Dr Cornelius Lucey, was another man of influence who had his suspicions about the new order in Ireland. He condemned what he regarded as the writing-off of backward and remote rural areas in attempts to develop an industrial economy. Dr Lucey was a romantic conservative and a populist, ever watchful for the interests of rural smallholders and the values which they symbolised. The idea that rural life was inherently superior to urban life went back a long way in the Irish Catholic consciousness. Its imagery and symbolism lay close to the heart of

Irish traditional music gained a whole new generation of adherents in the 1960s. This was due in part to an international revival of interest in folk music in the first half of the decade, in which Ireland, with its extraordinarily rich tradition, was well placed to participate. But more importantly, it was the work of Seán Ó Riada, who transformed the sound of traditional music through his Ceolteoirí Cualainn.

The ballad boom was another feature of the revival. The Dubliners, shown above in their original line-up, and the Clancy Brothers and Tommy Makem, were among the earliest and most enduring groups.

modern Irish nationalism, particularly to that sentimental Irish-Ireland school whose views had become the official popular ideology of de Valera's time. This view of the world regarded the flight from the land as a disaster, and lay behind successive futile schemes to arrest the process. Indeed, it survived in vestigial form into the 1960s — a bleak decade indeed for the Irish-Ireland movement — in the attempts to encourage industry to locate in the West, where, by and large, it did not want to go; there was, furthermore, the ludicrously half-hearted attempts to decentralise the civil service.

How closely did this official preference for the values of rural life actually correspond to the aspirations of ordinary Irish people? The Dutch rural sociologist, Dr J. H. W. Lijfering, detected a greater distance between ideal and reality than many would have desired. He told the 1960 Muintir na Tíre rural week:

My Irish experience has taught me that the wish to share in modern development and in urban culture is strong among the rural population here. I do not believe that it is a coincidental feature that Ireland has the highest rate per head per population in Europe for cinema-going. The rather limited interest of Irish people in Gaelic culture is a sign in the same direction. Urban influences in daily life, in the recreational pattern for example, like modern dancing and sport-mindedness, are not typically rural. I suppose that many of these cultural elements are partly influenced by the urban culture.

This is a most interesting judgment on Irish society at the start of the 1960s. It is important to remember that it was made *before* the advent of television in most rural areas, for television is usually blamed as the great eroder of rural values. It suggests a society receptive to the quickening of social change associated with a more restless and fluid urban culture. It helps to explain why Irish society accommodated itself with such surprising comfort to the tremendous changes of the sixties. Change meant not just increased material prosperity, but also a qualitative improvement in the lives of ordinary people. Or, to put it more plainly, people were getting what they wanted.

Lijfering's observations can have been of little comfort to Bishop Lucey, while the identification of modern dancing as one of the preferred rural recreations might have drawn a sigh from another prelate. In September 1960 the new Archbishop of Cashel and Emly, Dr Morris, issued a letter requesting dance promoters to observe certain principles in the archdiocese. Dances should end by 1 a.m. in the summer and midnight in the winter:

No dances [should be held] on Saturday nights, eves of holy days, Christmas night, or during Lent (except on St Patrick's night for traditional Irish dancing or where dancing has already been customary on that night).... Concern for the moral welfare of those who dance will surely be accepted as no more an interference with legitimate amusement than concern for their health and physical safety.... It has been customary in this archdiocese to refrain from organising dances on Saturday nights and on the other occasions mentioned above; departures from this custom are repugnant to the Christian outlook of our people and should not be accepted.... I urge the faithful not to patronise, and not to allow their children or others for whom they are responsible to patronise, dances which contravene these principles.

The days were numbered, however, for this particular type of episcopal interdict. Popular demand for Saturday-night dancing was irresistible, and by 1967 all the Irish bishops had rescinded their prohibitions.

Television was on everyone's mind at the beginning of the 1960s. A small number of houses along the east coast could already pick up BBC and ITV with the help of specially erected aerials. This technological intrusion, if nothing else, obliged the government to address itself to the question of a native television service.

The Broadcasting Act (1960) represented the legislative basis for Irish television. It also revolutionised Irish radio, because it established an independent broadcasting authority under whose aegis both television *and* radio would be run; hitherto Radio Éireann had been directly under the control of the Minister for Posts and Telegraphs, which in practice meant that it was under the dead hand of the minister's civil servants. The act provided for a nine-man authority, which would be advanced a loan of £2 million for capital purposes. They were to be appointed by the government, and in turn would appoint the station's director-general, as well as keeping 'constantly in mind the national aims on national language and culture', a somewhat platitudinous injunction which, right from the start of the television service, all Irish-Ireland groups felt was being flagrantly ignored.

Even before broadcasting began, conservative Ireland gave notice of its unease with the thing that was coming. During the Senate debate on the Broadcasting Bill, Professor P. M. Quinlan of University College, Cork, felt that the introduction of an Irish television service was 'premature by at least five years' and that the money could be better spent in building up rural organisations. He feared its effect on rural Ireland. In April 1960 the president of the Gaelic Athletic Association, Dr J. J. Stuart, in his address to the Association's annual congress, demanded 'constant vigilance' over the new service to ensure that it does 'for Irish games at least as much as English television is doing for English games'. He was concerned that the service might become a 'weapon for further anglicisation'. In a rather hand-wringing speech in June, Cardinal D'Alton trawled up the entire modern mass media in one cast. He said that, now more than ever, people needed the guidance of sound Catholic principles: we were living in a bewildered world where many ignored the gospel and were influenced rather by the confused and contradictory views presented to them on radio, television and in cinema performances.

Mr Eamonn Andrews was appointed first chairman of the authority, but not before a political row blew up in the Dáil. The act provided that if a member of the authority had an interest in any company which sought to make contracts with the authority, he should declare that interest and take no part in the authority's deliberations on the subject. In view of the new chairman's interest in Eamonn Andrews Studios, Dr Noel Browne felt that such a provision should be strengthened to oblige such members of the authority either to divest themselves of their commercial interests or to resign. He moved an amendment to the bill to this effect, which was lost. Mr Andrews's appointment was duly confirmed.

At the end of the year Mr Edward M. Roth, a thirty-eight-year-old Boston television executive of Irish extraction, was appointed the first director-general of the broadcasting service. New television studios were being built at Montrose, Donnybrook, and the first transmissions were scheduled for the end of 1961.

On 23 June 1959 Eamon de Valera relinquished the office of Taoiseach and moved to Arus an Uachtaráin, the old viceregal lodge in the Phoenix Park. Thus it was that, for the second time in his career, Mr de Valera became President of the Irish Republic. This time there was no problem of recognition by the rest of the world. Forty years earlier he had been the young revolutionary agitator; now, immensely straight and dignified, he seemed the very essence of restrained republican decorum.

He left behind in the world of active politics the Fianna Fáil party which he had founded, and which could hardly imagine life without him. He had led it from the very beginning in 1926; since he had first become head of the government of the Free State in 1932 he had contested nine elections and seen Fianna Fáil comfortably maintain its position as the largest party in all nine. On seven of the nine occasions he had been returned to government, and never once had he had to enter into a coalition with another party. Even on the two occasions when he had lost, it was only because the various factions opposed to him had cobbled together nervous and unstable coalitions, neither of which lasted more than three years.

Now, after thirty-three years at the helm, he was gone. The 1960s opened for Fianna Fáil under the leadership of another party founder and Civil War veteran, Seán Lemass. If de Valera had been thought of as the inspirational Chief, Lemass had acquired a reputation for practical hard work, attention to detail, and an unsentimental liking for efficiency. He was no orator. While de Valera had also been a poor speaker, he had had an immense presence; Lemass had little. He was sturdily built, moustachioed, and rather phlegmatic — the very essence of the plain, blunt man. He was in a tough position. De Valera had set a matchless standard, yet some time within three years of taking over Lemass would be constitutionally obliged to call an election; and since the war no party, not even Fianna Fáil under de Valera, had managed to win two successive general elections.

Lemass was sixty when he became Taoiseach. This was an additional handicap, as he was regarded as something of a stopgap leader, keeping the seat warm until one of the younger generation in Fianna Fáil could be groomed for the succession. After his retirement it was often said of Lemass that he got the top job ten years too late, that he had not had enough time left to him to carry through the transformation of Irish society that he desired. In fact Lemass became Taoiseach at just the right time, when the upturn in the Irish economy gave him a chance to show his mettle.*

He had long been impatient and frustrated at the lack of dynamism in Irish society. Although the architect of protection in the 1930s, he was one of the first in Fianna Fáil to recognise that by the mid-fifties it had outlived its use-fulness. His early attempts to change the direction of Fianna Fáil thinking foundered on the rocks of a financial orthodoxy no less dismal for being necessary in the circumstances. The stringency of the budgets of 1952 and 1956, for example, was proof of the need for a fundamental change of course. Lemass was fortunate that he did not have direct day-to-day responsibility for the Irish economy in the wretched circumstances of the fifties. By the time he became Taoiseach his expansionist views had been broadly accepted, and he could now give direction to a set of policies in which he truly believed.

Taking over in mid-term, he resisted the temptation to bring on too many younger men immediately. But he made it clear at an early stage that the opportunities were there to be taken by anyone with the required energy and ability. In May 1960 he appointed Charles J. Haughey, widely regarded as one of the party's most gifted and able young men, to his first government job as parliamentary secretary to the Minister for Justice. Lemass would, over the next five years, promote an entire new generation of Fianna Fáil ministers to high office, injecting vigour and energy into government at a time when such qualities were demanded by the accelerating pace of social and economic change.

In another, rather more symbolic way Lemass indicated a change of style. He stopped the practice of referring to Northern Ireland as 'the six counties',

*For a contrary view, from one who was well acquainted with Lemass, see C. S. Andrews, *Man of No Property*, 250.

an expression offensive to Unionists. So marked was this change that it prompted a rather mischievous Dáil question from Noel Browne and Jack McQuillan. Lemass replied that no firm decision had been taken by the government to use one term rather than another, nor did it intend to give formal recognition to the Belfast government. Significantly, he elaborated to the effect that while the government regarded partition as neither just nor durable, their aim was such essential unity of the Irish people as could be reflected in the country's institutions. He offered Unionists 'what Republicans have been prepared to see since 1921': a Belfast parliament within an all-Ireland context, with safeguards for the Northern Protestants. While cleverly underlining his sense of republican continuity, there was no doubting the softening of tone: Lemass placed the emphasis firmly on the unification of people rather than of territory.

Underpinning everything Lemass did was the political party he led, Fianna Fáil. It was, in its organisation and structures, the descendant of the disciplined mass parties that had been a central feature of the struggle for Irish freedom. Only seven years after its foundation, in 1933, a Fianna Fáil *cumann* had been established in every parish in the twenty-six counties.[2] As a vehicle for mobilising support, for turning out the vote at local and national elections, for keeping the party leaders in touch with local opinion, and for maintaining the enthusiasm of the party activists, it was among the most formidable and efficient political machines in the world. When it had shown signs of atrophy in the fifties, it had been comprehensively reformed and modernised. Since 1932 it had unfailingly delivered over 40 per cent of the nation's first-preference votes to the party in general elections. It was loyal and disciplined, an army of political shock-troops whose belief in the rectitude of Fianna Fáil and the turpitude of its rivals never wavered. Fianna Fáil seemed at times less like a political party than a people's crusade: drawing support from every element in the population; claiming to be not just a faction, but the nation itself in microcosm; stressing as its political objectives a pair of quite unrealistic ideals — the reunification of Ireland and the revival of the Irish language — but displaying a no-nonsense pragmatism in day-to-day affairs. For thirty years it had been the natural party of government, and the disunity and organisational disarray of its opponents gave it a clear advantage as the sixties began. It was an advantage it was to hold for the entire decade.

As the 1960s opened, Northern Ireland was still in the middle of the IRA border campaign. Since 1956 a desultory campaign of violence had been directed against RUC stations and customs posts along the border between

Seán Lemass about to open a new factory, the sort of activity which will always be linked with his name. After a generation of rhetorical moonshine, his intense practicality was just what Ireland needed. He put all his political muscle behind Whitaker's economic plans. Without this endorsement, and without his efficient sense of purpose as head of the government, Ireland's social and economic revival in the 1960s would have been a far less spectacular affair.

Northern Ireland and the Republic. The major cities and towns in the province were so little affected that the Unionist Party's hegemony over the Protestant working class, usually impregnable in time of serious nationalist agitation, was severely dented in the 1958 Stormont election: the Northern Ireland Labour Party (NILP) won four seats in Belfast.

Since the end of the war, membership of the United Kingdom had meant that Northern Ireland had benefited enormously from the effects of the welfare state and the UK's high levels of expenditure on roads, public housing and other utilities. Ironically, the Unionist Party had been opposed on ideological grounds to all the measures of the Attlee government that had led to Northern Ireland's prosperity. Unionism was undoubtedly a pan-Protestant movement, getting solid support right across the Protestant community. But its parliamentary representatives, both at Stormont and at Westminster, came overwhelmingly from the landed gentry and the industrial and professional middle class. Between these two groups there was a certain tension — the middle-class element, in classical fashion, resented the effortless ascendancy of the squirearchy — but the politics of sectarian solidarity kept it firmly within bounds. In a normal political society this grievance would long since have erupted in turmoil, as would the grudges of the Protestant working class. But Unionism was sustained by fear of the enemy within — the Roman Catholic nationalist minority who comprised one-third of the population — and the working class, as the most marginal, the least educated, and the most easily inflamed element in the Protestant population, had most to fear from Catholic advances. Protestants had chosen, therefore, to hang together, and the vehicle they had selected for this purpose was the Unionist Party. In 1943 the party had chosen Sir Basil Brooke as its leader and Prime Minister of Northern Ireland. Sir Basil was ennobled as Viscount Brookeborough in 1952, and in 1960 he was still *in situ*, the darling of the party.

Lord Brookeborough was an idle, charming Fermanagh squire with an adamantine dislike of Catholics. His suspicion of the Republic, natural enough for any Unionist, was carried to morbid lengths. It was one thing to rebuff political overtures from the South, but Brookeborough set his mind against the merest suggestion of economic or social co-operation. He refused to deal with the Irish Congress of Trade Unions — which appointed Billy Blease its full-time Northern officer in 1960 — because it was an all-Ireland body. Following the signature of the Anglo-Irish trade pact in April, Lemass had called for the formation of an all-Ireland economic council to deal with matters of mutual concern, like electricity supply. Brookeborough refused point-blank to have any truck with this idea. He told the annual general meeting of the Fermanagh Unionist Association in May that economic co-

Lord Brookeborough in old age. He was, from the very first, a bitter and uncompromising opponent of Irish nationalism. But he was immensely popular with Ulster Unionists, although the energy and drive that had characterised his early years as Prime Minister had faded away by the early 1960s.

operation with the South would be 'the thin end of the wedge'. His was a mind frozen in fear and suspicion, seeing plots and enemies everywhere.

He did, however, represent the overwhelming weight of opinion within Unionism. Within the parliamentary party at Stormont his leadership was hardly questioned, despite his advancing years. His government drew the occasional brickbat from Unionist backbenchers like Edmund Warnock, but the criticisms were directed at the inertia of the government overall rather than at the Prime Minister himself.

Warnock was a maverick, and a former Northern Ireland Attorney-General. In February 1960 he caused something of a sensation in Unionist circles by calling openly in Stormont for cabinet changes. Without saying so in as many words, he accused Lord Glentoran, the Minister of Commerce, of lacking vision and energy; he suggested that either Ivan Neill or Brian Faulkner would make suitable replacements. He further suggested that Captain Terence O'Neill was 'miscast' as Minister of Finance, and was of the opinion that he should swop with the Minister of Education, Morris May.

In July 1960 Warnock's *bêtes noirs*, Glentoran and Terence O'Neill, combined to fuel his anger. In the previous February MPs had been promised comprehensive legislation to correct the dreadful financial position of the Ulster Transport Authority. Nothing had happened by July, when Glentoran informed the House of Commons that the company was still not in a position to make its financial circumstances clear; he asked instead for approval to increase the UTA's borrowing powers by £2.5 million to see them through the parliamentary summer recess. The alternative, he said, was bankruptcy. Warnock and four other rebel Unionists then enquired why such a colossal sum was needed as a stopgap if comprehensive legislation to re-structure the UTA's capital base was imminent. They moved an amendment to reduce the amount ot £750,000. Glentoran stuck grimly to his guns, saying simply that if the full amount were not granted, the company would unquestionably fold in the autumn. But then, astonishingly, the Minister of Finance took a hand by announcing blandly that the amount was being cut in half, apparently without any danger to the immediate survival of the UTA. This intervention succeeded in making both ministers look foolish in the eyes of the dissenters, although the measure was finally approved in the amended form.

Captain O'Neill himself had been obliged, only the previous week, to deliver a stern rebuke to his cousin, the somewhat liberal Phelim O'Neill, MP, for a Stormont speech in which he had criticised the government's handling of current economic problems. It was, said Terence, 'outside the mainstream of Unionist thought'. What Cousin Phelim had done was to refer to a contribution made by Brookeborough earlier in the debate in which he had declared that his heart bled for the unemployed. Cousin Phelim quoted Ernest Bevin's reply to a similar remark from a gushing Tory lady: 'Madam, bleedin' hearts ain't no use; what we want are bloody brains!' He had also averred that Cousin Terence and his ministry between them constituted 'a damp squib'.

The sedate, patriarchal world of Unionist politics was, however, more accurately represented by the doings of another cousin of Captain Terence O'Neill. In late September Major James Chichester-Clark was returned unopposed as an MP to Stormont to fill the vacancy created by the resignation of his grandmother, Dame Dehra Parker. Grandmother had conveniently timed her resignation to coincide with James's leaving the army. He had not gone unopposed at the local Unionist Party constituency selection conference, but he had won, beating an urban district councillor and a former president of the Ulster Farmers' Union. It was this persistent Unionist tendency to select men of rank before practical men of affairs that caused most of the resentment within the party. It is important to remember, however, the backbench criticism was not necessarily a sign of liberal tendencies. Warnock, for example, the most vocal critic of the 'big house' Unionists, was probably further to the right than Brookeborough on some issues.

There were, nevertheless, hints of change in the air in 1960. Although the Northern Ireland economy went through a traumatic few years in the early sixties, the province was more prosperous than ever before, and it was felt that increasing affluence and universal secondary education would do much to destroy the immemorial hatreds and prejudices of Ulster. Brookeborough, who was quite correctly seen as the embodiment — at least on the Protestant side — of these malign legacies, could not last for ever; once he went, the tide would surely flow a little more freely for liberalism. The NILP's breakthrough in 1958 held out the hope of real class politics, which would shatter the Unionist monolith. On the Catholic side, there was the obvious lack of popular support for the border campaign, which seemed to toll the knell for the IRA and all other traditional insurrectionaries. In addition, the huge differences in welfare levels between the United Kingdom and the Republic of Ireland, combined with the hoped-for liberalisation of Unionism in the post-Brookeborough phase, opened the possibility that Catholics might yet become reconciled to the state.

Then there was *Over the Bridge*, a play written by a Protestant Belfast shipyard worker, Sam Thompson, which was searchingly critical of Protestant bigotry and intransigence. It pointed to reconciliation and forgiveness between Protestant and Catholic as the only way out of the North's historic impasse. It had been withdrawn by the Ulster Group

Theatre in 1959 after cuts in the more sensitive and outspoken parts of the script had been demanded. Then, in late January 1960, the uncut version opened at the Empire, Belfast, to an ovation.

But, in a pattern that was to be repeated again and again in Northern Ireland in the 1960s, every small gesture of hope was to be matched by a lurch towards the past. Six months after that Belfast audience had applauded Thompson's play, the new Altnagelvin general hospital in Derry was opened by the Governor of Northern Ireland, Lord Wakehurst. Because the dedicatory prayer was offered by a Church of Ireland chaplain, the Rev. Canon David Kelly, Roman Catholics refused to attend the ceremony.

The Northern Ireland economy gave every cause for concern in 1960. Traditional industries — shipbuilding, aircraft manufacture and linen — were in decline, and there was no sign of anything to replace them. In February Stanley Dennison, professor of economics at Queen's University, Belfast, said that unless new technological enterprises could be secured which would fill the gaps that were opening up, the outlook for Northern Ireland was bleak. Some short-term indicators were admittedly more hopeful. Harland & Wolff, the giant Belfast shipbuilders, were having their greatest boom since the war, and the *Canberra* went down their slipway in March. By September they had already beaten their previous annual record for output, measured in tonnage, set in 1946. By the end of the year three further launchings had pushed the 1960 total up to nearly 180,000 tons. But the effect of all this was to thin out the order book. Prospects in the medium and long term were poor. Seven thousand jobs were lost in Harland & Wolff alone in the first half of 1961. Short Brothers & Harland, the aircraft manufacturers, were hardly much better off. At the start of 1960 production was run down, although the management was sanguine about the immediate future and hoped that employment levels would pick up from January 1961. Bu August, however, 2,000 more men had been laid off. Finally, at Christmas, good news came. Shorts got the contract for the new RAF transport freighter, to be called the 'Belfast'. Since the initial order was only for ten, and Shorts needed to build thirty to break even, much lobbying remained to be done in Whitehall before the 'Belfast' became the saviour of the company. This process was to prove almost heartbreaking for the industrialists and politicians involved, and the whole episode, as we shall see later, very nearly sent Shorts to the wall.

As if the redundancies at the shipyard and Shorts were not enough, the Belfast yarn production firm of Forth River Mills announced that 1,100 men and women would be laid off in early 1961. The announcement was made, with an exquisitely gauche sense of timing, on 19 December 1960. Thus it was that, in Belfast alone, there were over 10,000 lay-offs announced in that year.

The launch of the 'Canberra' at Harland and Wolff in 1960. The ship has since become famous as a luxury cruiser and was requisitioned by the British army as a troop ship during the Falklands war.

In one area, education, Northern Ireland at the start of the 1960s might have felt a legitimate sense of pride. In 1948 the Northern education system had broken away from the traditional Irish system, dating from the nineteenth century and still operating in the South. The process had begun in 1923 with the introduction of local education authorities and of primary school rate-aid; previously only technical education had come under public control. The effect of the Education Act (NI) of 1947 was crucial. The 'eleven-plus' examination opened the way to a secondary education funded by the local authorities, except in the case of Catholic schools, which remained independent. In 1957 the school-leaving age was raised to fifteen, in line with Great Britain.

By 1960 the effect of all this was visible. In ten years the number of teachers had increased by 10,700; the number of schoolchildren by 50,000; in all, 100,000 new places had been provided. In 1959 alone, forty-four new schools had been built. There were nearly 700 Catholic students at Queen's University, an increase of 500 in a few years. The total education budget in Northern Ireland in 1960 was £21 million, compared with £19 million in the Republic, which had three times its population.

On 23 June 1960 Patrice Lumumba became the first Prime Minister of the Congo, which formally achieved independence from Belgium on 1 July. Eleven days later the rich copper province of Katanga seceded from the new nation and Lumumba called for United Nations troops to help prevent a civil war. The first UN troops arrived on the 16th; on the 18th they suffered their first casualties when three Moroccans were killed. On the same day the UN secretary-general, Dag Hammarskjöld, asked Ireland to supply troops for the peace-keeping force. Within twenty-four hours the government had agreed.

By the middle of August two Irish batallions of about 600 men each, under the command of Lieutenant-Colonel Mortimer Buckley and Lieutenant-Colonel R. W. Bunworth, were in the Congo. They were stationed in Kivu province, and although about 200 of them were moved up to the Katanga border on 11 August, it was stated that there was no intention of deploying them in the rebel province. By now, however, the Congo was in utter political chaos, for not only had Katanga seceded, but there was also a power struggle in full swing in the rest of the country between the rival tribal factions attached to Lumumba and President Joseph Kasavubu. On 28 July Irish troops were involved in a nasty incident at Goma when two US planes, flying in rations and equipment, were surrounded by aggressive armed troops of the anti-Lumumba *force publique* who confiscated the stores. A third plane, carrying the Irish advance guard, was diverted. It emerged subsequently that Commandant Joseph Adams had persuaded — 'blarneyed' in all the newspaper reports — the rebels to return the stores. It was a trivial incident, but it made the Irish public aware that, right from the start, their troops were in a danger zone, and the fact that they were on a peace-keeping mission was no guarantee against attack.

Then Irish troops were posted to Katanga after all. Lumumba had threatened to invade the province, and at the last moment an Irish contingent was diverted there. They were based at Albertville. It was nearby, at a place called Niemba, that eleven Irish soldiers from 'A' Company, 33rd Battalion, under the command of Lieutenant Kevin Gleeson, were ambushed by Baluba tribesmen on 9 November. Nine were killed, including Lieutenant Gleeson, and one of the bodies was never recovered. The remains of the other eight were brought home to a shaken country.

The word 'Baluba' passed into Irish colloquial speech as a synonym for barbarism, savagery, or plain oafishness. The real Balubas were a primitive tribe, known for their ferocity, who were opposed to the Katangan rebel army, which was reported to have employed brutal repressive measures against them. It was thought that large numbers of white mercenaries in the Katangan forces had made the Balubas regard all white soldiers as enemies, and that the Irish detachment was attacked for this reason.

It had been an exceptional year by any standards, an extraordinary one by those of the Republic of Ireland. After a generation of stagnation, the startling pick-up in the Irish economy which had begun in 1959 was sustained and accelerated. Economics may be the dismal science, but not so in Ireland in 1960. The catalogue of economic achievement in that year set the scene for the years to come. Industrial production up 7 per cent, on top of the 6 per cent rise for 1959; productivity per worker up 4½ per cent, on top of the 3½ per cent for 1959. Exports rose by £21.7 million to £152.4 million, and even with a record level of imports, the balance-of-trade deficit came down from £82 million to £74 million. The total national income rose by 5 per cent. The numbers employed in manufacturing industry rose by 7,500: still only 5 per cent up on 1958, but at least up, and showing every sign of rising further. The net value of agricultural output rose by 3½ per cent, and fat cattle exports went up by a dizzy 178 per cent.

Earnings from tourism were almost £43 million, an increase of 13 per cent on the previous year. The increase in the number of foreign visitors was even more gratifying. Out-of-state bed-nights rose by 17 per cent, the third successive year in which this figure rose by 15 to 20 per cent. The total volume of such business was up 58 per cent on the 1957 figure. More than a quarter of the country's foreign visitors were from outside the United Kingdom, and this figure too was rising.

The money was being spent, as well as being raked in. Spending by Irish people on foreign holidays, which had fallen by nearly £1 million between 1957 and 1959, rose by one-sixth in 1960 to £15.2 million. Rome and Lourdes were still the favourite destinations on the continent, but there was an enormous change coming in this area, as the combination of increased affluence, short-haul jet travel, and the development of the package holiday was soon to bring the gaudy — and distinctly secular — delights of Spain and Greece within the range of very ordinary people.

Chapter Three

1961

An overall minority

But in a well-constituted republic, nothing of this soldering, praising, and pitying, can take place; the representation being equal throughout the country, and complete in itself, however it may be arranged into legislative and executive, they have all one and the same natural source. The parts are not foreigners to each other, like democracy, aristocracy, and monarchy. As there are no discordant distinctions, there is nothing to corrupt by compromise, nor confound by contrivance. Public measures appeal of themselves to the understanding of the Nation, and, resting on their own merits, disown any flattering application to vanity. THOMAS PAINE

Why should she give her bounty to the dead?
What is divinity if it can come
Only in silent shadows and in dreams?
Shall she not find in comforts of the sun,
In pungent fruit and bright, green wings, or else
In any balm or beauty of the earth,
Things to be cherished like the thought of heaven?
WALLACE STEVENS

THE new year opened in style. The recently married Princess Margaret and Mr Anthony Armstrong-Jones arrived at Birr Castle on New Year's Day to an enthusiastic welcome. For the public, the highlight of the visit was a *guignol* worthy of Somerville and Ross. Her Majesty the Queen rang her sister, and instead of getting connected to Birr 23, which was the Castle, she found herself talking to Birr 32, which was Dooley's Hotel. Séamus Brady, the *Daily Express* man in Ireland, was standing by the phone awaiting a call from his London office, and when it rang he answered. A man's voice asked to speak to Princess Margaret, and when Brady enquired who was calling, a woman's voice said: 'This is the Queen.' Brady said in reply: 'Your Majesty, I am sorry. You seem to have got the wrong number.' The man's voice cut back in rather testily to know who was speaking. 'This', said Brady, 'is Dooley's.' Delivery of this piece of intelligence caused the line to go dead.

It was the year of Yuri Gagarin, the first man in space, and of John F. Kennedy, inaugurated as President of the United States in January. At home Seán Lemass called an election which led to his famous 'overall minority' in the Dáil. The economic boom continued in the South, which could now even consider itself a prospective mining nation: the Irish Base Metals Company found large deposits of lead, silver and zinc at Tynagh, Co. Galway, a startling piece of news for a country which traditionally thought of itself as deficient in mineral wealth. But in the North the persistent industrial crisis brought even more pressure to bear on Lord Brookeborough from within the ranks of Unionism.

The Electricity Supply Board launched its complete new home-heating system. Indeed, central heating was being promoted heavily, with one advertisement showing a smiling, pleased-with-herself housewife called 'Mrs 1970', the last word in snug modernity. The ESB also gave notice in 1961 of its intention to demolish sixteen Georgian houses in Lower Fitzwilliam Street, Dublin, and touched off a new era of impassioned environmental protests. Their case rested on the fact that over six years previously the Dublin Corporation's dangerous buildings department had reported the entire block to be in a critical condition, while Sir John Summerson, the Georgian expert whom the Minister for Transport and Power had invited to inspect the buildings, had reported that rebuilding to an entirely new design was the only reasonable course. The town planning expert, Sir Patrick Abercrombie, had reached a similar conclusion some years previously, according to the ESB. In time the conservationists were to marshal their own experts to offer a contrary view.

The first troops came home from the Congo in January, and those from Dublin found their city provided with new postal district numbers. The city fathers considered an offer of £1,000 from a group of pious businessmen to replace Nelson with St Patrick on the Pillar. They thought it better, on balance, to leave Nelson where he was. The Lane pictures arrived at the Municipal Art Gallery, in conclusion of the long wrangle with the British government over the unsigned codicil to Sir Hugh Lane's will. In Galway they welcomed home the ceremonial sword and mace, which had been lost to the city in 1840 when the impoverished Corporation gave them to the mayor in lieu of salary. They were returned from the maw of the William Randolph Hearst Foundation, into whose possession they had come at a London art auction some years before.

Mr Hamilton Tanney of Pittsburgh, Pennsylvania, thought that Ireland should become the fifty-first state of the United States, and arrived in Dublin to put his plan to Seán Lemass. He argued that social security rates in the US would leave Irish people better off than if they were in full employment here; he invited us to consider the example of Puerto Rico. Besides, he continued, there were more Irish people in America than in Ireland, and, as for the Northerners, they would want to join because, in their hard-headed Presbyterian way, they would know that prosperity was a-staring them in the

The centre of paralysis: Dublin city in the final years before the avalanche of new buildings and cars overwhelmed it. 'The Thing' is still proudly in situ on O'Connell Bridge, there isn't a traffic light in sight, traffic is two-way everywhere, and, still perched aloft, Admiral Nelson is keeping his good eye on everything below.

face. Ergo, the end of partition! The only burden that would be placed upon Ireland would be the location of US missile bases along the west coast. What Lemass, a man notoriously disinclined to suffer fools gladly, made of Mr Hamilton Tanney of Pittsburgh, Pennsylvania, is happily unrecorded.

In the United States a controversy blew up about the new US embassy in Dublin, to be located at Elgin Road, Ballsbridge. Its circular design was described by some as 'an architectural monstrosity'. Representative John Rooney (Dem.) of the House Appropriation Committee, who had seen the site some years before when it was first chosen, delivered himself of the view that it was 'in a slum area'.

Aer Lingus reached its twenty-fifth birthday with a fleet of twenty-two planes. Over the vital summer season of 1961, from March to September, its operating surplus reached a new record of £500,000, of which the trans-atlantic contribution was £320,000. Passenger numbers for the period rose by a staggering 55 per cent to over 35,000, while transatlantic cargo volume trebled. No wonder Aer Lingus celebrated its silver jubilee by announcing an ambitious new winter schedule, offering 30,000 economy and 3,500 first-class transatlantic seats, twice the total number of passengers carried from Ireland to North America by *all* airlines in the previous winter. Aer Lingus was by now carrying three out of every five passengers who flew from Ireland to America, and in July it announced that it planned to open its seventh US office, in Dallas, Texas. It employed 2,500 people, and eleven years had passed since it had received a subsidy from any source.

In the summer, CIE decided to resume its mystery tours which had been cancelled owing to persistent vandalism, which was all the more shocking in a country where, for the second year running, there was a fall in the overall crime rate. The company also opened a new sales bureau in O'Connell Street, Dublin, the main feature of which was a large stained-glass window by Evie Hone entitled 'The Four Green Fields'. Meanwhile, across the street, Clery's spring sale offered 'ladies good-looking interlock knickers in full women's sizes with elastic at waist and knee, in assorted shades' for 1s 11d, knocked down from 3s 11d.

The Royal Canal, written off as a 'total failure' as long ago as 1862, and hardly used since the Emergency, was finally closed. The Commission on Taxation recommended that all farmers whose land — apart from buildings — was valued at £100 per annum or more be made to pay income tax on their profits, like shopkeepers; and furthermore, that the valuation limit should be reduced annually until, within ten years at the most, every farmer who made a profit in excess of the taxable minimum would be liable for tax. It was reckoned that this would bring between thirty and forty thousand farmers into the tax net.

Had that report been carried into action, the budget of 1961 would have done something to lessen the howls of the farmers, for the minister, Dr James Ryan, managed a reduction of 8d in the standard rate of income tax, bringing it down to 6s 4d in the pound. That provision, plus an increase in social welfare payments and £1 million in subsidies to farmers, was the clearest signal yet of a general election to come.

The 1961 census report was hardly encouraging. The Republic's population was the lowest ever recorded in the twenty-six-county area at 2,818,341. This reflected in large part the massive emigration of the second half of the fifties and was a salutary reminder of the amount of ground to be made up in the economic boom. The total drop in population since the 1956 census was just 3 per cent, with even Leinster, which had shown a rise in population in every census from 1926 to 1956, registering a slight loss. Unexpectedly, it was not the western seaboard which experienced the greatest decline in population, but the three Ulster counties still in the Republic: Cavan, Monaghan and Donegal. The severity of the problem in these areas can be gauged from the fact that, as Garret FitzGerald wrote,

Every part of the region between the border and a line running south of Castleblayney, Cavan, Mohill, Castlerea and Swinford, except for the coastal area of Co. Sligo and also Co. Donegal north of Donegal town, has experienced a decline in population of more than 15 per cent during the past decade — and throughout a large area comprising northern Leitrim, the northern part of Cavan, and the southern tip of Donegal the drop ... has been in excess of 21 per cent.[1]

A move began against one of the most scandalous manifestations of national backwardness when the government announced a plan to extend piped water to over a quarter of a million rural dwellings at a cost of £35 million. In 1958, out of 300,000 rural dwellings in the Republic, barely one in eight had piped running water, and fewer still had water-borne sanitation. On the other hand, the rural electrification scheme was already very well advanced by international standards, and was to be triumphantly completed by the end of 1962.

At the United Nations Mr Frederick Boland completed his year as president of the general assembly in the autumn, having had to cope with a turbulent Mr Khrushchev during his year in office. In one well-remembered incident, the Soviet leader had taken off his shoe and banged it on his desk to indicate his displeasure. Ireland joined UNESCO in October, and was to become a member of the UN Security Council for the first time in 1962. In the Congo over 180 Irish troops were held prisoner by the Katangans for more than five weeks; by the end of 1961, after a year and half in the Congo, the Irish death toll in the peace-keeping force had risen to twenty-two.

In Dublin the German Cultural Institute opened in November and within a week had to rent extra accommodation to facilitate all the people who wanted to take language lessons; clearly the European future was beckoning to many. The boom in European language classes did not, however, survive the collapse of the British and Irish applications for EEC membership, and by late 1963 demand had slumped.

The early 1960s found the Irish Catholic Church much as it had been for the best part of a century. Its stern authority over the faithful went without challenge; even in urban areas, where one might expect to discover signs of a truculent anticlericalism, there were none that were in any way representative of a concerted popular movement. The ecclesiastical structure bore some striking similarities to the political structure, in particular to that of the Fianna Fáil party: an organisation that reached to the most remote parts of the country; sensitive to the demands made on it, and efficient in satisfying them; receiving the unswerving loyalty of its partisans; brutally impatient with dissidents; and, for all the intimacy of its local units, subject to strong and authoritative direction from the centre.

No more than the political parties, it was not a congenial institution for troubled intellectuals. The habit of authority and obedience came too easily; consequently the Irish Church was weak on theologians, but strong on briskly efficient bishops who got things done and were usually afraid of nobody. It was a church well suited to an authoritarian, rural society.

It was proud of its achievements: its missionary endeavours in the twentieth century were on a heroic scale, while at home it could argue that it discharged its primary responsibility — the salvation of souls — more efficiently than any other national church in Europe outside the Iberian Peninsula. Attendance at Sunday mass and at the sacraments was almost universal. In rural parts, especially, failure to attend Sunday mass was a sensational social lapse, which could quite seriously — and on occasions quite correctly — lead to questions being asked about the mental stability of the miscreant.

Proud it might be, but not complacent. For an institution that commanded the obedience of its followers so thoroughly, it was extraordinarily sensitive to the danger of moral corruption. It was eternally vigilant, and like every sentry it often mistook a shadow for an enemy. Bad as were the dangers within, these were nothing to the manifold hazards without; the Irish Church tended to see the country as a sacred reservation — not perfect, to be sure, but at least insulated from the horrors of a modern world characterised by atheism, indifference, the rampant instrusions of the secular state, and a gravely weakened sense of morality.

Every spring, at the start of Lent, the Irish bishops addressed pastoral letters to their flocks. The letters contained pastoral advice, especially for the penitential period; specific diocesan regulations to be observed by the faithful; and the animadversions of their lordships on a variety of subjects, sacred and profane, on which they wished their voices to be heard. As a formal, considered exercise, pastoral letters are as good a guide as we are likely to get to the state of mind of the concerns of the Irish hierarchy at any given time. The spring of 1961 was no exception.

The dangers of communism were stressed by three prelates: Archbishop McQuaid of Dublin and Bishops O'Doherty and Murphy of Dromore and Limerick respectively. As a political force in Ireland, communism was as good as non-existent; no candidate brave enough to declare his communism openly had ever as much as saved his deposit in an Irish election.

Dr McQuaid further stressed the duty of Catholic parents to ensure a full Catholic education for their children. He reiterated his long-standing prohibition on Catholics in the archdiocese of Dublin attending Trinity College. It was necessary, he said, for the pluralist and secular influences in much modern thought not to go unchallenged, especially in third-level institutions suitable for Catholics.

Bishop McNeely of Raphoe was concerned with 'snares for youth'. 'What passes for amusement and pastime is not always the harmless thing it was a generation ago.' Was this the latest manifestation of the bishops' obsessive and persistent suspicion of dancing and other occasions on which the young of opposite sexes might meet? Irish Catholics were, as far as anyone could determine, among the most chaste people in the western world; illegitimacy rates were low by international standards, and since contraception was almost unknown, it was reasonable to suppose that extra-marital sexual intercourse was therefore not widespread. Besides, what Bishop McNeely described as the harmless amusements of a previous generation were not so regarded by his episcopal predecessors, who were as vigilant as he in denouncing the entertainments of their own times.

Cardinal D'Alton of Armagh and Dr Philbin of Clonfert — soon to be translated to the important see of Down and Connor, which included Belfast — wrote on different aspects of a similar point. The Cardinal noted that

The faithful are living in a world in which some denied the existence of God, while many ... took little or no account of him in their daily lives. In the face of such unbelief ... we need to have a sound intelligent grasp of our faith.

Dr Philbin agreed that we were living in an age of licence:

In Ireland we are protected against some at least of the most offensive and dangerous influences which circulated elsewhere with the hallmark of approval from the makers of public opinion; thank God we have made these defences and maintained them in the face of so much ridicule and abuse. But we are not immune ...

The pastorals of 1961 were not untypical. The following year brought similar concerns and anxieties. Cardinal D'Alton wrote in 1962 that

We no longer enjoy [*sic*] our isolation of former days. We are living in a world where many seem to have forgotten God.... In this distorted world, through the medium of the press, the radio and the television, we are subject to the impact of views wholly at variance with Catholic teaching.... In these days when the question of the reunion of our separated brethren is being widely discussed we should have some knowledge of how the unity of the Church was disrupted ...

Following a potted account of the Eastern Schism and the Reformation, he observed that

However much the Protestant reformers disagreed, they were united in their anti-papal hostility. Their principle of private scriptural interpretation has led inevitably to the multiplicity of religious bodies so much at variance with Christ's ideal of one fold and one shepherd. At the present time we should in all charity pray earnestly for our separated brethren that, enlightened by the Holy Spirit, they may find their way to the one fold of Christ.

Also in 1962, the Bishop of Derry stressed the moral dangers of dances after midnight and urged 'moderation' in the number of dances attended. Archbishop Walsh of Tuam identified the twin aims of the forthcoming Vatican Council as a statement of the faith in the face of modern errors and the adaptation of the Church to the modern world through disciplinary reform. Dr Hanly of Elphin spoke of the Council in the context of a Catholic Church which was the only bulwark against militant atheism. Dr Murphy of Limerick noted that Ireland was going to become more involved with the outside world and stressed the need to preserve those valuable features of our heritage, of which the Catholic faith was foremost. Dr Michael Browne of Galway saw the Church everywhere confronted with hostility and contradiction. Even in the democratic nations atheism and materialism determined the atmosphere of universities, schools and the entertainment media.

Not just in pastorals but in speeches also, the bishops maintained their relentless line. Speaking at the opening of a new national school at Oranmore, Co. Galway, in November 1961, Dr Browne complained of the very strong influences working against Christian morality: materialism was not confined to Russia; in newspapers, paperback novels and the radio, young people were exposed to demoralising influences. Public opinion had the greatest effect on the young, and one of the chief moulders of public opinion was drama. The bishop deplored the fashion of using 'filthy language' in plays, as well as that of representing Irish people as playboys and morons. Nor did he approve of the dramatic practice of representing Irish homes as places of squabbling. Irish people were not playboys; Ireland was 'a nation of saints and scholars', and the country had a noble tradition to put before the young, the tradition of the Irish saints.

On 11 November Archbishop Morris of Cashel had told an assembly of the Catholic Boy Scouts of Ireland in Thurles that Ireland was 'a Christian country surrounded by paganism'. The day before, Bishop Lucey of Cork, speaking on the occasion of the 150th anniversary of the city's first Christian Brothers' school, had noted the many changes that had taken place over those years: 'the alien ascendancy is no longer ascendant and Catholic Ireland is coming into its own'; while we must engender change in education, we should ensure that the changes are not dictated 'by the noisy few who, speaking in the name of liberalism and progress, were in fact anti-Irish, anti-Catholic and out of touch with the common people'. Addressing a Muintir na Tíre meeting the following week, he added that 'small farmers are the backbone of the rural community' and charged that an atmosphere hostile to them was being created by 'economists, industrialists, and lineal descendants of the old landlord class'.

It was a melancholy list. The Irish bishops, on the questions that seemed important to them, were generally defensive and conservative, placing a strong emphasis on tradition and discipline. They were, as men of the cloth, properly suspicious of the material world, although one could be forgiven for feeling that their suspicion inclined towards a morbid fixation with the evils of modern life. They were certainly happy with the idea of an Ireland cocooned from the modern world, and generally regretted the fact that this was now becoming a thing of the past. They were predictably suspicious of the mass media; television they found to have a particularly insidious capacity for mischief. Meeting at Maynooth in October 1961, the bishops issued a statement on the forthcoming Irish television channel. Although stressing the potential for good in the medium, they were careful to emphasise:

But it can do great harm, not merely in the diffusion of the erroneous ideas of those who were lacking in deep or accurate knowledge of religious truth, but also in the broadcasting of programmes which offend all reasonable standards of morals and decency.

The contrast in tone and content between the pastoral letters of the Irish bishops and the encyclical letter of Pope John, issued in July 1961 and entitled *Mater et magistra*, was unmistakable. The encyclical appealed for 'politically disinterested aid' for underdeveloped countries; it warned

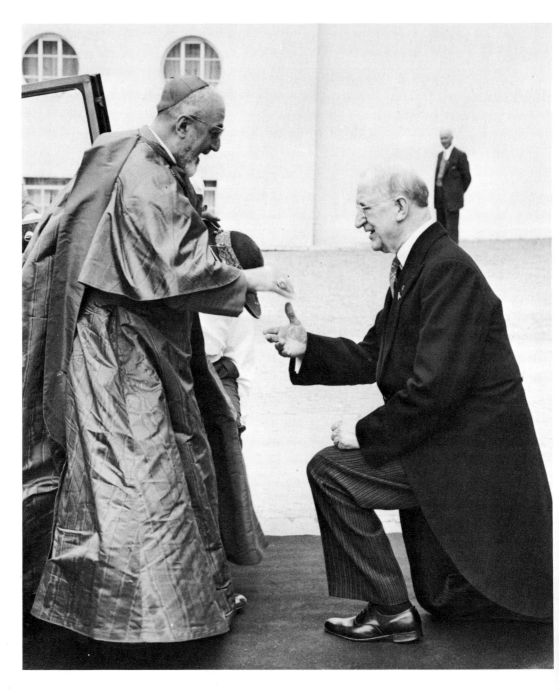

The Patrician Congress of 1961 was the last great public triumph of pre-conciliar Irish Catholicism. Above, President de Valera gets the relationship of Church and State about right as he welcomes Cardinal Agagianian, the Papal Legate, who is seen talking to Cardinal D'Alton (right above). Archbishop McQuaid of Dublin, the chief organiser of the Congress, stands behind the Cardinal and seems pleased with things. Croke Park was the setting for the mass which closed the Congress (right below).

against what it called the 'new colonialism'; it held that social progress should march side by side with economic progress; it pleaded for the proper use of scientific and technological breakthroughs, lest they be used to provide 'terrible instruments of ruin and death'; and while it insisted on the right to private property, it accepted that a certain degree of socialism was equitable.

It would hardly be an exaggeration to say that in 1961 the papacy was somewhere to the left of the Irish Church. That church now inhabited a country which was already beginning to feel the effects of the materialist culture which its pastors so deplored. No one was in any doubt that there was more of the same to come. Television alone would see to that.

But for the moment the Church could glory in the past a while, before facing the storms ahead. The year 1961 was reputedly the 1,500th anniversary of the death of St Patrick, the founder of Irish Christianity, from whom the Irish Catholic Church claims descent in unbroken ecclesiastical succession. To celebrate the event the Church declared 1961 to be Patrician Year, and numerous ceremonies were planned. Cardinal McIntyre of Los Angeles was nominated papal legate to the Patrician Year, and he arrived in Dublin to a twenty-one-gun salute from the army on 17 March, St Patrick's Day. But the principal ceremonies revolved around the Dublin Congress of the Patrician Year, which ran from 17 to 25 June and comprised an elaborate series of public liturgical events culminating in a mass celebrated before a congregation of 90,000 souls in Croke Park, the headquarters of the Gaelic Athletic Association.

The Congress had its own papal legate, the bearded Armenian Cardinal Agagianian. His arrival on 17 June was marked by a liturgical reception in the Pro-Cathedral which coincided with the lighting of a symbolic candle and the raising of the Congress flag in O'Connell Street. During the week the cardinal legate laid the foundation stone in Ringsend Park for the port of Dublin's proposed statue of the Virgin Mary. He was granted the freedom of the city of Dublin, as well as an honorary degree by the National University of Ireland.

It was the most public manifestation of Dublin's Catholicism since the famous Eucharistic Congress of 1932. Protestant churchmen received no invitations to participate in any of the events.

But all voices in Irish ecclesiastical affairs did not sing in exactly the same key. The Maynooth Summer School on Christian Unity met at the end of June, and while its deliberations were cautious — Father Bernard Leeming, SJ, for example, hoped that 'our separated brethren will accept papal infallibility and supremacy' — the fact that it took place at all, and in the epicentre of the Irish Catholic world at that, was significant.

There was enough sense of change in the air for Canon R. R. Harford of the Church of Ireland to observe the increasing friendliness and courtesy which now obtained between every Christian denomination, 'not least between ourselves and our Roman Catholic countrymen who represent something like 93 per cent of the people of this country'. Canon Harford, regius professor of divinity at Trinity College, Dublin, was proposing the adoption of a report from the diocesan Committee on Christian Unity, just two weeks after the end of the Patrician Congress.

Two weeks before the Congress, the Presbyterian General Assembly met in Belfast. The newly elected Moderator, Dr W. A. A. Park, told the Assembly that Christian unity was desirable and necessary. The recent visits of the Archbishop of Canterbury and Queen Elizabeth to Pope John in Rome proved that Protestants were not bigoted, he said, but they would not accept obedience to Rome as a condition of unity. They would, nevertheless, be glad to see Roman Catholics somewhat keener on the Bible: 'The Bible is dynamite, and when read and inwardly digested, no one knows what may happen.' The Presbyterians, themselves no lovers of modernity, nevertheless appointed a television and radio working party and stressed the necessity for a positive attitude towards the media, which was described as a 'powerful ally' of the Church. Perhaps familiarity with television had helped them overcome any anxieties they might have had: by then an Ulster Television training course for clergy had already been in operation for a year and a half.

As everyone had been expecting, it was an election year. Fianna Fáil faced the disturbing prospect of having to fight without the legendary de Valera at the helm. While the government had been carried on very smoothly by Lemass, his ability as a national vote-puller was unknown and could hardly be expected to match that of 'the Chief'. Moreover, the party had received a particularly large vote in 1957, and some loss of support was almost inevitable. In Fianna Fáil's favour, however, was its incomparable machine, the success of the government's economic policies, and the prevailing sense of optimism in the country. The other factor that assisted it was the state of the opposition parties.

Fine Gael had been unconvincing. Like Fianna Fáil, they had a new leader. James Dillon, colourful, florid in the old-fashioned oratorical way, and probably the outstanding ministerial success — along with Noel Browne — in the two coalition governments, assumed the parliamentary leadership of the party from Richard Mulcahy in 1959. In February 1960 he was formally elected party president at the annual Ard-Fheis. Like Lemass, he can hardly be said to have represented a generational change. Although younger than

Mulcahy, he was still nearly sixty. In his first presidential address he enunciated a series of objectives that Lemass himself might have heartily endorsed: protection having failed, we must now ensure that we are not isolated from both large European free trade groups; the Control of Manufactures Act should be repealed; industrial development should be based on private enterprise; we should not insist above all else on a balanced budget if this involved taxing bread. Only on agriculture did Dillon differ significantly from Lemass. He doubted if the thirty-five-acre farm had much of a future, and he wanted a review of Land Commission activities accordingly. Whatever Lemass may have believed privately — and he was more than once accused of a townie's insensitivity to agriculture — such a suggestion would have been political suicide for any Fianna Fáil politician, given the party's reliance on the small farmers' votes. Fine Gael, with its traditional big-farmer support, could afford to contemplate the disappearance of the thirty-five-acre farm.

Dillon made one other statement in his speech which, while it had the sound of ritual about it, revealed a party attitude that was to do it little good over the course of the decade. It was a fundamental principle of policy, he said, that the country's prime reliance must be placed on its principal resource of 'twelve million acres of arable land'. It was plain to see, however, that the conditions for an economic boom based on agriculture did not exist in Ireland in the 1960s. But Fine Gael, perhaps out of a natural desire to woo the farming vote at a time when farmers resented their exclusion from the country's increasing prosperity, hammered at the point so hard that they allowed Fianna Fáil to become the 'industry party', almost by default. Time and again over the next few years Fine Gael gave the impression, rightly or wrongly, that their hearts were not really in the new industrial drive. They tended either to make little of its achievements or to ignore them. They were undoubtedly in a fix, because opposing the party responsible for the most successful economic boom in the history of the state was no easy job. Nevertheless, on one of the two major issues where they distanced themselves from Fianna Fáil, they allowed themselves too easily to be characterised as a stuffy, conservative party, wedded to the interests of large farmers and small rural businessmen.

A few weeks after his Ard-Fheis speech Dillon addressed the Dáil in the debate on the vote on account. There was, he said, a pall of gloom over the country. (If so, Mr Dillon was almost alone in detecting it.) Rural businessmen were pessimistic about the future, he went on, because the removal of food subsidies had led to the sixth and seventh round of wage increases 'and more than one small business in rural Ireland has had to close as a result'. This protest may have brought some comfort to small rural businessmen, but was unlikely to impress industrial workers who had benefited from the effects of the pay rounds and among whom support for Fine Gael was already very low.

It was this failure to broaden the appeal of the party which may be considered the chief defect of Dillon's leadership. When eventually the 'Young Tigers' forced the 'Just Society' document on the party before the 1965 election, the elders made it abundantly clear that they disapproved of it. Unlike Lemass's Fianna Fáil, Fine Gael was not a party in which an energetic and restless younger generation was going to get much encouragement.

For Fine Gael was immobile. It tended to react to Fianna Fáil's actions rather than formulating positive policies of its own; its intentions were stated negatively. The personal attacks made by party leaders on Lemass — that he was an irresponsible gambler and a nepotist, the latter charge arising out of his promotion of Charles Haughey, his son-in-law, to junior office — impressed nobody. Attacks on the government for allegedly not doing those very things which it was in fact doing weakened the party's credibility. For example, Gerard Sweetman, effectively the deputy leader, accused the government in March 1961 of not hitching a ride on the unprecedented world economic boom. And in the following July he told a party meeting that the government stood indicted for not alerting the people sufficiently to the implications of EEC membership.

This really was preposterous. Hardly a week passed in which a senior cabinet minister, usually Lemass himself, did not make a minatory speech on the subject, and that very month the government established the Committee on Industrial Organisation to survey the entire range of Irish manufacturing industry. The CIO was to adjudicate on the degree of preparation for free trade conditions in each industry and make recommendations for adaptation.

Lemass expressed the view that the only constructive criticism of government policy was coming from outside the Dáil; inside, he said, Fine Gael simply 'belittled' the government. When, for example, Dillon voiced the familiar Fine Gael complaint about industrial expansion coming at the expense of agriculture, Lemass replied tersely: 'No country can sit on its posterior and slide downhill into prosperity.' It might have been a watchword for his whole career. He spelled out his attitude even more plainly to the Fianna Fáil Ard-Fheis in November 1960:

This is a time to push forward, to experiment, to gamble if need be, a time when the country needs Fianna Fáil enterprise and initiative. The difference between Fianna Fáil and Fine Gael is that the former is dynamic and positive, while Fine Gael is fundamentally conservative and negative.

Even when all allowances have been made for the partisan manner and setting of that remark, it is hard to disagree with it. Fine Gael remained a deeply conservative collection of comfortable, part-time politicians, attached to the notion that an expanding agriculture was the motor which would most efficiently drive the engine of Irish prosperity. They started the 1960s as they intended to go on: a party condemned to second place in Irish politics for want of dynamic leadership and national organisation and a clear, coherent philosophy which distinguished them from Fianna Fáil.

The Labour Party still had some years to go before it lost its fear of socialism and gave itself the intellectual elbow-room to offer a major critique of Fianna Fáil policy from the left, as well as attracting an enthusiastic influx of new young members and supporters. In the electoral sense, it was not even the party of the working class: Fianna Fáil got the majority of the working-class vote, a point Lemass was always glad to rub in to Labour Party spokesmen. Not even in the formal, organisational sense could Labour claim to be the political voice of the trade union movement, for neither the Irish Transport and General Workers' Union nor the Workers' Union of Ireland — the two largest unions — were affiliated to the party. There were, however, stirrings beneath the surface. In March 1961 the Irish Congress of Trade Unions and the party founded a joint council of action and thus began a process that eventually led to a closer and more fruitful collaboration between the unions and the party, culminating in the affiliation of the ITGWU and the WUI later in the decade.

On 1 March 1960 Brendan Corish was unanimously elected leader of the Labour Party in succession to William Norton. The most striking thing about Corish was his age. At forty, he was twenty years younger than the other two new party leaders. Nearly a year after taking over the leadership Corish gave a long interview to the political correspondent of the *Irish Times*. He declared that he would not lead the Labour Party into coalition without the party's annual conference reversing its repeated preference for a go-it-alone policy; he insisted that they still adhered to 'the ideals of James Connolly', but added hastily that 'Of course, the things that Connolly stood for have been distorted and misrepresented.' The shadow of the crozier still fell on the party, and Corish was enough of a realist to know the necessity of avoiding allegations of 'atheistic socialism'. Questioned about the party's differences with Fianna Fáil, the new leader said that 'While Fianna Fáil are prepared to go a small way on social welfare and health legislation and industrial organisation, the Labour Party would go much further.' They would provide an insurance-based no-means-test comprehensive health service, and would also favour more public enterprise: the government should not rely 'so much on foreign interests'. He also stressed the point that his was the only party in the state which had been founded by a 1916 signatory.

The interview ran across five columns, and yet not once in this conversation between two men of the left — the interviewer was Michael McInerney — did the word 'socialism' pass. Or if it did, it did not appear in print.

Labour's dramatic opening to the left, when it eventually came from 1967 onwards, owed less to its union connections than to a surge of new, often middle-class enthusiasts. In the early 1960s what the unions could offer the party was a sounder basis to its finances and organisation. They were unlikely to nudge the party to the left, for the unions were, in the main, conservative protest groups within the overall structure of Irish capitalism, suspicious of socialist ideologues because of the damage they could do the movement in a country which shared the bishops' unflattering view of socialism. There was a straightforward class prejudice at work here as well: most theoreticians of the left were, regrettably, middle class. *Liberty*, the official organ of the ITGWU, summed up the negative union view of the radical left in a rather intemperate leader in January 1961. With a vigilant eye worthy of any bishop, it detected small active groups of communists at work, most particularly in Belfast but also in Dublin, Cork, Limerick and Waterford. But that was not all: in addition to 'the red core', it also noted the presence of

the usual pale-pink fellow-travellers who would like to be considered of the brethren so long as they are not required to contribute to the party funds or to undertake any active work for the cause.... What do they add up to? ... Just a handful of pseudo-intellectuals with a few rejects from office in the trade union movement, the usual odd characters who like to be looked upon as different, and the residue, the riff-raff of undesirable hangers-on that attach themselves to most newly formed revolutionary organisations.

The most important political fact in 1961, and the one which had a decisive effect in the election, was the estrangement between the two major opposition parties and erstwhile coalition partners. Neither Fine Gael nor Labour had any enthusiasm for another coalition. Fine Gael aimed to form a majority government — rather improbably, since it would require a near doubling of the party's Dáil strength — while Labour sought to achieve a significant increase in its parliamentary representation. In consequence the inter-party transfers never materialised, and despite the fact that the two parties together got about the same share of the first-preference votes as Fianna Fáil, their total of seats was seven less.

Polling took place on 4 October. Fianna Fáil lost its overall majority, but Lemass was still able to form a government with the support of

The sixties is commonly thought of as a decade of street protest but in fact it took the authorities a long time to come to terms with such untraditional manifestations. Here Dr Noel Browne TD is in a spot of bother with the law outside the American Embassy at the time of the Cuban missile crisis in 1962.

independents. The party strengths in the new Dáil were: Fianna Fáil 70 (78 in the 1957 Dáil); Fine Gael 47 (40); Labour 16 (12); Clann na Talmhan 2 (3); National Progressive Democrats 2 (—); Clann na Poblachta 1 (1); Sinn Féin 0 (4); others 6 (9). So the result, while gratifying for Lemass in the sense that he was returned to office, was by no means a triumph for Fianna Fáil. Presiding as they were over an unprecedented economic boom, they might have expected better than to lose seven seats, while watching Fine Gael and Labour gain eleven between them. This was all the more surprising when one recalls how threadbare Fine Gael were for policies: only the promise to abolish compulsory Irish distinguished them sharply from Fianna Fáil on a major issue.

Fianna Fáil did well in Dublin, increasing its total of first preferences there to almost 110,000; Fine Gael could only manage 78,000. More suggestively, the Labour Party secured only one seat in the capital, despite an unprecedented call from ICTU for trade unionists to support the party. As it was, Michael Mullen won the party's lone Dublin seat without reaching the quota.

Fianna Fáil's decline in rural constituencies was due in part to the absence of the patriarchal figure of de Valera, partly to a certain rural suspicion of Lemass, and partly to the incessant Fine Gael emphasis on the primacy of agriculture. The minor fringe parties began the inexorable decline characteristic of them in the 1960s. Clann na Poblachta, which barely a decade before had seemed the bright new star in the political constellation, was reduced to a single seat, and the leader, Seán MacBride, was once again defeated. Clann na Talmhan, never much more than a marginal parliamentary pressure group for the interests of the small western farmer, held two seats without showing any signs of political development. Sinn Féin disappeared from the scene, an appropriate response from the electorate to their abstentionist policies. More tellingly, their eclipse was characteristic of a constant tendency in Irish politics, to recoil from 'out' groups and extremists in times of calm and prosperity. The IRA border campaign, which may have appeared heroic in the depressed circumstances of 1957, was now generally regarded with indifference and disdain in the South. The occasional outrage still made front-page headlines, but the country had already had a glimpse of more material opportunities than the recovery of the troublesome fourth green field. The IRA's squalid and ineffective campaign sputtered on for barely another year, and with its demise, militant republicanism was thought to have disappeared into history.

When the Seventeenth Dáil met for the first time a week after the election, Lemass had a comfortable majority of four in the contest for Taoiseach, thanks to the support of two of the independents. He made only one major cabinet change, promoting Charles Haughey to be Minister for Justice in place of Oscar Traynor, who had retired from public life. Almost immediately a problem arose which gave Lemass an opportunity to show his mettle and his style.

The weeks of the election campaign had seen some of the worst autumn storms for years. Farmers stood to lose over £2 million as a result of extensive damage to wheat crops just at the moment when the harvest should have been in full swing. Barely 50 per cent of the normal crop had been delivered to mills, and it was claimed that unless the government bailed the farmers out, thousands could face ruin. The National Farmers' Association urged the government to make good the loss to farmers whose wheat was not millable, but the proposal was turned down. Fine Gael immediately put down a Dáil motion urging that the decision be reversed. Lemass, speaking against the motion in the house, said that the government had deliberately avoided taking the politically easy course because of the absence of any real intrinsic merit in the proposal:

We examined these proposals carefully and with the utmost sympathy because there is a natural desire on the part of the government and a party such as ours to help the farmers.... But because we did not believe that these proposals were justifiable, or supportable on their merits, we rejected the idea of buying for ourselves an immediate relief from political pressure by adopting them.... If we did accept them, we would have created still greater difficulties of a political character at other times and in other sectors.

He added that the storm damage had occurred against a background of an over-production of wheat, and that while everybody sympathised with the farmers, acceptance of the NFA proposal that they should be paid for unmillable wheat as though it were first class would be tantamount to telling them that they need never take care of their wheat again. But the heart of his remarks came in the following declaration:

When I was elected here ... I said that the government would proceed in all matters in precisely the same way as if we had an overall majority. We would do what was right in our judgment in the circumstances and let the political consequences look after themselves.... This is how we dealt with this proposal from the NFA.

Thus did Lemass set the tone of his government from the very start. It was a brave, almost reckless, policy for a man without an overall parliamentary majority, especially in view of the political influence of the farming lobby and the naturally high level of public sympathy for a group of men who faced severe financial loss through a vicissitude wholly beyond their control. But Lemass was above all else a doer, and he would not be baulked by a gaggle of independents and minor party men. He had little time for the eccentricities of political virgins, and he had a sound knowledge of the cost of fighting elections; he calculated that few independents would relish another contest so soon, and that they realised that the voters might not thank them for pre-cipitating one. The independents got the message, and never lost it all through the course of the Seventeenth Dáil. The Fine Gael motion on the wheat farmers was lost by 68 votes to 54. Lemass had established his 'overall minority' and on the back of it proceeded to lead one of the most energetic and creative governments in the history of the state.

The government's policy on free trade and on membership of the European Economic Community had been abundantly clear for some time. The Taoiseach's personal commitment to the ending of protection was well established; like many other Irishmen, he had been convinced by the dreadful crisis of 1956, if by nothing else, of the imperative necessity to abandon traditional economics. De Gaulle's first veto on British membership of a European free trade area at the end of 1958 pushed the question into the background for a few years, because not even the most besotted European imagined that we could join such a body unless and until Britain joined as well.

Lemass had hammered away, in speech after speech, at the need to adapt quickly to the radical changes ahead. More than any other theme, this dominated the first four years of his period as Taoiseach.

On 31 July 1961 the United Kingdom formally applied for membership of the EEC. The Republic of Ireland followed suit the next day.

It is unnecessary to dwell on the symbolic significance of this. It merely fixed in time the central pillar of the new economics. Of course, the application lapsed eighteen months later when de Gaulle once again slammed the door on the British. But nobody at the time imagined that this was any more than a hiccup. The European movement — and it really was a movement in the sixties, with some of the starry-eyed zeal that the word implies — appeared to have a touch of historical inevitability about it. The idea that we were on the threshold of European membership was a constant for most of the decade. That marked a profound change, particularly for the generation that came to maturity in the 1960s.

The older image of Ireland had been dominated by the struggle for independence and the attempt to recapture in the new nation the lost threads of a hidden Ireland. The country's physical isolation, the simplicity of its economy, the overwhelmingly rural disposition of its population, the absence of large deposits of wealth, its wartime neutrality: all these forces had turned Ireland in on itself; Irish people looked to their own country and traditions for the standards that gave value to their lives.

But the fifties had finished all that. The pursuit of the hidden Ireland was abandoned with the collapse of the old Sinn Féin ideal. The new men of the sixties thought in terms of recovering the European corner of the Irish mind and enlarging it. Even in traditional music, the most marvellous rediscovery of the decade was the work of Turlough O'Carolan, in whose hands the classical European and the Celtic Irish modes of composition had mingled so happily. The impassioned struggle to save Dublin's Georgian heritage, the supreme achievement of the European mind in Ireland, enclosed the decade at either end: Fitzwilliam Street at the beginning, Hume Street at the end.

Ireland's re-engagement with Europe would have happened without the application for EEC membership; there were other cultural forces working in that direction. But the economic impetus quickened the process. The farmer, the industrial worker, the businessman, the student, the civil servant: all of them, thousands of ordinary Irish people, gradually came to realise the material implications of Europe, and acquired the habit of looking outward, in a mixture of expectation and apprehension, at the wide, complicated, dizzying world beyond.

Chapter Four

1962

Citizens of the world

For every hour and every minute his mind was always full of those battles, enchantments, adventures, miracles, loves, and challenges which are related in books of chivalry; and everything that he said, thought or did was influenced by his fantasies. As for the dust-cloud he had seen, it was caused by two great flocks of sheep, which were being driven along that road in opposite directions, but owing to the dust they were not visible until they drew near. So emphatically, however, did Don Quixote affirm that they were armies, that Sancho came to believe him and asked: 'Sir, what must we do now?'

CERVANTES

At the high speeds of electric communication, purely visual means of apprehending the world are no longer possible; they are just too slow to be relevant or effective. MARSHALL McLUHAN

IN the 1960s tourism became a major Irish industry, and by the middle of the decade it was already the country's largest single source of revenue. Between 1961 and 1969 tourist earnings more than doubled, and the number of hotel beds increased by a half, roughly in line with the rise in the number of tourists. In particular, Ireland established itself as a holiday centre for continentals and North Americans; the number of visitors from these areas increased fourfold.

This influx of foreign holidaymakers made new demands on Irish standards of accommodation and catering, especially outside the Dublin area. The restaurant trade, in particular, began to develop in those parts of the south and west which attracted significant numbers of continental visitors. Sleepy provincial towns, where nothing much had stirred for years, realised the potential of these new seasonal visitors: festivals sprung up like mushrooms in the most unlikely places, usually based on a local theme which had been happily neglected for generations. There was nothing traditional about these festivals. They were opportunistic and usually vulgar, being no more than vehicles to attract large crowds to spend money in the one place for a week or so. But the energy and enterprise that lay behind them was altogether typical of the sixties.

In the early years of the decade a great deal of the tourist industry's attention was concentrated on the business of raising standards. Whereas ten years earlier all but a few hotels in the country were small, with central heating and private bathrooms regarded as exceptional, things had changed in the face of tourists' expectations. A substantial investment programme was launched in new and refurbished hotels, and the Bord Fáilte 'Better Hotels Plan' accounted for the provision of over 3,000 new hotel bedrooms between 1961 and 1963. Moreover, international hotel chains established themselves in Ireland. The Intercontinental group, for instance, opened in Dublin, Cork and Limerick in May 1963. This corrected one of the most glaring shortcomings of the industry — the simple inability to satisfy an increasing demand. At the end of 1962 CERT (the Council for Education, Recruitment and Training in the hotel and catering industry) met for the first time and thus institutionalised the drive for higher standards.

In the previous June Mr William Cormack, the publicity manager of Thos. Cook & Son, had volunteered his opinions on what needed to be done to keep the Irish tourist industry going forward. He suggested the development of major resorts around existing beaches where there was already a nucleus of one or two hotels and a village:

I have in mind two places in Donegal — one at Gortahork and the other at Port-na-Blagh. The potential for development in either area is first class, but it will be necessary to change their names by deed poll. Suitable brand names for seaside resorts are now an essential part of tourist promotion. Local feeling can be met by re-naming the beaches and not the actual place.

He was particularly critical of the lack of entertainment in Irish resorts. There was little to do in the evenings; he said that during a motoring trip through Irish towns in 1961 he found that amenities were exactly the same as they would have been before 1914:

the dirty, grimy little bars into which you daren't take a lady, which break up the monotony of grey, humdrum shops, the complete lack of public lavatories, the limitation of entertainment to one-horse cinemas, the limitations of eating ...

He cited Bray, Co. Wicklow, in evidence of his view that Irish tourism would be greatly helped if local by-laws were to insist on light, gay colours for the painting of houses, especially along drab seafronts.

Mr Cormack was not alone in disapproving of Irish visual insensitivity. Even the government — who were to remain, in spite of all their achievements in other areas, outstandingly philistine in questions of aesthetics — were beginning to fret on this account. In February 1961 Jack Lynch, the Minister for Industry and Commerce, opened an exhibition of posters sponsored by the Dublin Rotary Club; in his speech he stressed the contribution that creative artists could make to industrial progress. In modern commerce, he observed, packaging and design was of paramount importance. But there was no proper school of design in the country, and when Córas Tráchtála (the Irish export board) looked for a means of tackling the whole industrial design deficiency in Ireland, it was obliged to go to Scandinavia for five experts who agreed to survey existing facilities, to advise on design problems, and to help develop Irish design to international standards. The Scandinavian team arrived in April 1961.

Their report was published in February 1962 and was severe in its criticisms. Ireland had to make a substantial improvement in its standards if it proposed to face seriously into the EEC. Pending the establishment of an Irish Institute of Visual Arts, a small working party should be set up to collect the data necessary for its formation. The Institute should have its own premises with facilities for summer schools. No other body could cope with the problems, least of all the National College of Art, whose existing methods the committee held to be hopelessly outdated. It judged the first priority to be the provision of industrial designers; it recommended that selected craftsmen and artists be trained as designers, and that the state make funds available for design education. Attention should also be paid to the primary and secondary schools: 'To set up a new school of design and at the same time ignore the fact that the Irish schoolchild is visually and artistically among the most under-educated in Europe, would appear to us unwise.'

The committee praised some sections of industry, particularly traditional crafts and glass-making. Their main criticisms were levelled at textiles, machine-made carpets, ceramics, pottery, metalwork and furniture. Not surprisingly, they hammered the souvenir trade.

They made a specific study of postage stamps. From a random selection of forty-one, divided into three groups (portraits; figures, landscapes and buildings; and symbols) they made a classification based on the following criteria in descending order of priority: the need for a clear indication of value (where twelve out of the forty-one got a low rating); easy visibility of the name of the country (where seven failed to reach an acceptable standard); and ease and balance of composition (where ten issues were unsatisfactory).

The following September an industrial design school was opened at the National College of Art. The central recommendation of the Scandinavian committee led to a much more important development in the following year: the establishment of the Kilkenny Design Workshops, one of the truly outstanding Irish achievements of the 1960s, not least for its effect on the visual sensibilities of the Irish public. In addition, the government announced a programme of grants and consultant advice to firms who wanted to improve their design standards. About ninety firms showed some initial interest, but in the first year of the scheme only twenty-five made any real effort to employ consultants or improve their own designers' abilities.

In the two critical areas of emigration and employment, the news continued good in 1962. Net emigration had been cut by over 70 per cent per annum since 1957, and employment in non-agricultural pursuits was up by 30,000 since the end of 1959. This contrasted neatly with a fall of similar dimensions in employment between 1955 and 1958.

As in any period of economic expansion in Ireland, the construction industry was flourishing. Although the demand for housing was no greater than in the peak of post-war building, it had changed in character. According to the Minister for Local Government, Neil Blaney, more viable economic conditions for the builders, together with a general rise in living standards, had altered the balance in the provision as between public and private housing. Now five private houses were being built for every one local authority dwelling, and the building boom in the Dublin area was sufficient to create the danger of a labour shortage.

The most significant news of the year came from the Shannon Free Airport Development Company just before Christmas, when they announced a 'stay-at-home-in-Ireland' campaign. In a new town which already employed 2,500, they now found themselves, like the Dublin building contractors, running short of workers. For the West of Ireland, accustomed to generations of under-employment and emigration, this was sensational. The campaign aimed to encourage workers home from England for the Christmas holidays not to return, but to take up employment opportunities at Shannon instead. By August 1963 the Irish embassy in London was handling sixty to seventy enquiries a month from Irishmen wanting to return home because of increased economic opportunities in Ireland. This was double the rate of enquiry for 1958.

Still, some traditional fixations remained undisturbed. *The Empty Canvas* by Alberto Moravia and Joseph Heller's *Catch-22* were banned by the Censorship Board, a kind of curious, inverted literary prize; it seemed that while prize committees abroad ignored or overlooked the occasional literary aspirant, the Irish censorship was infallibly comprehensive. Bishop Lucey of Cork, however, did not agree. He felt that censorship was not stringent enough, and called for open trial by jury of prosecutions which could be brought either by the state or an individual. He resented the fact that the existing legislation was presented to the world by 'our liberals, anti-Catholics and pornographers as a censorship destroying all real freedom of expression'.

Some kind of advance was registered by the successful production in the Eblana Theatre, Dublin, of Tennessee Williams's *The Rose Tattoo* without any of the constabulary antics which marked the Pike's production of the play five years before. The largest variety theatre in Britain or Ireland, Dublin's Royal, closed for the last time at the end of June. In November the sixteen-year-old schoolgirl pop star, Helen Shapiro, who had a huge hit in 1962 with 'Please Don't Treat Me Like a Child', played to an excited Dublin audience, whose whole world was about to be revolutionised by a funny-looking Liverpool quartet who had released a single called 'Love Me Do' a few weeks before.

The *Evening Mail*, first published in 1823, went out of business in 1962. It was speculated that Harland & Wolff, in deep financial trouble, was about to be taken over by Aristotle Onassis. Prices, as always, went to hell: the small whiskey up to 2s 2d; the cost of posting a letter up a penny to 4d; the pint of stout, after two increases in a few months, up to 1s 10d. A new, economical car, the Renault 4, was launched at £489 10s 0d. Hire purchase was a major growth area, with the total HP indebtedness rising to a staggering £30 million. Materialism was upon us with a vengeance.

One of the more bizarre controverises of the sixties gathered speed in 1962. The Minister for Health, the doughty Seán MacEntee, proposed to legalise the artificial increase of fluoride in drinking water to a level of one part in one million in the public supply. A body called the Pure Water Association had been formed to oppose what they regarded as 'a grave hazard to health'. The legislation was enacted in December 1961, and the ministerial order enabling fluoridation to proceed was duly signed. Dublin Corporation was not so sure. They were sensitive to the views and votes of the Pure Water Association, and in October 1962 they met to discuss the issue. MacEntee made it plain before the meeting that he was not impressed by their deliberations; suspecting an anti-fluoridation majority, he decided to head them off at the pass: 'Where the public health is concerned, a partisan majority in a subordinate authority cannot be allowed to flout the law and defy the Oireachtas.' In the event, the fluoridation proposal was carried by twenty-two votes to fifteen, but not before one of the most outspoken opponents of the scheme, Mr Richie Ryan, TD, had shouted of the fluoridators: 'Let them stand up and be counted with the murderers of the children of Dublin.' More reasonably, Mr Ryan could not understand why those who wished to take fluoride for their teeth could not be offered fluoride tablets, without forcing the entire community to ingest the substance along with them. There was a breach of personal rights involved here, in Mr Ryan's view. Mr Ryan, in his non-political incarnation as a solicitor, was acting for Mrs Gladys Ryan (no relation) in an action against the Attorney-General in which she sought a High Court declaration that the Fluoridation Act was unconstitutional. We shall hear more of the fluoridation saga in due course.

On 26 February 1962 the Irish Republican Army formally abandoned the border campaign begun in December 1956. The decision, in the words of the Irish Republican Publicity Bureau's statement, was taken

in view of the general situation. Foremost among the factors motivating this course of action has been the attitude of the general public whose minds have been deliberately distracted from the supreme issue facing the Irish people — the unity and freedom of Ireland.

This was a rhetorical death-rattle. The futile military antics of the IRA belonged to the blighted Ireland of the fifties. In a country where reality had offered nothing but despair and emigration, the fantasy of destroying partition was a comforting opiate. It was exciting: all those old shibboleths. It was idealistic: the recovery of the fourth green field. A fierce tribal innocence informed the border campaign, but by 1962 the culture which had bred the IRA was moving beyond innocence. The South was growing prosperous; it was bidding for a place in Europe. Ireland in the early 1960s had no use for these juvenile *banditti*. It wished to conduct itself like a mature nation state, not like a turbulent offshore island. It seemed that the shadow of the gunman had disappeared at last from Irish life, for, as one historian of the IRA wrote,

The Army was a husk — its strength eroded, its purpose lost, its future unclear. Sinn Féin lay shattered on the far shore of Irish politics, without power or prospects, still a captive of the principle of abstentionism. ... In Dublin the *United Irishman* faced rising debts and declining circulation. ... In the spring of 1962 the greatest danger to the Movement was not despair but disintegration.[1]

The most important new event in Irish life in 1962 was the inauguration of the domestic television service. The service began transmission at 7 p.m. on New Year's Eve 1961, with an address by President de Valera. Thus did the presiding spirit of an older, safer Ireland usher in the troublesome and unpredictable medium which — even if all other considerations were put aside — would ensure that his vision of a rural arcadia was about to be dashed for ever. Television was to prove a steady conduit for a predominantly urban and cosmopolitan set of images, not as individually powerful as its detractors feared, but insidious in their cumulative effect. There was, certainly, a note of apprehension in the President's opening remarks:

I must admit that sometimes when I think of television and radio and their immense power, I feel somewhat afraid. ... Never before was there in the hands of man an instrument so powerful to influence the thoughts and actions of the multitude. A persistent policy pursued over radio and television, in addition to imparting knowledge, can build up the character of a whole people, including sturdiness and vigour and confidence. On the other hand, it can lead, through demoralisation, to decadence and dissolution.

In the very first hour of the new year Cardinal D'Alton of Armagh appeared on the screen to welcome the new service. He was, like the President, in his late seventies, and a living symbol of a passing world. He too sounded an anxious note. He warned parents not to allow their children to become television addicts, no matter how meritorious a particular programme might be. He had been relieved, along with others, he said, when Mr Eamonn Andrews had been named chairman of the Radio Éireann Authority, in view of Mr Andrews's declaration, in the course of an address on Irish television at the Gormanston Summer School, that he would be very unhappy to sponsor anything which might be corrupting or could cause scandal. The Cardinal was sure that Mr Andrews and Mr Roth, the director-general, would as far as possible provide programmes which would be enlightening, entertaining, would reflect high ideals, and would not present viewers with a caricature of Irish life 'such as we have had from our writers in recent years'.

Lemass, on the other hand, appeared to have few qualms about the new service. Speaking to the guests at a celebration banquet in the Gresham Hotel, he offered the view that the Irish people were citizens of the world as well as of Ireland, and that there were standards, aims and values which transcended national frontiers and were universal in their application. The reasonable needs of the Irish people, who looked forward to receiving information and cultural programmes of merit as well as entertainment from the national broadcasting service, would not be satisfied by programmes of local origin. He believed that it was now generally accepted that world events, new ideas, and developments everywhere — including such things as sporting events and new trends in fashion — would be of direct and immediate interest to Irish people. In satisfying the understandable and healthy demand for information on these subjects, the Taoiseach hoped that the television service would adhere to proper standards and would have a proper regard for our national values.

The contrast in tone between the Taoiseach on the one hand and the President and the Cardinal on the other hardly needs to be underlined. Traditional Ireland had been uneasy at the coming of television, and its chief political and ecclesiastical voices had now articulated their worries on the opening night. Once regular programmes began, it was quick to discover that its suspicions were justified.

Within a fortnight of the opening of the service, the first complaint that there was an inadequate number of programmes in Irish was voiced, in the Irish-language paper *Comhar*. There was no future for Telefís Éireann, in

Ireland first entered the Eurovision Song Contest in 1965 with a song called 'Walkin' the Streets in the Rain' sung by Butch Moore **(above)** *. The Nolan family of Tolka Row* **(right below)** *became Ireland's first television soap opera family, while the Late Late Show* **(right above)** *has been running for so long now that it is possible to reproduce a picture of Gay Byrne with no grey hairs.*

Comhar's view, if it merely continued to imitate British and American television.

On the other hand, it was difficult to see what future the service might have if it were to rely on a programme-planning policy which would meet with the approval of *Comhar*. Telefís Éireann inhabited the world of commerce, where cultural prescriptions, however desirable in the abstract, had to be dispensed very sparingly, lest they kill the patient. It relied on advertising revenue; the larger concentrations of population lay along the east coast, where British television could already be received; the necessity to capture a large, popular audience and to demonstrate to advertisers that it could be held firm was of primary importance to Telefís Éireann. Cultural proselytism would have ruined the service, because it would have alienated the viewers. The first Television Audience Measurement (TAM) ratings were issued in May 1962; since not all the booster stations throughout the country were ready, the survey was confined to the area covered by the Kippure transmitter, including Dublin. Apart from the main evening news, which was the most popular programme, only one other home-produced programme, Paddy Crosbie's 'The School Around the Corner', featured in the top ten. For the rest, sadly but unsurprisingly, it was canned American stuff all the way: 'Dr Christian' and 'Dragnet', for example, were in second and third positions respectively. Nor did this relationship of home- to foreign-produced programmes change greatly during the decade: popular imported drama and situation comedy continued to hold a commanding position in Irish TAM ratings. 'The Fugitive' had the whole country by the ears in the second half of the sixties, and there were remarkably few people out of doors on the night when the final episode was broadcast.

In time TE developed its own skills in episodic popular drama. 'Tolka Row', set in a Dublin working-class suburb, was its first success, and it followed this with 'The Riordans', set on a farm in Co. Kilkenny, which ran until the late 1970s, when it was taken off amid storms of protest. Both series were distinguished by fine writing and acting and a habit of raising awkward social and moral issues of the kind that seldom got discussed before a mass audience in the age before television. The unique 'Late Late Show' started on Friday nights in the summer of 1962, and in October 1963 transferred to the Saturday-night position which it still occupies — and which it seems set to continue occupying when every other chat show in the world is one with Nineveh and Tyre.

Successful home-produced programmes tended to be local variations on an international theme. The platitudinous injunction contained in the Broadcasting Act (1960), that the Authority would 'keep constantly in mind the national aims on national language and culture', proved impossible to carry into practice. This point was candidly acknowledged by Edward Roth, in his final interview as director-general, in January 1963. There was, he observed, a wide divergence between the requirement of the act and the necessity to provide a commercial service. Furthermore, the tension between ideal and reality was to lead in time to the resignation of the other founding father of the television service, Eamonn Andrews. When he quit as director-general in May 1966, he said that the emphasis being placed on Irish-language programmes could lead to a loss of communication with audiences.

This question led to the first highly publicised resignation from the new service. Within six months of the opening of TE, Ernest Byrne, the only Irish person employed in a senior production position, resigned because he was unable to urge a 'distinctly Irish flavour' on his superiors. This affair drew an oblique comment from Micheál Mac Carthaigh, president of the Gaelic League, at a special Ard-Fheis held by the organisation in June 1962 to reaffirm its television policy. Deploring the absence of a positive policy in TE towards Irish language and culture, he wondered if the right sort of people were in charge, people who understood the traditions of the country.

But the brutal fact was that TE was a commerical television service, and the Irish language and culture were simply not popular. As ever, there was an ocean of goodwill towards the language, exceeded only by a determination not to speak it or to listen to anyone else speaking it if that could be avoided.

The protests from Irish-language supporters gathered force in the course of 1962 and have rumbled on consistently ever since. Some of these — as in the case of Dónall Ó Moráin, president of Gael-Linn — had as much to do with the vulgarity of commercial television and a defence of the principles of public service broadcasting, but in the main were concentrated on the central cultural point. Unflattering comparisons were made between TE and BBC Wales. And TE could certainly give ammunition to their critics. Daniel Corkery, author of *The Hidden Ireland* and a passionate Gaelic revivalist, died at the end of 1964. When, in April 1965, Seán Ó Tuama of UCC asked a TE researcher if the station proposed to broadcast a memorial tribute, he was met with a simple question: 'Who is Daniel Corkery?' Ó Tuama was moved to denounce TE as

a smooth strip of cosmopolitan desert where suave gentlemen congregate who know more about what makes the Beatles pop than what makes the pulse of Ireland beat.

It was a bitter experience for *gaelgoirí*. They had had every reason to fear television as an agent of anglicisation, and while their rush to criticism suggested a defensive mentality born of extreme suspicion, it did appear that their worst fears were being confirmed. Television was a new technology, and in 1962 Ireland did not have sufficient trained personnel to man the new operation. The service was obliged to draw on many foreigners or returned exiles, particularly in senior positions: the first director-general and the first two controllers of programmes were foreigners. Like any new technology, television bred a rather clannish *esprit de corps* among its practitioners, while outsiders regarded it with a mixture of fascination and resentment wholly conducive to the discovery of plots and conspiracies against whatever it was that the observer held dear. Finally, the native personnel employed by the station tended to be of above average education; TE became a 'glamour' employer and quickly conformed to an established international pattern by creaming off the brightest university graduates, particularly among editorial and production staffs. In Ireland in the 1960s this meant a disproportionate number of people from an urban, middle-class background, precisely the background reckoned to be least friendly to Gaelic culture.

The television service was the most obvious example of a pattern that ran through the decade. Before the 1960s a great many of the country's bright and enterprising people had emigrated, in the absence of any future for them at home. Now there *was* a future for them at home, with an expanding economy and a genuine sense of optimism about the future. The vigour of Irish social and intellectual life in the 1960s owed much to their staying. Busy, restless, ambitious people, well educated and more impressed by the frankly materialist cultures of the major capitalist countries than it was thought proper for Irish people to be, they were unlikely to be satisfied with the complacent certainties that had passed for social thought in Ireland for two generations.

Mr Oliver J. Flanagan, TD, summed it up a few years later in the best-remembered Irish bull of the decade. He told the nation on 'The Late Late Show' that 'there was no sex in Ireland before television', and everyone knew what he meant.

The treatment of Irish on television remains a delicate and potentially explosive subject. It is not reasonable to suggest that there was a deliberate conspiracy in TE against the language. Indeed, a substantial case can be made out to the contrary, not least in respect of programmes designed to bring modern language learning techniques to bear on the teaching of Irish to a mass audience. But the circumstances of the time in which the station was established, combined with the international orientation of the medium itself, made it inevitable that it would be perceived by Irish-Irelanders as a hostile force. The most that can be fairly charged against it in respect of the language is that it hastened a process of decline that had been visible and unbroken since before the foundation of the state. As against that, it would be a mistake to underestimate the role of television in promoting the extraordinary revival in traditional music — the most accessible area of Gaelic culture — during the 1960s.

Television was a metaphor. It was the most blatant, and yet the most intimate, agent of that international culture which offered a direct threat to the official culture of Irish-Ireland. It was cast in a commercial mould and, in order to survive financially, was forced to give people what they wanted. People made it clear what they wanted from the start, and their choice revealed the gap between the official image of the Irish people and the reality. That revelation was the critical achievement of Irish television in the 1960s. It forced us to look at ourselves anew. We may not have liked all we saw, but at least we saw ourselves as we actually were, making real choices in the real world. It was a painful business for the cultural acolytes of traditional Ireland, wedded as they were to a view of the Irish that owed more to the characterisations of nationalist intellectuals than to the living behaviour of real people. Out of that conflict came the possibility of national self-knowledge and national maturity.

On 24 January 1962 Paul Singer was acquitted on eight counts of fraudulently converting moneys invested in Shanahan's Stamp Auctions. After a trial of forty-seven days in the Central Criminal Court, Mr Justice Walsh directed that the prosecution had failed to prove its case beyond a reasonable doubt, and Singer walked out of the Four Courts, a free man. It was a sensational verdict, for the public had long considered Singer guilty of a massive fraud.

Shanahan's Stamp Auctions Ltd was founded in October 1954. The Shanahan family had been in the furniture business, but decided to venture into a new and, it was to be hoped, more profitable, enterprise upon meeting Singer, a philatelist. Money invested by the public would be used to buy stamps abroad. These would then be sold by public auction at the company's Dún Laoghaire premises. The profits generated from the sales would benefit both company and investors. Singer was the technical expert; he produced the catalogues and other publicity inducements to the public aimed at securing new investors or encouraging existing ones to increase their investment. He dealt with the company's accountants and did all the stamp buying abroad.

The company collapsed in May 1959. In the following January three of the four principals were returned for trial on two charges of conspiracy and thirty-seven of fraudulent conversion. They were Singer, his wife Irma, and the company secretary, Arthur D. Shanahan. Shanahan's father was released, it being held that there was no *prima facie* case against him.

Arthur Shanahan was tried and found guilty on seventeen counts of fraud and conspiracy in the summer of 1960. The jury, having deliberated for just over six hours, added a rider recommending leniency. The summing up of Mr Justice McLaughlin had been suggestive. He noted that the prosecution alleged that from an early date the company had carried on a colossal fraud in a barefaced manner; but he added that the jury had to consider the state of mind of Arthur Shanahan, having regard to his capacity, intelligence, statements, evidence and actions. Regarding Paul Singer's personality, the judge observed that the jury might find him very domineering, and very forceful and brutal in some of his acts. They should bear these facts in mind in reaching their verdict. Clearly judge and jury were of one mind, for although Shanahan was held to be technically guilty, he received a sentence of a mere fifteen months on all counts, to run concurrently, although the total sum involved in the charges was £846,000. The judge offered his quite explicit opinion, when pronouncing sentence, that Shanahan had been unduly influenced by Singer, into whose criminal schemes he had been inexorably sucked.

There was considerable public sympathy for Shanahan, a young man with a family, and the lenient sentence was applauded. Singer, by now established as the villain of the piece, was confidently assumed to be facing a long prison sentence. His trial came on in November 1960, and he was found guilty and sentenced to fourteen years' penal servitude. Sentence had been deferred for a week after conviction to give Singer the opportunity of informing the liquidator of Shanahans Ltd about the whereabouts of the money, to which, in the opinion of Mr Justice Haugh, Singer alone had access. It was established in court that £1,086,794 was paid to Singer out of investors' money and lodged by him in various foreign banks, mainly in Zurich. A further £388,930 was given to him by the company over the same period, and no proper explanation of why all this money was transferred from Dublin was offered by the defendant. Singer claimed that all the money had been used for legitimate company business, and that since there were, therefore, no huge sums lying in foreign banks, he could not be of any help to the liquidator. Thus defiant, he was led off to Mountjoy, and proceeded to lodge an appeal.

His conviction was overturned in the Court of Criminal Appeal in June 1961. Incredibly, the foreman of the original jury had been a victim of the alleged offences, and in consequence Singer was held not to have had a fair trial. He had claimed, as his grounds for appeal, that the foreman had not only been an investor and a claimant on the company's assets, but that he was also a member of a firm of accountants whose senior partner was the liquidator of the company! A retrial was ordered, and Singer was released on bail.

The Singers and the Shanahans at one of the
lavish parties which Shanahan Stamp
Auctions used to throw in the days before the
bubble burst. Also in a party mood (right),
Paul Singer appears to be enjoying himself at
the 1959 staff party. A few weeks later, the
company was in the hands of the liquidator.

The second trial took place in the final days of 1961 and the start of 1962. This time there were only eight counts, as there was judged to have been a considerable amount of overlap in the original list of charges. The sum involved in the first trial had been similar to that in the case of Shanahan: the principal charge referred to an amount of about £800,000. But since the count which included this main sum of money was one of those which duplicated other counts in the indictment, it was quashed by the court as 'bad for duplicity'; in other words, it was inadmissable because of duplication. So Singer was never tried a second time on this critical central issue. As Seán Lemass admitted in the Dáil when the whole affair was over, the matters concerned were not properly tried on their merits. This monumental piece of legal incompetence formed the backdrop of the Singer retrial.

Even when the trial came on, the prosecution was unable to prove beyond reasonable doubt that investors' money had been misappropriated. Their case was entirely circumstantial, and Singer was accordingly released. There was a howl of outrage from the public, many disturbed editorials, and questions in the Dáil. There was a widespread feeling that a foreign shyster had twice escaped justice on a technicality, while his duped Irish accomplice had been sent to prison. The legal profession had been made to look ridiculous, for they had appeared to mismanage the prosecution of Singer from first to last, while he had brought his defence — which he conducted himself, pleading poverty — to a triumphant conclusion.

He basked in his triumph. Certainly he would co-operate fully with the hearings of the Bankruptcy Court, which was investigating the affairs of Shanahan's Stamp Auctions Ltd. Of course he wanted to stay in Ireland, 'if the people will have me', although he did first expect to visit his aged mother in Canada. He expressed the hope that the investors in the company would all eventually be paid off as the stamps still held in Ireland and some that had been recovered abroad were sold off by the liquidator.

When the Shanahan liquidation hearing came on in the Bankruptcy Court on 12 February, there was no sign of Paul Singer. His Canadian address was given. A week later there was still no sign of him, and Mrs Irma Singer, who had remained in Dublin, was ordered to attend the court on 5 March. The day dawned, but, as if by sorcery, Mrs Singer had now also disappeared! Two months later the examination of Paul Singer was adjourned indefinitely.

On that very day, 7 May 1962, by a macabre coincidence, Arthur Shanahan was the subject of another conviction. He had completed his sentence in Dublin and taken his family to England in the hope of a fresh start. But their lives had been blighted and a pall of tragedy fell upon them. Their two young children were neglected to the point where they had to be taken into care, for they were 'just skin and bone', in the words of a hospital sister. The parents were tried for child neglect and convicted. And so, on the very day that Irish justice finally despaired of reaching Paul Singer, Arthur and Diana Shanahan were sentenced to six months each by a court in Kingston, Surrey, for the neglect of their children.

All through 1962 Lemass and his cabinet hammered relentlessly at a single point in their public speeches: the necessity to readjust every aspect of national life in order to meet the challenge of free trade and Europe. On 26 April the Taoiseach told a conference held by the Institute of Public Administration in Killarney:

The industrial producer whose equipment, organisation and sales methods may have been good enough in the conditions of a protected market and who fails to adjust to the new conditions with sufficient speed and thoroughness; the farmer who still thinks of farming only as a traditional way of life and not as a business enterprise in which the maximum utilisation of resources, modern productivity techniques and new methods of marketing his output are as as essential as in any other kind of competitive business; the trade union leader who is still thinking in terms of the defensive campaign of the Victorian era and not of labour's vital interest in productivity and expansion — all these by 1970 will have become anachronistic relics of a dead past.

Speeches in a similar vein followed: to the Irish Management Institute in May; at the opening of the Wavin Pipes factory in Balbriggan, Co. Dublin, in June ('it is good to be alive at this period in the history of the world . . .'); to the annual dinner of the Cork Chamber of Commerce in November, when he suggested plainly that company directors who viewed rapid change with distaste should 'consider whether they have not outlived their usefulness and decide to pass their responsibilities over to younger men'; and to a succession of industrial and political meetings in every corner of Ireland.

But would our European commitments have any political or military aspects? This was a highly sensitive point. Ireland had remained neutral during the Second World War, in what was the clearest possible confirmation of the country's independence from Britain. Since the end of the war we had pointedly refrained from having anything to do with the North Atlantic Treaty Organisation. It was not that Ireland was neutral in the ideological sense as between East and West. On the contrary, the country was ferociously anti-communist, as might be expected of a staunchly conservative Catholic people. But as long as partition existed, Ireland felt unable to join any military alliance which included the United Kingdom. The question now was: would the EEC extract concessions on political and military sovereignty from Ireland as a pre-condition for membership? If

Ireland joined, she would be the only country in the Community which was not a member of NATO. As things were, the Irish case was proceeding slowly in Brussels, and a majority of member countries felt that there was a *prima facie* case against full Irish membership on the grounds of economic under-development.*

Was there a possibility that, in the hard bargaining to come, neutrality would be forced onto the table as a negotiating point? It seems that Lemass at least considered the possibility. He took the trouble to fly a kite in order to test public reaction to the idea that neutrality might no longer be considered non-negotiable. On 5 February 1962 the Minister for Lands, Micheál Ó Moráin, addressed the Chamber of Commerce in his native Castlebar, Co. Mayo. He said that while the economic implications of EEC membership had received much attention, the political implications had not. It would be unrealistic, he said, to ignore the fact that all the members of the Community were in NATO and that neutrality in the face of post-war East/West divisions had never been envisaged by the Irish people. In the context of the divisions between communism and the free world, 'neutrality ... is not a policy to which we would even wish to appear committed'.

Not surprisingly, public reaction to this was heated. There was an assumption that Lemass had put Ó Moráin up to it, for the Taoiseach was a past master of testing public opinion in this way. Besides, Lemass was a cabinet disciplinarian and had little time for ministers who made public statements on matters outside their departmental concern. It is inconceivable that he would not have known and approved of Ó Moráin's speech, hinting as it did at a fundamental change in Irish foreign policy.

Having thus raised the issue, the Minister for Lands then disposed of it in the classic manner associated with kite-flying. He claimed to have been misreported. For good measure, he blamed the *Irish Times*, never a bad move for a West of Ireland Fianna Fáil TD. He denied that he had said or suggested that the government was going to take the country into NATO, and he pointed out that an EEC spokesman had categorically stated that NATO membership was *not* a prerequisite for EEC membership. All he had said (he said) was that there were no countries in the EEC who were not members of NATO, and that Ireland was not neutral on the question of communist imperialism. And was not that merely a statement of the facts? What was all the fuss about?

But the matter did not die there. Eight months later Lemass himself took a hand. He told a West German audience that Ireland's reasons for applying to

---

*It was significant that the original letter from the ministerial council of the EEC to the Irish government, suggesting talks on the Irish application, did not 'welcome' the application. Only Germany and Holland favoured the inclusion of such a word; the other four nations were opposed.

join the EEC were primarily political: 'Our desire is to participate in whatever political union may ultimately be developed in Europe. We are making no reservations of any sort, including defence.' This caused the furore to revive. Members of all political parties, not least the traditionalists in Fianna Fáil itself, were alarmed; the Labour Party tabled a series of Dáil questions on foreign and defence policy. In reply to these, Lemass blandly assured the house that there was nothing in the Treaty of Rome which entailed any defence obligations, and that Ireland had not been requested by member states to join any military alliance.

It was an indication of the extent to which the ground was moving under the feet of traditional Ireland that a Fianna Fáil Taoiseach could publicly contemplate bargaining with the country's neutrality. Whether it would have happened, or been allowed to happen, or whether it would ever have been raised in serious negotiations, are now purely speculative questions. Two months after Lemass's statement to the Dáil, de Gaulle's veto on Britain's application for EEC membership rendered the whole affair academic.

Finally, the event which, in the opinion of many, was to have the most profound and pervasive effect on Irish life and the Irish mind in the 1960s began on 11 October 1962. Like so much else in the decade, it came from beyond our own shores. On that day, amid the incomparable splendour of St Peter's in Rome, Pope John XXIII opened the Second Vatican Council.

Chapter Five

1963

Faith and fatherland

Among those who cling to their opinion are some who are called 'obstinate', being people on whom argument is more or less wasted. They bear a general resemblance to the incontinent such as the reckless spender bears to the liberal man, and the hotheaded to the brave. But at several points they differ. The continent man is not driven from his position by passion and desire; he will on occasion prove open to conviction. The obstinate man, however, is not influenced by argument.   ARISTOTLE

> Royal Charlie's now awa,
> Safely owre the friendly main;
> Mony a heart will break in twa,
> Should he ne'er come back again.
>   Will ye no' come back again?
>   Will ye no' come back again?
>   Better lo'ed ye'll never be,
>   And will ye no' come back again?
>   ANONYMOUS

THE winter of 1962-63 was one of the worst on record. The new year began with a massive cold spell enveloping the whole of Europe, extending as far as Madrid and Greece. It gave the Irish, with their national weakness for discussing the weather, some new themes beside 'soft day' and 'sure, the rain might keep off'. Powerscourt waterfall froze over, and there were skaters on the pond in Dublin Zoo for the first time since 1947. Snowdrifts cut off thousands of people in isolated areas and finally convinced the government of the necessity to introduce the country's first helicopter relief patrols.

The government itself survived two major crises in 1963, both of which had seemed likely to topple it. On 8 February it published a white paper entitled *Closing the Gap*, in which it proposed to consult the National Employer/Labour Conference on ways of relating future income rises to increases in productivity. 'An obligation rests on all sections of the community not to jeopardise economic progress by pressing for higher incomes or profits until national production can support such increases.' A peremptory halt was announced to all claims for better pay and conditions in the public sector 'which would arouse expectations of similar increases in other employments'.

The reaction of the trade unions was swift and hostile. They claimed that the government should have consulted the National Employer/Labour Conference in advance, rather than unilaterally setting the agenda for later meetings; they pointed out that no country in the world had succeeded in pinning wages to productivity: the ICTU was sufficiently angered to withdraw all its representatives from government-sponsored bodies. The white paper, it claimed, was 'weighted against workers'. Furthermore, ICTU charged the government with disrupting the recognised machinery of bargaining, conciliation and arbitration.

This caused Lemass to retreat. He had worked hard to integrate the leadership of the trade union movement into the national decision-making process and had no wish to drive them back to the margins of Irish political life. He described ICTU's statement as constructive, and he offered to meet representatives of Congress and the employers to discuss 'any practical alternative' to the white paper. He was quick to deny any suggestion of a general wage freeze. Before February was out he was telling the Dublin Chamber of Commerce of the necessity for profit restraint *pari passu* with wage restraint; it was a speech directed less at his immediate audience than at trade unionists outside. At the end of April he made a highly publicised Dáil speech in which he said that the time had arrived for national policy to take 'a shift to the left'; he called for more positive measures of government intervention to ensure that economic progress was converted into social progress. This was just talk, but it served its purpose of mollifying the unions.

Both sides had left the door open. As the year went on, the pressure increased for a settlement of the wage problem; Lemass was to find himself, in due course, moving a long way from his position of February, when his main concern had been to arrest the inflationary wage increases that had been a feature of 1961 and 1962. But by budget day, in late April, another, related, problem had arisen.

Since 1959, government spending had been rising at a faster rate than tax revenue. The cost of public services rose to record levels in 1963, and the Minister for Finance was faced with a budget deficit of £13 million; in those days this was considered an alarming prospect. In the budget the minister, Dr James Ryan, introduced a $2\frac{1}{2}$ per cent turnover tax on retail sales and services. It was expected to raise £10.5 million in its first full year.

The proposal drew a lot of criticism. Some economists argued that a considerable degree of tax buoyancy could be expected anyway in 1964 and that to add the turnover tax to this would leave the government awash with money which it might be tempted to spend in an electorally popular way. Trade union and general opinion focused on the fact that more than half the revenue which the tax would generate would come from essentials, like food, clothing and fuel.

The Dáil vote on the turnover tax came in the second half of June, and there was much talk of a government defeat. It was felt that the independents, on whom Lemass relied, would abandon the ship rather than court the sort of unpopularity attached to support for the new tax. On the Saturday before the vote one of them, Frank Sherwin, declared for the government. Immediately Dublin members of RGDATA announced that they would march to his house in Linenhall Street to protest. 'They can come if they like,' said Frank. 'I won't be in. I'm never in on a Saturday night.' A couple of days later another independent, Joe Leneghan, a colourful and flamboyant character from West Mayo, also declared his support for the government. The turnover tax proposal was carried by one vote.

Its effect was immediately felt. Between August and November alone the consumer price index rose by 5 per cent. The Labour Party put down a Dáil motion of no confidence in late October, and this time, for a while, there was something approaching certainty that the government was finished. Labour were so sure that the best Fianna Fáil could possibly hope for was a tied vote that they took the unprecedented step of telling the Ceann Comhairle, Patrick Hogan, a member of the Labour Party, to vote against the government in such circumstances. Hogan was non-committal; his office was above politics, and there was no way he could be made subject to a party whip. In the event, support for the motion evaporated, four independents stuck by Fianna Fáil, and that was that.

But the increase in the cost of living meant that the attitude the government had first struck in *Closing the Gap* was no longer realistic. Talk of wage restraint was bound to fall on deaf ears. Instead Lemass made a novel suggestion in November when he proposed discussions on a general wage increase, to be negotiated nationally, whose terms would take account of the effects of the turnover tax as well as of the expected rate of economic growth in the coming year. But the thinking behind the white paper had not been abandoned; Lemass still hoped to avoid the sort of inflationary increases which had weakened the competitive position of Irish industry in recent years. The leading authority on the events that followed has written of Lemass's feelings at this time:

It is clear from his statements in Dáil Éireann on the adjournment debate in December that he saw in such an agreement a beginning — a beginning of an orderly system of national bargaining which would keep wages and expectations within the limits of national production.[1]

The trade unions were still suspicious and resented what they regarded as yet another unilateral intrusion by the Taoiseach into the area of wage bargaining. But the tide was running against such resistance. There was a widespread feeling that an 8 per cent rise would be proper; economists, the Federation of Irish Industry, and the Irish Exporters' Association had all endorsed such a figure. The negotiations began.

ICTU said that it would recommend 14 per cent to its member unions. This alarmed the employers, who were prepared to go to 10 per cent but no further. Their real fear was that the unions were not really of a mind to settle, that the talks would collapse, and that the sort of percentages under discussion — which were quite large by contemporary standards — would become the unions' base figure for the free-for-all that would follow. This would give the employers the worst of both worlds: a high settlement *and* industrial trouble. By mid-December things appeared to have reached an impasse. But just before Christmas the two sides agreed to return to the table, the employers having been coaxed by Lemass. In returning, they implicitly sold the pass on the 10 per cent. On New Year's Day 1964 agreement was reached at 12 per cent, to run for two years, with a further six months for review.

There was much confidence that a new era had dawned in Irish industrial relations. Here, it seemed, was a rational, ordered structure for the determination of wage and salary levels. The unions, for all their chagrin during 1963, had ended by making a very good bargain; the employers, although unhappy at the way the extra money was squeezed out of them in the end, could look forward to two and a half years of industrial peace and assured continuity of production; the government was best pleased, having achieved its coveted national wage agreement and mended its fences with the unions. The agreement, said Lemass, signalled the end of the old idea of class war and the start of a new era of partnership. He added that he was confident that it would change the mainly defensive attitudes of the trade union movement.

Just how cruel a disappointment the agreement proved to be for all sides will be seen in future chapters.

For the Catholic Church in Ireland, 1963 was a year of readjustment. Cardinal D'Alton died in February and was replaced as Archbishop of Armagh in September by William Conway. The new Primate's first message to his people was couched in language not usually associated with Irish bishops: he spoke of 'a certain sense of spring in the air through the Church as a whole and, if I mistake not, in Ireland also'. The Vatican Council was moving towards concepts strange to the Irish Church. The introduction of lay involvement in the liturgy and the proposed use of the vernacular were to have far-reaching consequences, not least in the area of church architecture, where the traditional, Victorian Gothic style was quickly to be superseded: it

Cardinal Conway, seen here with the Church of Ireland Archbishop of Dublin, Dr George Simms (left). Meetings of this kind became more and more frequent as the spirit of ecumenism spread through the Irish Churches. Cardinal Conway was an enthusiastic ecumenist, at least by Irish episcopal standards, and his open, courteous and informal manner did much to break down traditional barriers and allay traditional suspicions. Not all his brother bishops were quite as enthusiastic as he, however, and the tendency to regard Protestantism as a hydra-headed heresy was only slowly put aside by the more conservative members of the hierarchy. But in general the 1960s was a good decade for ecumenism in Ireland, and for this Cardinal Conway is due a great deal of the credit. He also presided over the subtle adaptation of the Irish Catholic Church to radically altered social circumstances. Within his own sphere, he was very much a moderniser.

raised too many acoustic problems and visual distractions to be suitable for an age of liturgical mass participation. There was a noticeable softening of tone in the Lenten pastorals of 1963: Bishop O'Doherty of Dromore praised the world media for its coverage of the Council; Bishop Rodgers of Killaloe deplored the 'scandal' of Christian disunity and quoted the Pope on the brotherhood of all Christians; Bishop Ahern of Cloyne noted the ecumenical intention of the Council, although he was at pains to stress that it was not its only aim. His neighbouring prelate, the redoubtable Bishop Lucey, was, however, not impressed, doubting if the Council would produce 'anything sensational' and failing to see where the Catholic Church had room to compromise in the interests of ecumenism on fundamental matters of faith and morals.

Ecumenism was the issue on which divisions between progressives and conservatives in the Irish Church were most readily discernible. Differences in language and tone of voice were suggestive, and in this regard the accession of Cardinal Conway to the see of Armagh was a watershed in the history of the Catholic Church in Ireland. In January 1964 the first octave of prayer for church unity following his consecration emphasised the differences neatly. In the archdiocese of Dublin Archbishop John Charles McQuaid, the most formidable and intelligent of the conservatives, summed up the octave thus:

Catholics throughout the Church unite in what is called the octave of unity at this season to pray for the intentions of the Holy Father that Christians separated in doctrine and discipline from the Holy See may, at length, by the Grace of God, rejoin the true Church of Christ.

Cardinal Conway's observations on the octave were less flinty. Although affirming that the Catholic Church 'is deeply conscious of the fact that . . . Christ has entrusted the fullness of divine truth to her', he stated his own desire to lessen misunderstanding and prejudice, and spoke of disunity not in terms of schism or heresy but of 'neighbours falling out'. He noted the virtues of Protestants: 'They have the mark of Christ upon them from baptism. . . . How could we do otherwise than feel kinship with them?'

One should not, of course, exaggerate the extent of Cardinal Conway's liberalism. In November 1964 he told the Vatican Council that mixed marriages 'are not desirable and . . . people should be dissuaded from them'. Liberalism is relative.

The changes that were already visible over the horizon would increasingly leave the more conservative bishops beating the air. Not that a new liberalism and populism was about to sweep unopposed through the Church in Ireland; but the atrophied, authoritarian, changeless face of Irish

Catholicism, which had reflected so much else in the society in which it had been most comfortable, had begun to pass away. Lay participation, churches built in the modern style, folk masses, a revolution in seminary life, a listening clergy as well as a preaching clergy, and, most significant of all, the progressive softening of the old ecclesiastical voices, with their jeremiads about the moral corruption of the world: there lay the immediate future for the Church.

Pope John XXIII, the author of this revolution, died, in great suffering, in June, mourned by the whole world for his holiness and joy-in-life. Less than two months earlier his final encyclical, *Pacem in terris*, had been published. It had called for a ban on all nuclear weapons, condemned all racism and the settlement of disputes by force, and endorsed without the least ambiguity the rights of workers all over the world. It repeated the approval, first stated in *Mater et magistra*, for the general principles of the welfare state, and acknowledged that doctrines which have their sources in error (such as socialism) can in time change and 'contain elements that are positive and deserving of approval'.

The effect of John XXIII's brief pontificate on the Irish Church was explosive. It transformed the context of Church life, emphasising ecumenism, change and renewal, and open discussion. It humanised the Church, but robbed it of that mantle of Olympian authority which had been its outstanding characteristic. Henceforth the Church would be contending with other, secular, voices of authority in Ireland. The success with which it maintained its pre-eminent position in Irish life, despite the shattering of its old *persona*, is one of the most instructive features of the second half of the decade.

The pace of change in Irish life was quickening. In June the first section of the Dublin/Naas dual carriageway was opened, the first such road in the Republic. The number of cars on Irish roads had doubled since the mid-fifties. Esso developed an enormously successful advertising campaign ('Put a Tiger in Your Tank') aimed at the ever-growing motor market; the slogan was later picked up by James Dillon, TD, who dubbed the Fine Gael liberals the 'Young Tigers', a name that stuck. Road freight also expanded, especially in the Dublin area, following the end of a dispute about containerisation in Dublin port which had lasted for years. While the Dublin dockers had kept their backs to the future by banning all container traffic through the port, the little port of Greenore, Co. Louth, had exploited the opportunity by equipping itself to do what Dublin would not, with remarkable success.

The funny-looking quartet from Liverpool who had recorded 'Love Me Do' in the autumn of 1962 had become the most famous young men in the world a year later. The Beatles were in Dublin in November, playing at the Adelphi, while fans who could not get in rioted in Abbey Street and O'Connell Street. The Dublin which they visited was a city on the brink of major physical changes. Already the builders were at work on the new Liberty Hall, on Hawkins House which was rising on the site of the old Theatre Royal, and on O'Connell Bridge House. None of these buildings did anything to enhance the beauty of the city; they emphasised yet again the deplorable visual illiteracy of the Irish. And for the most valuable element in the city's architectural heritage, time was running out. In July general permission was given to the ESB to rebuild on the site of its Georgian houses in Fitzwilliam Street; the permission was confirmed by the Minister for Local Government, Neil Blaney. The Pembroke Estate, the ground landlords, indicated their disapproval, so the ESB gave notice of its intention to acquire the houses by compulsory purchase. Although the streets committee of Dublin Corporation fought a rearguard action against the ESB, by the autumn of 1964 the battle was over: the minister had overruled the Corporation, and the compulsory purchase of the freehold had been completed. The houses were demolished in May 1965.

Georgian architecture was an issue that generated a lot of passion, but it was — and remains — overwhelmingly a concern of the professional middle class and the few surviving members of the Anglo-Irish aristocracy. Their view of Georgian Dublin as something authentically Irish, albeit part of a larger British and European tradition, cut little ice with the mass of the population. The Irish nationalist tradition was substantially one of exclusive tribalism, and the great Georgian builders — the Earl of Charlemont, Lord Mountjoy, the Duke of Leinster, Viscount Fitzwilliam of Merrion — were not of the tribe. The popular nationalist view of Georgian Dublin was that it had been built by the English, and that it was no part of the Irish nation's business to preserve monuments of the oppressor.

And so it was that the longest continuous Georgian streetscape in Europe was despoiled. It was a shameful act of vandalism. Dublin had been a decaying city for decades, and the prospect of architectural renewal was one of the brightest hopes of the sixties. It was a chance lost: much of real value was gratuitously destroyed, while the more delapidated areas were untouched by renewal. Most of the new architecture of the decade lacked any distinction.

There was an enormous boom in private suburban housing as well as in corporate city-centre buildings. Here too styles were both derivative and mediocre. One of the biggest firms of private housing developers, Wates Builders, took a report on Dublin suburban development from a London architect, K. W. Bland, in early 1963. He argued that Dublin was making all the mistakes made by London between the wars:

The traffic might still be flowing both ways on Eden Quay, but there are big changes on the way, none more out of proportion or ugly than the new Liberty Hall, seen here in the early stages of its construction. Even though it is only half way up at this point, it still towers over everything else around it.

Uneven spread in all directions of dull, two-storey, low-density housing. . . .
It seems incredible to me that there should be no body of public opinion
sufficiently strong to force action that would stop the spread of the present
type of development.

Architects might wring their hands, but two-storey, low-density houses in
the suburbs, with gardens back and front, were apparently what people
wanted. There was indeed no body of public opinion mobilised against this
kind of development. Private house ownership was popular; for a great many
people, a house in suburban Dublin was simply a mark of upward social
mobility, echoing a movement all over the western world in the prosperous
post-war years. There was, of course, rather more to explain the nature of
private housing development than a simple response to public demand: the
speculators and builders had their own reasons for taking the courses they
did. It was clearly in a builder's interest to crowd as many houses as possible
into the space at his disposal. Fortunately for the convenience of Irish
builders, the public's environmental expectations were low.

The severity of the crisis in public housing was underlined in June. Dublin
had been notorious for its tenements, and despite an extensive, and at times
heroic, programme of slum clearance and re-location of tenement dwellers in
suburban public housing estates, there were still large pockets of mouldering
city-centre tenement houses by the early 1960s. A government white paper
on housing, published in November 1964, stated that nearly 13,000 houses
per annum would have to be built if bad and overcrowded housing was to be
eliminated. The total built in 1963-64 was 7,500.

On Sunday 2 June an old house collapsed in Bolton Street, killing two
people. Ten days later there was a terrific thunderstorm in Dublin, the worst
for years, and on the following day another house collapsed, this time in
Fenian Street, on the other side of the city. Two little girls, aged eight and
nine, were killed beneath tons of rubble.

While the Republic of Ireland was enjoying an unprecedented boom in the
early 1960s, Northern Ireland was still in the grip of economic palsy. Despite
expansion in the British economy overall in the 1950s, the province
remained in a stagnant rut. Unemployment rose from 26,922 in 1950 to
39,040 in 1963.[2] The failure to attract new industries to the province to
compensate for the contraction of the three traditional industries, shipbuilding, aircraft manufacture and textiles, was the root of the problem.

The scale of the decline in traditional industries is easily forgotten,
especially as there is a tendency to think that Northern Ireland's economic
troubles began only with the revival of its political troubles. Shipbuilding,

the proudest of all Northern enterprises, was the most cruelly hit. Employment in 1960 stood at 16,185; by 1963 this had dropped to 7,076; by 1969 it had fallen again to 5,571. In other words, employment in Harland & Wolff, the province's largest single employer, fell by two-thirds in a decade. The boom year of 1960 was followed by a vicious slump. By March 1961 shipyard workers were organising marches in Belfast to protest against job losses. In October 1961 the launch of the guided missile destroyer *Kent* left the shipyard without a Royal Navy keel for the first time in twenty-five years. By the middle of 1962, however, the order book had begun to fill up again, and employment levels were relatively stable from then until the next serious crisis in 1968, but at only half the level enjoyed in 1960.

For the other major Belfast employer, Short Brothers & Harland, the aircraft manufacturers, the start of the decade was just as bleak. They were, however, to weather the storm more successfully than Harland & Wolff, but not before they had gone very near the brink. The crisis year was 1962. In June it was announced that 7,000 jobs were at risk if the order book did not fill up quickly. Since defence contracts were Shorts' life-blood, Unionist MPs at Westminster were made to lobby hard in the corridors of power. Not that there was universal confidence in their ability; the most vocal internal critic of the Unionist establishment, Edmund Warnock, Stormont MP for Belfast St Anne's, accused them of timid fawning on the Tories. They were, he said, little more than 'the barren limb of the Conservative Party'. Incredibly, Lord Brookeborough refused to lead a delegation from Belfast itself, claiming that it would be wrong and useless to bring a deputation to browbeat a London cabinet minister. Useless, maybe: he had led such a delegation in 1961 and had returned home with nothing to show for it.

The crucial order needed was for the RAF freighter plane, the 'Belfast'. As already noted, ten had been ordered and a further twenty were needed for Shorts to show a profit on the undertaking. A gleam of hope appeared in September 1962 when the company was given an assurance by the Ministry of Defence that 'Means will be found, if necessary, to enable full and satisfactory completion of the current "Belfast" contract.' It was not an order, but it was better than nothing. In November Shorts announced that the 7,000 threatened jobs had been saved for the moment.

In February 1963 the British government gave Shorts £10 million to enable it to complete orders for the 'Belfast' and the 'Seacat' guided missile, on condition that its financial position was reviewed again when these orders had been completed. But in the following month a contract for a new RAF short-range aircraft, which Shorts had hoped to win, went to Hawker-Siddeley instead. It was a bad blow, which emphasised Shorts' junior position in a rationalised British aircraft industry. The stability which followed for the rest of the decade was largely the consequence of decisions by the London government, which had a two-thirds shareholding in the company, to keep it going for political reasons. The extra twenty orders for the 'Belfast' never came, but at least the company's losses were underwritten. More and more the company came to depend on subcontract work from aircraft manufacturers across the water. It was unsatisfactory, until one contemplated the alternative.

The third traditional Northern staple, textiles, also suffered a decline in the 1960s, but it was merely the continuation of a chronic pattern that went back to before the war. Employment fell from 77,870 in 1939 to 57,964 in 1960; by 1969 it had fallen still further to 43,507.

In general, the closing years of Brookeborough's premiership was a time of anxiety in Northern Ireland, in which the province seemed to have left itself badly prepared for the future. The announcement in November 1962 that Michelin were to build a £14 million factory outside Belfast was the first really good economic news of the decade.

The behaviour of the Northern Ireland government during this time was abjectly lazy. It is best summed up by an exchange in the Stormont House of Commons on 27 June 1961, at the height of the employment crisis in the shipyard. Desmond Boal (Unionist) and David Bleakley (NILP) put down a motion which regarded the dismissal of 7,000 workers in Harland & Wolff 'with disquiet' and called on the government to announce its plans for the creation of employment. Replying to the debate, the Minister of Commerce, John Andrews, told MPs 'to look on the bright side'! There were, after all, he said, now more people employed in the shipyard, even after allowing for the 7,000, than there had been in the 1930s.

In the face of this sort of thing, it is hardly surprising that the NILP held its four Belfast seats with increased majorities in the 1962 Stormont election. Indeed, it nearly captured a fifth from the Unionists. Of course, the Unionists were returned to power once again, but with three seats less than they had at the dissolution.[3] It is worth noting that no less than twenty Unionist MPs, out of a total of thirty-four, were returned unopposed.

So 1963 opened with Lord Brookeborough back in power, but with a paltry record of achievement to show for his recent years in office. Unemployment, at just under 10 per cent, was still the highest in the United Kingdom, and the UK Prime Minister, Harold Macmillan, told Unionist MPs at the end of January that while he and his colleagues had a 'special concern for Northern Ireland and would always be anxious to help in overcoming its difficulties', there was actually nothing that they could do for it just at the moment. It was, incidentally, productivity year everywhere in the UK — except in Northern Ireland, owing to the failure of the regional government so far to establish a productivity council.

The pressure that brought Brookeborough's resignation built up suddenly in the early months of 1963. There had been rumblings within the Unionist Party for some time, usually led by Warnock. But even he hesitated to attack the Prime Minister openly. The nearest he had come to that was during the shipyard crisis of 1961, when, along with excoriating the Unionist MPs at Westminster, he had said that a lot of people would like to see Lord Brookeborough 'take off his coat and fight' for jobs for Northern Ireland.

In February 1963 Desmond Boal went one better. He called openly on Brookeborough to resign and voted against the government on an NILP motion of censure on unemployment. Brookeborough said three days later that he would not resign. But in the meantime another issue was increasing the pressure on him.

Government ministers in Northern Ireland were still allowed to hold company directorships, and Lord Brookeborough had set his face against changing this rule on the grounds that if it were changed, it would be impossible to get 'sound businessmen' into government. But it had emerged that Lord Glentoran, Minister of Commerce from 1953 to 1961, had allowed advance factories which had been built by the ministry to be insured by an insurance company of which he was a director. The storm on this issue grew so great that Brookeborough had to yield some ground, and he agreed to the listing of cabinet directorships in *Hansard*. The printed list revealed that five members of his cabinet held private directorships, and this caused the Unionist dissidents to push for a final victory on the issue by having the practice outlawed altogether, as in the rest of the United Kingdom.

All this pressure was telling on the Prime Minister. He was almost seventy-five, and beset by difficulties on every hand. Michael Farrell describes pithily what happened next:

Shortly afterwards ten backbenchers also signed a memorandum calling for his resignation. Brookeborough had a diplomatic duodenal ulcer operation and resigned on 25 March 1963.[4]

He was succeeded by Captain Terence O'Neill.

The new Prime Minister was forty-eight. He was a 'big house' Unionist in the established mould: Eton, the Guards, an English accent. Although an MP since 1946, he had never had to fight an election in his Bannside constituency. He had lost two brothers in the Second World War, just as Brookeborough had lost two sons. He lacked Brookeborough's common touch and charm; he was rather remote and aloof.

He was not elected leader of the Unionist Party. In those days, even in Britain (as events later in the year were to prove so dramatically), Tory leaders did nothing so vulgar as get elected. They emerged.

Terence O'Neill (right) with the British Prime Minister Sir Alec Douglas Home outside 10 Downing Street. Having spent seven years as Minister of Finance, O'Neill knew which side Northern Ireland's bread was buttered on and was always careful not to antagonise London, unlike some of the wilder spirits on the Unionist Party's right wing.

The circumstances of Terence O'Neill's emergence were to colour his premiership, so it is instructive to set them out here. It appears that undertakings had been given by Brookeborough to the late Morris May, MP, former Minister of Education, and to other Unionist leaders that the succession would be decided by a vote of the full parliamentary party.[5] This undertaking was not honoured; instead there was a late-night meeting between Brookeborough, John Andrews and O'Neill at which the principal arrangements were made. William Craig, the chief whip, spent the following day generating support for O'Neill among Unionist backbenchers. By 6 p.m. on 25 March O'Neill had been announced as the new Prime Minister. His principal rival, Brian Faulkner, who was in the United States in search of industrial investment for Northern Ireland, arrived home to a *fait accompli*. The fact that O'Neill was the beneficiary of what many Unionist MPs regarded as a dishonourable transaction weakened his moral position from the beginning. Faulkner, in particular, felt aggrieved. He was the most able middle-class Unionist, and he would have welcomed an opportunity to test his standing openly in an election. Indeed, he might have won: his reputation as a former 'hardline' Minister of Home Affairs would have done him no harm with backbenchers. On the other hand, political correspondents had marked out O'Neill for the succession for some months before Brookeborough's resignation, so the suggestion that the new Prime Minister was somehow 'imposed' on an unwilling party by a 'big house' cabal is probably an exaggeration.

However, it is no exaggeration to say that the 'big house' Unionists suited themselves in the business. The fact that Terence O'Neill became Prime Minister as the result of a 'secret deal' was remembered with bitterness in some quarters. It was to be recalled at a critical moment in his premiership, when, in an atmosphere surrounded by as much secrecy as had attended O'Neill's original 'emergence', Seán Lemass drove through the gates of Stormont on the morning of 14 January 1965.

O'Neill's succession to the premiership was assumed to mark a new era. In fact he made a quiet start — so much so that some journalists were complaining towards the end of 1963 that it was simply business as before. There was a widespread view that he was a prisoner of his right wing, and the *Belfast Newsletter*, the principal voice of Unionist opinion, was never enthusiastic about him. In April 1964, when he had been Prime Minister for over a year, two leading Catholics — J. J. Campbell, senior lecturer at St Joseph's Training College, Belfast, and Brian McK. McGuigan, a solicitor — made public the contents of three letters which they had sent to the Prime Minister on the subject of 'religious apartheid'. No reply had been received to any of them, although the writers had subsequently been in touch with the cabinet secretary, who had promised a reply 'when the Prime Minister has had a chance to consider the matter'. The letters had stressed two complaints: the Prime Minister's proposed economic council for Northern Ireland, announced in the autumn of 1963, contained no Catholic member; similarly, the Lockwood Committee on higher education was an all-Protestant body. The writers expressed general disappointment with the new dispensation, expressed the willingness of Catholics to participate in the public life of the province, and indicated their frustration at being excluded. Messrs Campbell and McGuigan were hardly representative of the Catholic population and had no mandate from anyone, but their letters, and the fact that they had not even received the courtesy of a reply, were indicative of the depth of the Ulster malaise. The *Belfast Telegraph* commented:

The government, for all its brave new ideals, carries a millstone of old prejudices and fears, and makes hardly an attempt to gain its intellectual freedom.

What evidence was there for brave new ideals? Within a month of assuming the premiership, O'Neill had got rid of Billy Douglas, for twenty years secretary of the Unionist Party and Brookeborough's right-hand man. More dramatically, he had sent a message of sympathy to the acting head of the Catholic Church in Ireland on the death of Pope John in June (the Pope died in the period between the death of Cardinal D'Alton and the elevation of Cardinal Conway). Brookeborough would not have communicated directly with a Catholic ecclesiastic; he would have sent a note to the leader of the Nationalist Party. Moreover, in the very month that the letters from Campbell and McGuigan were made public, O'Neill took the unprecedented step of visiting a Catholic school: it is hard to convey the effect that this had on public opinion in a state as rigidly sectarian as Northern Ireland. It was at least deemed worthy of sharp criticism from Unionists. At the end of the same month, April 1964, the Prime Minister finally recognised the Irish Congress of Trade Unions, something which Brookeborough had always refused point-blank to do because it was an all-Ireland body with its headquarters in Dublin. O'Neill's motives may not have been purely idealistic: his economic council would have been a nonsense without ICTU participation.

So there had been a cautious change of direction by O'Neill, especially once he had got 1963 behind him. Nevertheless, some of his decisions had been in the old style: the Lockwood Committee, in particular, would do him immense damage in the Catholic community. This was the pattern of O'Neill's government: the outward symbols of reform and reconciliation balanced by the expedient maintenance of Protestant supremacy. This is not to say that Terence O'Neill was a cynical opportunist: symbolism was as much as he could allow himself in the way of liberalism, and it had the virtue of costing nothing; he could not allow himself, however, to alienate his own backbenchers, some of them very rough diamonds indeed and not disposed to forfeit any of the realities of Protestant power. Additionally, O'Neill was inclined to regard Catholics *de haut en bas* and never really made any effort to attain a sensitive understanding of the Northern Catholic mind. There was always an air of the pious squire about him, doing the decent thing by the tenantry.

Finally, what of the party O'Neill now led? It was, *par excellence*, a party of tribal solidarity. Its instincts were authoritarian, defensive, and marked by a streak of real brutality. It was notorious for the manner in which it had institutionalised a spider's web of discrimination in favour of its own supporters across the province. It was almost unique in the political world. Only the Nationalist Party of South Africa bore comparison with it.

Its absence of subtlety was breathtaking. In March 1961, for example, at the height of the unemployment crisis in Belfast, an ambitious young lawyer, Robert Babington, told the Ulster Unionist Labour Association:

Registers of unemployed loyalists should be kept by the Unionist Party and employers invited to pick employees from them. The Unionist Party should make it quite clear that the loyalists have the first choice of jobs.

In January 1964 Senator J. E. N. Barnhill was of a similar opinion when he addressed the Rural Unionist Association in Derry:

Charity begins at home. If we are going to employ people, we should begin with Unionists. I am not saying that we should sack Nationalist employees, but if we are going to employ new men we should give preference to Unionists.

Northern Ireland was the only place in Western Europe where the government controlled absolutely the entry of workers to the state, under the Safeguarding of Employment Act. Brookeborough had long been unhappy at the thought that the United Kingdom might enter the EEC, thus compromising Unionist control of employment; presumably he feared an avalanche of Catholics from the South. Like many other Unionists, he certainly dreaded the potential for North/South co-operation implicit in any European agreement. As for Northern Catholics, they were beyond the pale. In 1959, in a fit of enthusiasm, the Young Unionists attempted to discuss the possibility of Catholics joining the Unionist Party. They drew down upon their heads the wrath of senior party members, including Brookeborough, who left them in no doubt as to their heresy.

In July 1962 ITV broadcast a television programme on the 'Twelfth', the annual day of Orange parades in Northern Ireland. Brian Connell, the commentator, described the celebrations as an occasion when 'militant Protestants of the Orange Order made a gesture of defiant intolerance against their fellow Roman Catholics [*sic!*]'. He interviewed Brian Faulkner. The Minister of Home Affairs pooh-poohed the abusive and vulgar anti-Catholic wall slogans in Protestant areas as the excesses of exuberant youths. Not only that; some slogans and banners merely referred to 'false doctrines' of the Roman Catholic Church, and the Minister of Home Affairs felt that Orangemen had a right to advert to these if they held them to be false. Mr Faulkner was generally credited with one of Unionism's more subtle minds.

The Unionist Party was steeped in this kind of casual, reflexive bigotry. It was the tribal party of Ulster Protestants, a talented, capable and determined people, but neurotically aware of their marginal status in Ireland as a whole and determined to cleave to the greater Protestant world of the United Kingdom. Because theirs was a culture ultimately grounded in fear, their political vehicle, the Unionist Party, was always a hostage to its own extremists.

This, then, was the party of which Terence O'Neill found himself the leader in the spring of 1963.

On 26 June 1963 President John F. Kennedy of the United States of America arrived in the Republic of Ireland and was received like a conquering hero. He was the descendant of a Famine emigrant from Co. Wexford.

It was the supreme Irish-American dream. The country which his great-grandfather had left in the middle of the nineteenth century was broken by natural disaster. Millions took a similar course over the next hundred years, abandoning a country that had nothing to offer them except isolation and poverty. And now one among them had gained the supreme prize and had returned, like an envoy to the old country from the world of action and achievement. It is tempting to see Kennedy's Irish visit as the end of an era, the final apotheosis of that traditional Ireland which had looked to America as the land of opportunity where Irish energy could prosper in a manner impossible at home.

He spoke to Irish people in traditional terms. What gave Ireland's experience a special significance, he told a cheering crowd in Wexford, was that after hundreds of years of foreign domination and religious persecution she had maintained her identity of loyalty to faith and fatherland. This was the authentic self-image of post-Famine Ireland, a nation in eternal and tenacious communion with its past.

Kennedy spoke to an Ireland that was passing away: the inert, defeated country which never ceased to contemplate its own miseries and keep warm its old resentments. But the image he employed was one that went very deep

John F. Kennedy at Arus an Uachtaráin with President de Valera **(opposite and below).**
What passed for Irish 'society' disgraced itself at a presidential garden party held in a
downpour in the grounds of Arus an Uachtaráin **(above)** *by mobbing Kennedy like a pop*
star.

in the Irish psyche, and which was impervious to the effects of modernisation. For what Kennedy had stated was a definition of nationality, in terms which echoed de Valera's famous reply to Churchill in 1945.[6] It was unhistorical, as all such definitions are, but it had great emotional power and popular appeal, for this was how the Irish nation saw itself in history.

It may have seemed anachronistic in a decade when Ireland was hastily importing new value-systems and standards of authority. But a nation's sense of identity is not an ephemeral thing, and will only be modified slowly over time. Kennedy described the Irish to themselves as a nation who had survived by stubbornly refusing to conform to the ways of others. Almost everything that was happening in Ireland as he spoke was tending to pull the country in the opposite direction. In the 1960s Ireland increasingly conformed to the ways of others while still nurturing the myth of resistance in its heart.

In de Valera's Ireland the national culture had been a seamless garment, with a palpable similarity between theory and practice. In Lemass's Ireland theory and practice moved apart, but the new Ireland could offer no alternative definition of nationality as comprehensive or as comforting as that which John Kennedy recalled in the last days of June 1963.

Chapter Six

1964

The past is another country

We are prepared: we build our houses squat,
Sink walls in rock and roof them with good slate.
This wizened earth has never troubled us
With hay, so, as you see, there are no stacks
Or stooks that can be lost. Nor are there trees
Which might prove company when it blows full
Blast: you know what I mean — leaves and branches
Can raise a tragic chorus in a gale.
                                    SÉAMUS HEANEY

Are you right there, Michael, are you right?
Have you got that parcel there for Mrs White?
Oh! You haven't? Oh, begorrah!
Say it's comin' down tomorra',
And it might now, Michael, so it might!
                                    PERCY FRENCH

THE heroic period in the revival of Irish social and economic life ended in 1963. The First Programme for Economic Expansion produced a growth rate which was double the original forecast. National income rose by nearly a quarter. The public investment programme achieved a total of £78.5 million against a target of £44.5 million; crucially, most of this money was invested productively. Both national output and the purchasing power of wages rose by more than 20 per cent. The number of cars on Irish roads doubled in a decade. The level of unemployment dropped by over 30 per cent, and the rate of emigration slowed dramatically, to the point where its final cessation could be contemplated. It was an extraordinary transformation in a few years.[1]

From 1964 onward, however, the euphoria of the early sixties began to dissipate. The country continued to flourish, and there were remarkable achievements, especially in education and in relations with Northern Ireland. But the steady advance on all fronts was halted. The Second Programme sought to continue the rate of expansion of the First, but it was soon apparent that its targets were unattainable. Agriculture, which alone had lagged behind in the First Programme, continued to languish, and farmers were to turn to futile street politics in 1966 and 1967. Industrial relations deteriorated to the point where moralists — most of them employed, it seemed, as newspaper leader-writers — wondered if there was not some self-destructive quality in the Irish character. Trade unions failed to reform themselves, and a dangerous gap opened up between the leadership and the ordinary members.

At the start of 1964, as we have already seen, there was a widespread feeling that the national wage agreement marked a major step forward. However, at 12 per cent, the increase was inflationary, and there was an alarming series of price rises in the first half of the year. Some trade unions naturally grew restive in the face of this and chafed at the thought that, under the terms of the agreement, they could do nothing about it until the middle of 1966. The feeling began to grow that the ICTU leadership had developed rather too cosy a relationship with the establishment. Seats on the National Industrial Economic Council and the Employer/Labour Conference were a long way from the shop floor; and in a movement which had for so long occupied a place in Irish life far removed from the councils of power it was natural for men to wonder if their leaders had not simply got into bed with the enemy.

The building workers had had reservations about the national agreement. Traditionally they were used to annual agreements, and they also feared that their long-standing claim for a forty-hour week would be compromised. But clause 5 of the agreement did allow for specific improvements in hours and holidays, while forestalling a general review. It was designed to cater for groups which had received no improvements in these areas, even though other comparable groups had. But, fatally, clause 5 did not define how one could identify those groups of workers who might benefit from its provisions.

In the early summer of 1964 craft workers in the Dublin building trade lodged a claim for a forty-hour week. It was rejected by the employers as being in breach of the national wage agreement. The case went to the Labour Court, which could find no special circumstances under clause 5 to justify the claim. But then the Plasterers' Union decided that if the claim were not conceded, they would not return to work after the end of the annual holiday in mid-August. They were supported by the other craft workers, and a two-month strike ensued which brought work to a standstill on building projects worth a total of £15 million.

The unions had expected the employers to capitulate, but the Federated Union of Employers saw the floodgates opening if the claim were conceded. They stood firm. They accused the craftsmen of bad faith and of attempting to wreck the national agreement once it had served their purpose. The ICTU, in reply, charged the employers with inflexibility and argued that the building workers were a special case.

The employers were in the position of having to break the strike completely or make some concession. When, in October, the Minister for Industry and Commerce intervened and appointed a Labour Court conciliation conference, it became likely that they would yield some ground. And in fact they did so. The conference settled the strike by recommending an improvement in winter working hours, and it appointed an independent commission to adjudicate on summer hours. The commission eventually decided that summer hours should be amended along the same lines as winter hours. The employers were livid at this, claiming that while the winter concession could be justified by bad light and poor weather, there were no extenuating circumstances in the case of the summer and that this was a flagrant breach of the national agreement.

Whether or not the terms of the agreement had been breached, one of its primary aims had been. It had failed to prevent a major strike. The employers were very bitter, having reluctantly agreed to a high national settlement as the price of industrial peace. Now the ICTU had failed to deliver through an inability to police one of its own member unions. It was, however, naïve to expect the ICTU to discharge such a role: it was not a highly centralised body whose members were likely to take dictation about what they might or might not do. The tradition of independence in individual unions ran too deep for that.

The employers were not displeased merely with the ICTU. They were most unhappy with the government. It was the Taoiseach himself who had cajoled them into signing the original 12 per cent; now Jack Lynch, the Minister for Industry and Commerce, had made the decisive intervention in the building workers' strike which ended so badly for the employers. It seemed to the employers that every time the government took a hand in industrial affairs it benefited the unions.

More than the employers were of this view. Fine Gael had accused Lemass of railroading through the original agreement in order to win two forthcoming by-elections. (If this was true, he was successful: Fianna Fáil won the Cork and Kildare by-elections in February 1964.) But that sort of thing was the normal currency of political abuse. Now, sensationally, a dissenter appeared, not just within the Fianna Fáil party, but within the cabinet itself. On 8 October the Minister for Agriculture, Paddy Smith, resigned in protest at Lynch's intervention in the building strike. Smith deplored the unions' attitude to the national agreement and described them as 'an incompetent, dishonest tyranny' who wanted for leadership and with whom negotiations were a fraud.

Smith was one of the Fianna Fáil old guard, and he had never been happy with Lemass's weakness for the unions. Moreover, he was a staunch defender of agricultural interests, and his affection for the trade union movement may be supposed to have been on a par with that of the average small farmer. Farmers were bitterly resentful of the way in which wage and salary earners were prospering while rural Ireland was stagnant. Nevertheless, Smith's action was highly unusual in a country where ministerial resignations on a point of policy or principle are practically unknown.

The new Minister for Agriculture was Charles Haughey. Whatever awaited him in his new department, nothing was likely to be as bizarre as a controversy that had enlivened his final months in the Department of Justice. In March it was reported that ban-ghardaí were acting as decoys in order to capture gallant gentlemen in search of prostitutes. The ban-gharda on one particular beat was instructed to delay her randy punter by haggling about the price until reinforcements arrived. The country was not in the way of regarding ban-ghardaí as conspicuous sex objects, and the whole arrangement seemed rather ... improbable.

To clarify matters there stepped forward the inimitable Joe Leneghan, TD (West Mayo), who put down a Dáil question for Haughey. The minister read a carefully worded reply: 'The statements are totally false, and I regret that they should have been published without any evidence to sustain them.' He explained that there had been complaints of harassment from 'respectable women' in certain areas and that ban-ghardaí had then been assigned to patrol these areas, since 'the respectable women would be unable to give evidence that would sustain a conviction'. The ban-ghardaí were 'fully aware' that their job was to apprehend accosters and that 'it was essential that they should not give any one passing by reason to think that they were women of easy virtue, but that they should represent the average respectable girl walking along the street'. These instructions had been scrupulously observed. The minister took exception to Mr Leneghan's description of the ban-ghardaí as 'decoy prostitutes'.

In June a new series of advanced Boeing 707s began service with Aer Lingus and a few months later the last Douglas DC-3 in the fleet left Dublin to join the Royal Nepalese Airlines. In November the government finally yielded to a political clamour of some years' standing when it introduced legislation to tighten control over the sale of land to foreigners. It was a cautious measure, designed only to close a loophole whereby the heavy stamp duty payable on such transactions could be avoided by using an Irish buyer as a 'front man' for the real purchaser. The government was determined to go no further than this, and as long ago as 1961 had voted out a bill to impose more comprehensive restrictions on such sales as damaging both to the tourist industry and to our image as putative free traders.

Television came to Irish schools in April, when Telefís Scoile began.

Physics and chemistry were the subjects chosen, and once again the language problem rumbled in the background. RTE decided, reasonably enough, that since the overwhelming majority of schools which taught science did so through English, it could not justify a bilingual transmission. Within a month Telefís Scoile had established itself. No less than 87 per cent of all secondary schools in the Republic which taught science were receiving it; this represented about 300 classes in 169 schools. A less useful form of television appeared for the first time in February: the party political broadcast was born, a permanent and boring legacy of the Cork and Kildare by-elections. Not content with that, the politicians strangled at birth Ireland's first pirate radio station, Radio Juliet, in Cork. Pirate radio was one of the wonders of the age, and the most glamorous and successful of all, Radio Caroline, was owned by an Irishman, Ronan O'Rahilly.

The middle years of the 1960s swept away a whole gallery of outstanding Irish writers. Louis McNeice had died in 1963, and on 20 March 1964 Brendan Behan died at the age of forty-one. His life had been set on a destruction course for years, for he lived on the exposed outcrops of experience. Yet, like many other self-destructive artists before and since, he was loved by thousands not just for himself but for the quality of his life, as if they were living vicariously, through him, a more intense and exciting existence than they dared contemplate in reality. His native Dublin loved him and paid him Dublin's greatest tribute: his funeral was the biggest in the city for forty years.

Seán O'Casey, twice Behan's age, died as he had lived, fighting. In 1957 he had forbidden any professional production of his plays by Dublin companies, a ban that bore heaviest on the Abbey Theatre.*[2] He finally relented, and in 1964 he lifted the ban in order to allow the Abbey to perform in London at the celebration of the Shakespeare quatercentenary. Standards in the Abbey had been a source of controversy for years; the focus of criticism was Ernest Blythe, the company's managing director. He was a Gaelic enthusiast and former Minister for Finance who acquired a reputation for ferocious financial orthodoxy, becoming famous for actually cutting the old-age pension in one budget. In the Abbey his artistic policy favoured popular but profitable dross. He was not the sort of character likely to be beloved of creative artists, and when the Abbey's London performances of 1964 received poor notices, O'Casey added his voice to the complaints of low standards by enquiring: 'What the hell does Blythe know about the drama?' He was supported in his view by Micheál Mac Liammóir, speaking at the

---

*The Abbey was caught in the middle of a dispute between O'Casey on the one hand and an unlikely coalition of Archbishop McQuaid and the Dublin Council of Trade Unions on the other.

Yeats Summer School in Sligo at the end of August. But by then O'Casey had suffered a heart attack complicated by severe bronchitis, and he died on 18 September. But in what might almost now seem like a form of symbolic succession, a new star appeared in the Irish dramatic firmament before September was out, when Brian Friel's *Philadelphia Here I Come* opened at the Dublin Theatre Festival.

The consumer revolution edged closer. In February Quinn's Supermarkets, later to become Superquinn, announced that they were to open an American-style out-of-town shopping centre in Finglas, on the north-western edge of Dublin. The grandiose plans did not quite come off: instead Superquinn bought up an old and failing cinema, the Finglas Casino, and opened a supermarket pure and simple. This was to be the fate of a lot of suburban cinemas in the sixties. The first comprehensive shopping centre in the country was developed, not by the Quinns at Finglas, but by a British property company in the more affluent purlieus of Stillorgan, on the south side of the city. But, as ever in Ireland in the 1960s, new rubbed shoulders with old. Just as these radically new retail operations were being announced, the chief medical officer of the Dublin Health Authority was criticising the timeless Dublin practice of selling foodstuffs from open street stalls. Sooner or later, he said, the capital would have to follow 'practice in enlightened cities' where such trade was confined to covered or enclosed markets.

Supermarkets effected a subtle but decisive change in urban lifestyle. Not only were the intimacy and credit facilities of the neighbourhood grocer superseded, but the habit of shopping by the day, a strong one in working-class areas, was weakened. Supermarkets made sense, and saved money, if one bought by the week and stored perishables in refrigerators; but this transformed shopping from a partly social activity, a daily round of contact and gossip, into a purely consumer one. The main attraction of supermarkets was their prices. By the middle of 1965, for example, they had captured the retail market in toothpaste and toilet soap from the chemists. Toothpaste which cost 3s 8d in a chemist's shop was only 2s 1d in a super-market. While the chemist took the traditional profit margins and sold at the recommended retail price, the supermarket settled for a lower margin — although it got a longer discount for bulk purchases — and sold in high volume to compensate.

Finally, one of the longest-running sagas of the 1960s ended in July. The Supreme Court dismissed an appeal from Mrs Gladys Ryan against the High Court judgment that the Health (Fluoridation of Water Supplies) Act (1960) was not unconstitutional. Mrs Ryan had claimed that fluoridation of water violated the constitutional rights of herself and her children under Article 40.3, the authority of the family (Article 41), and the family's right of

Gaelic games were dominated in the mid sixties by Galway footballers, seen above in the 1964 all Ireland final against Kerry, and Tipperary hurlers, photographed below before the hurling final of the same year.

physical education of the children (Article 42). The court held that the state had the right to protect public health. In this case fluoride was the only effective preventive for dental caries; its interference with the constitution of the body was minimal, and it had no effect on the wholeness or soundness of the body. The Minister for Health was less judicious than the Supreme Court. For Mr MacEntee, the anti-fluoridation lobby were 'flat earthers' and 'outback Amazons'.

The new prosperity of the 1960s was disproportionately concentrated in the south and east of the country. The impoverished West of Ireland continued its decline. The West held a special place in nationalist mythology as the repository of those qualities most incorruptibly Irish, and its poverty had been a reproach to successive governments since the foundation of the state.

The population of the five counties of Connacht plus Co. Donegal fell by over one-third between 1901 and 1961. Even in the early 1960s, with emigration rates falling in the rest of the country, this region was still losing its population at a rate of 4,000 persons a year. Every 100 people of working age (15 to 65) had 78 people dependent on them. In Roscommon a survey by the Department of Agriculture found that, of 372 houses on 17,000 acres, nearly half the farmers were over sixty years old. Only 2 per cent of farmers in Co. Mayo and 7 per cent in Co. Galway were under thirty. Out of 23,000 agricultural holdings in Co. Donegal, 2,500 were less than one acre in size.

The West apparently lacked the material resources to sustain a decent quality of life. In one Co. Clare parish, the subject of the most compelling study available on a small West of Ireland community, approximately one house in three was inhabited by a 'chronically isolated' person, that is, somebody without any close relations nearby other than possibly an elderly brother or sister with whom the farm was shared.[3] The possibilities for a more commercially viable agriculture were restricted by the poverty of the soil, the small average size of the holdings, the conservatism and inertia of the inhabitants, and the prevailing sense of demoralisation which was the product of generations of decline:

The young who remained at home used to inherit a farm, but today they inherit more isolation than land. The Inishkillane community is intensely demoralised. The new gereration ... is composed ... of people who are likely to be exposed to the loneliness and hopelessness which ineluctably confront the last to be held within an eclipsed tradition. The present structure of the population shows a spiral of decline which has not been checked. Demoralisation has become a feature of this spiral, accelerating it and then being accelerated by it. Population decline and depression among the people have become elements in a single and unremitting process.[4]

The life described in that passage was typical of hundreds of small communities west of the Shannon and in Counties Donegal and Kerry. The conventional wisdom among the economically orthodox in the east was that there was no hope for the western smallholder, and that small farms there should be consolidated into economically viable units. Father James McDyer in his autobiography recalls one government minister telling him that the West 'should be allowed to find [its] own level of depopulation'.[5] This prescription was passionately opposed by those who were emotionally involved in the West of Ireland, whether because they were natives of the place, or believed in the moral superiority of the life of the rural smallholder, or because they simply could not stomach the measures required to disperse the surplus population. Very few champions of the West of Ireland actually had any idea of how the existing social structure was going to be made viable, least of all the Fianna Fáil party, who had presided over the last thirty years of decline while never ceasing to declare their special concern for the region.

Then, in the early 1960s, a gleam of hope appeared. Glencolumbkille is a remote and beautiful valley in south-west Co. Donegal. Late in 1952 Father James McDyer had come there from Tory Island.[6] He found it without electricity, decent roads, or even a parish hall. There were 250 families in the place, who between them supplied twenty young people for the emigrant ships each year. But there was also a parish council, which McDyer managed to galvanise into action. He lobbied the county council and got the roads re-surfaced; he helped overcome the suspicion of electricity among his parishioners; he built a weaving factory and a hall and laid out a sports ground.

He knew, however, that the vital necessity was for a stable economic environment in Glencolumbkille which would provide a decent living for its inhabitants. His first idea, for a market-gardening enterprise, faltered for want of a government grant. Then he looked to the possibility of growing vegetables, which he knew was feasible in the sandy soil. But the market for fresh vegetables was uncertain; what was needed was a canning plant to process the harvest. He tried, without success, to induce a Dublin canning factory to locate in Glencolumbkille.

Then he got in contact with General Michael J. Costello. Costello was the general manager of the nationalised Irish Sugar Company, which had established a special division precisely to ensure that Irish vegetable produce would generate as much added value as possible in Ireland by being processed in the country according to the most modern techniques; this division later developed into Erin Foods. Costello was a rare type in Irish life: he both cared about the West of Ireland and actually had practical ideas about how its decline might be halted without stripping it of its remaining population. He was sympathetic to what McDyer was trying to achieve.

At a series of meetings in Co. Donegal in early 1961 Costello and McDyer urged farmers from six different parishes to grow forty acres of vegetables each on a trial basis; Costello warned that a total minimum of 200 acres was needed to make the experiment feasible for canning purposes. It didn't work: the farmers responded with a mixture of caution and lassitude, and the minimum acreage was not attained.

McDyer now turned back to his own people in Glencolumbkille and the two adjacent valleys, Carrick and Kilcar. What happened next was almost miraculous. He persuaded the families of the three valleys to lease 190 acres of land to a co-operative which he proposed to establish. Moreover, the 700 families put up £8,000 between them in £10 shares towards the initial capital of the enterprise. It was an astonishing act of trust, all the more so when one thinks of the legendary close-fistedness and proprietorial instincts of the western smallholder. But £25,000 was needed. The Donegal Association in Dublin, encouraged by Costello and Peadar O'Donnell, put up £2,000; the Guinness Workers' Employment Fund, £1,200; the London and Birmingham Donegal Associations, £2,000. McDyer raised the rest of the money in America. He made a seventeen-day tour to Chicago, Philadelphia, Boston and New York which raised $36,000.

Errigal Co-operative was established. The state, in the form of An Foras Tionscail, now added a grant of another £25,000 to the co-operative's own capital, on condition that half the produce was exported. In the first full year of operation, 1962, eighteen of the twenty-one members of the executive committee were under thirty years of age. Land was fenced, and a central pool of machinery and fertiliser was organised. The Irish Sugar Company built and equipped a processing factory in Carrick, the cost of which was to be repaid to them by the co-operative. The Sugar Company also trained local young people in the skills they would require in the future, and provided guaranteed markets for the produce which could not be sold locally by the co-operative. It was hoped that Errigal would show a profit in the third year of production.

By 1964 the emigration rate had been cut by 75 per cent, from twenty to five. The co-operative was diversifying into sheep rearing, weaving, knitting and tourist organisation. 'Glencolumbkille ducklings' were being reared and supplied to hotels in the area.

McDyer's ambition was to prove that there was a future and a decent living to be got from the small family farm in the West of Ireland. In April 1964, addressing the Christus Rex conference, he listed four vital prerequisites for the salvation of such farms: co-operation, education, capital, and, crucially, a spirit of enterprise. He dismissed comparisons between Irish conditions and those in developing countries: Ireland had modern utilities and infrastructure. Our output was low because the level of farming techniques was low; because production was for home consumption, not for cash; because of the dead weight of custom and tradition; because the marriage rate was too low and the marriage age too high; and because the age of farm inheritance was too high. Here was an unsentimental critique of what was wrong with the West, born not of a desire to depopulate, but to conserve and revive. McDyer could afford to analyse. As he observed in August,

This great experiment is paying off. From an area where farming was far below subsistence level, our sales have increased from £12,000 in the first year to just over £40,000 this year. Over 80 per cent of our produce has been exported. The area cropped by private owners on contract is double what it was last year, and more than quadruple what it was in the first year.

'Save the West' became a national catch-cry, and Father McDyer became an evangelist for the cause. But could the rest of the West of Ireland follow where he led? The neglect and defeatism of generations were not to be swept away by one brave experiment, no matter how successful. For one thing, there was not a McDyer in every western parish. Nor was there a coherent national policy, based on his or anyone else's ideas, for the development of hundreds of thousands of acres of marginal hill land in the West. National agricultural policy, despite all Fianna Fáil might claim to the contrary in election manifestoes, was dominated by a concern for the farm of at least forty-five acres in size. The government's eye was on the EEC, and in the opinion of the EEC's farm modernisation scheme, big was beautiful.

The other chronic problem in the West was the absence of any heavy concentration of industry. Here again, there was a single beacon of hope at the edge of the region. By 1962 employment at Shannon had risen to 1,300. In 1963 it increased to 2,109, and by 1966 had risen to 3,293. Many companies which had established there had already expanded their premises, in some cases by actually doubling their factory space. A rigorous screening process had been established by the Shannon Free Airport Development Company, in collaboration with the Industrial Development Authority, to weed out companies who were simply looking to exploit the system of inducements. Like Father McDyer in Glencolumbkille, SFADCO was animated by a desire to revitalise the social fabric of a whole region. To this end it deliberately encouraged certain kinds of enterprise, in particular those which promised a high male labour content, in an effort to staunch the flow of seasonal male emigration, one of the most insidious features of traditional western life.

'Save the West' was one of the great rallying cries of the 1960s. A man and a town between them symbolised what was possible in pursuit of this goal. Father James McDyer of Glencolumbkille was the very incarnation of the movement to save the West by utilising existing resources efficiently, while Shannon was an example of what could be created almost out of nothing.

One of the increasing number of American companies at Shannon was the Standard Pressed Steel Company of Pennsylvania. The head of its Shannon plant, Armin Frank, Jr, offered an astute outsider's observation of the industrial estate in the autumn of 1964. Addressing the annual conference of the Engineers' Association in UCD, he pointed out that Shannon was an artificial creation, stimulated by economic incentives which would burn out in twenty years. He explained that his own company had located at Shannon because of the low cost of facilities, the relatively cheaper cost and ready availability of labour, and the twenty-five-year tax holiday. In the long run he recognised that taxes were an essential part of any economic system and had to be considered as a normal business cost. Low labour rates were but a temporary advantage for industry, and how could they sustain a high standard of living? 'Ireland has to develop something unique besides tax forgiveness and low labour rates to sustain industrialisation in the long run.' Here he had touched on the fatal flaw in Ireland's programme for regeneration. It *had* nothing else unique to offer, and was therefore exceptionally vulnerable to a world recession. Shannon, in his view, however, had two basic advantages: it had 'an intense and inspired attitude', supported by action, on the part of the SFADCO executives; and its relatively unskilled workforce was highly adaptable. But he was concerned that wage increases were now outstripping productivity increases and that the peripheral necessities of industrialisation, like housing, were not being provided in sufficient quantity or at sufficient speed. Most particularly, there was a problem with engineers. His own company had no trouble finding scientists and engineers who were capable of doing research work, but it was proving impossible to discover an engineer who knew how to run a manufacturing operation or to determine the method by which a part was made.

The problem with production engineers was to be overcome in time; it was a legacy from the pre-industrial days, when engineering graduates who wanted to make a career in manufacturing almost automatically thought of emigration. So too was the housing difficulty, as a whole new town grew up around the estate. In sheer scale and novelty, nothing in Irish life this century could even approach the development of the town of Shannon.

Despite problems and uncertainties, Shannon and Glencolumbkille both exuded an air of confidence and success in the autumn of 1964. Both were radical and imaginative departures; in each a whole society examined itself unsentimentally and refused to make comforting excuses for itself; both demanded a mixture of vision and common sense. Between the two places lay the snipegrass and bog of the West, where the burden of defeat was still being borne, with precious few signs of people determined to relieve it.

107

Nineteen sixty-four was the final year of a five-year period, designated under the Transport Act (1958), in which the national transport company, CIE, had been set the task of a major internal reform. It is worth looking at the progress of CIE in those years, for it epitomised some notable features of Ireland at the time: a dynamic and confident semi-state company; a high degree of government support for a public enterprise; and finally, the collapse of high — many would claim later, exaggerated — hopes.

The 1958 act had stipulated that CIE would be given an annual subvention of £1.175 million for each of the five years, at the end of which period, in March 1964, it would be expected to have balanced its income and expenditure on day-to-day operations. It was never expected to make a profit in all divisions: the railways were always going to lose money, but the intention was to discard the more obviously unprofitable parts of the railway system, to the point where the losses on the remaining sections could be covered by profitable parts of the company, such as the Dublin city bus services.

It was an audacious undertaking. No public transport system in the world operated without a government subvention, and the danger was that the utility aspect of CIE would be sacrificed to accounting success. But the fact that such a programme was entered upon at all spoke volumes for the new spirit abroad in Ireland. It was, inevitably, Lemass's doing.* He was convinced that the snug monopoly of CIE in public transport had enervated the company, and, as with everything else in the national life, he was determined to blow the cobwebs out of the corners.

There was no shortage of cobwebs in CIE. The new chairman of the company, Dr C. S. ('Todd') Andrews, has described the conditions he found on his first tour of inspection:

The exterior of the buildings bore evidence of decay, office equipment was mostly obsolete, and in some cases the premises appeared not to have been cleaned for years. In an office attached to one of the larger stations there was a wall full of cubby-holes stuffed with delivery dockets dating from before the First World War. At every station there were masses of valuable scrap material including in some cases obsolete steam engines of which the copper alone would fetch a high price. At Inchicore we had the largest engineering workshop in Ireland. It was just like a scrap yard. Even the latrines were open-ended which meant that the backsides of the men at stool were visible to anyone. The stores had stacks of material which had not moved for generations. They included hot-water bottles which had been used to heat the feet of first-class passengers before the introduction of central heating.[7]

---

*The 1958 act was one of Lemass's last major pieces of legislation as Minister for Industry and Commerce, shortly before he became Taoiseach.

The company embarked on a major reorganisation of its management structures, with an emphasis on decentralisation. From the start it had not only the support of Lemass but the enthusiasm of Erskine Childers, the Minister for Transport and Power. In January 1960 he described the changes in CIE as 'the greatest reorganisation campaign ever conducted by any business organisation of this country'. In April he singled out the company as a symbol of the new, revitalised Ireland. For a quarter of a century, he said, those who believed in scientific progress had been battling against cynics and fatalists who revelled in the idea that the Irish people were incapable of dynamic decisions. CIE was proof that they were wrong, and it was setting a headline to industry.

In his speech of January 1960 Childers touched on another point which was central to CIE's plans in these years. He said that facts had to be faced in the cases of grossly uneconomic railway branch lines. He quoted the examples of one where only 266 lorry-loads per annum would be needed to replace the rail facility, and of another where only 142 passengers per day travelled on four trains. Such lines had to be closed, he said.

In fact CIE was closing branch lines already. The first to go had been the moribund Harcourt Street line in Dublin, and while its closure became a matter of controversy as the sixties progressed and commuter pressure built up in Dublin, there was hardly a murmur on this account at the time. Most of the early branch-line closures were accomplished quietly; there was a public realisation that many such lines were simply a hopeless burden on CIE.

The first major controversy arose over a proposal to close down all the stations on the main southbound suburban line in Dublin between Westland Row (now Pearse Station) and Blackrock, except for Lansdowne Road, which would have one train each way per day plus a service for rugby internationals. The full route from Westland Row to Bray was losing £137,000 a year, and it seems that CIE had actually considered closing the entire service. The arrangements proposed in May 1960 entailed fewer trains, offering express times, to Blackrock and points south. The existing service was to conclude on 11 June.

The day, a Saturday, duly arrived, and the Bray train made its last call at Sydney Parade, Sandymount, Booterstown and Salthill. At Sydney Parade a carriage-load of young men and women dressed in Edwardian costume had entrained, and the Last Post was sounded by a gentleman in full military regalia.

Then there arose a nasty legal snag for CIE. Under the terms of the 1958 act, it was necessary to give two months' notice in *Iris Oifigiúil* (the official gazette) if it proposed to close a railway station. This had not been done, and so CIE undertook to postpone the closures and restore the old service until the end of the summer schedule. In fact the new plan lapsed, although three of the five stations were phased out at a later stage. A well-organised public lobby had developed in opposition to it, under the auspices of a body styling itself the Suburban Railway Committee.

Despite this embarrassing reverse, CIE was able to look back with satisfaction on the first year of the new dispensation. The annual accounts for the year ending in March 1960 showed that the deficit had been reduced from just under £2 million to just over £700,000. The loss on the railways had been more than halved to just over £500,000. Revenue overall increased by £800,000. In the autumn of 1960 the company announced what it said would be the last substantial branch-line closures under the five-year plan. The West Clare, Waterford/Tramore and West Cork lines were to go in the first half of 1961.

The West Clare railway was the last narrow-gauge line in Ireland, and had been immortalised by Percy French's song, 'Are You Right There, Michael?' It closed on 31 January 1961. It was a highly sentimental occasion, and such numbers of people were present that CIE officials feared that too many would attempt to travel on the last train. So they cancelled it! The earlier train had already been packed to capacity, and huge crowds had gathered at each of the twenty-one stations along the fifty-three-mile route from Ennis to Kilkee. Among the passengers was an old gentleman named William McInerney, aged eighty-five, a retired civil bill officer from Kilrush. He had travelled on the very first train to Kilkee over seventy years before, five years after Parnell had turned the first sod for the West Clare with a silver spade. Mr McInerney took a poor view of CIE:

I think it's a disgrace to close the branch line, as it could be made a great tourist attraction and be the means of attracting foreign tourists during the summer season. CIE thought to fool me and hundreds of others by cancelling the late train, but I anticipated their move and travelled on the earlier one which proved to be the last.

The whimsical ghost of Percy French pursued the West Clare to the end. The information office at Kingsbridge (now Heuston) in Dublin had informed enquirers, with an appropriate sense of paradox, that 'Officially there will be no last train on the West Clare.'

By now public opposition to branch-line closures had gathered momentum to the point where both Lemass and Childers felt obliged to give support to CIE. They pointed to the astonishing improvement in the company's fortunes and emphasised that only 420 miles of line had been closed, despite a recommendation from the Beddy Committee — whose original report formed the basis of the 1958 act — to close over 1,000 miles.

They repeated the assurance that the present closures would be the last under the five-year plan, a point Childers stressed yet again in the Dáil in July.

By then the Cork and Waterford branches had been closed, not without a bitter campaign of protest in the case of the West Cork. But in spite of the government's pledge, these proved to be by no means the last of the closures. At the end of June 1962 Andrews told a meeting at the Institute of Public Administration of CIE's intention to close another twenty-three branch lines before the end of the five-year plan, thus reducing the railway system by a further 500 miles. All through the second half of 1962 and 1963 the announcements tolled like a bell as yet more charming and unused stretches of railway were finally abandoned.

The battle to modernise the railways had been won, and the aura of success in CIE was reflected in the continued improvement in the company's accounts. In the year ended March 1961 the deficit was reduced again, to just under £250,000 despite a bus strike that cost the company over £70,000; in other words, a reduction of seven-eighths in two years. It seemed that the company, if it could hold its course, would actually make a profit in the coming year, two years ahead of target. By any standard this was an astonishing performance.

But now the focus shifted abruptly from the railways to the buses. There had been an unpleasant dispute with the busmen, involving a lock-out by the company following a weekend strike by the men over a pay claim in March 1961. It did little to help labour relations in the company, which had been placid over the preceding three years. Once the dramatic improvement in CIE's finances became apparent, there followed the inevitable wage claims, and the management took to issuing worried statements about the recovery being threatened by excessive demands.

To all this was added the question of one-man buses which the company had been trying to introduce since 1960. Discussions had dragged on, without any real progress being made, until 1962, at which point CIE decided to force the issue. They announced that one-man buses would be operated from 1 May. They realised that there would be trouble over this, but reckoned that at least it would break the log-jam and hasten a final settlement. The ITGWU, to which a large majority of busmen belonged, told the men not to work the one-man buses in the absence of an agreement with the company. When six ITGWU men at Broadstone garage in Dublin followed their union's instructions, they were dismissed on the spot by CIE management. An immediate unofficial strike followed as the incensed bus workers ignored the cautious advice of ITGWU officials that seven days' notice of strike action should be given in accordance with established pro-

111

All the Roses! Early sixties contestants for the title of Rose of Tralee, the centrepiece of the Festival of Kerry, which started in 1959 and quickly became one of the most successful of the dozens of local festivals which sprang up throughout provincial Ireland in the 1960s. The Rose of Tralee competition is relentlessly wholesome, however, and is in no sense a beauty contest: there is never a bathing suit in sight. Judged purely as a commercial venture, which is basically what it is, the Festival of Kerry has been a runaway success.

cedures. For the men this was a simple issue of principle: six union members had been sacked for obeying a union instruction. The union, in turn, should not pussyfoot in its response.

Eventually two priests intervened in the dispute, and a formula was put together whereby the six men would be reinstated, the union would accept the principle of one-man buses, and the company would not implement any such scheme in advance of an agreement with the union. The dispute was to be sent to the Labour Court.

The Labour Court recommendation, that one-man buses be introduced at once for day-tour and private hire coaches, was rejected by the men by a large majority. Dublin busmen, in particular, were resolutely opposed to it. The Labour Court had also recommended bonuses, training for conductors, and an absolute guarantee against redundancies, all of which were accepted by CIE. In July, but only after considerable pressure had been brought to bear on the men by the ITGWU, they agreed to allow the introduction of one-man buses on the limited scale provided for in the Labour Court recommendation.

There were two more or less simultaneous developments in the autumn of 1962. First, CIE aimed to extend the one-man bus operation to other areas, but the unions would not negotiate on this without first receiving guarantees of improvements in pensions, sick leave and privilege travel. The company rejected these claims as irrelevant to the question of one-man buses, and their position was supported by the Labour Court.

Secondly, the union moved against the leaders of the unofficial strike of the previous May. They suspended them from holding office in the union for periods ranging from two to five years.

The spring of 1963 arrived. CIE were hoping to widen the breach already made on the issue of one-man buses. The unions were determined to drive a much harder bargain than before. And the men were suspicious of the very concept of one-man buses, which they had only agreed to accept under great pressure, and resentful of the ITGWU's action towards the unofficial strike leaders.

The paranoia of the men was the distinguishing feature of what followed. Once again, CIE increased the stakes by announcing their intention of extending one-man buses to twenty provincial routes. An immediate strike was averted by the intervention of Jack Lynch, the Minister for Industry and Commerce. His main proposal was for a form of compulsory arbitration to settle the unions' ancillary conditions claim. The men rejected this by a margin of three to one, despite a recommendation from the unions to accept. The idea of compulsory arbitration had been too much for the men to take; moreover, they had in mind the Labour Court's finding on the issue. In desperation the minister now suggested a commission, whose recommendations would not be binding, to examine pay and conditions. The men rejected this too, and on 8 April an official national bus strike involving all CIE unions began.

It ended on 12 May. By a narrow majority the men accepted a formula which allowed the company to extend its one-man operation to the twenty nominated provincial routes, but only under the stringent conditions agreed in respect of the previous year's settlement. Anyone becoming redundant as a consequence of the new operation would receive compensation comparable to that offered to railwaymen due to branch-line closures.

It seemed that the men had lost. The company had widened the breach they had first made in the men's resistance to one-man buses in 1962, albeit at a price. The men looked for a scapegoat and were not long in finding it in the ITGWU. They felt that it had dragged its heels on the issue; it had been too willing to play by the book when the company was obviously unafraid of confrontation; it had been happy to concede the principle of the one-man operation when the men disliked it intensely, no matter what the conditions might be. Now, to cap it all, the ITGWU refused to lift the suspensions on the leaders of the unofficial strike. CIE, in contrast, had not made the men re-apply for their jobs after the strike, as was the traditional practice. It seemed to the men that on the issues where the union should have stood firm, it yielded, and on those where it might have yielded, it stood firm.

The men were fed up with the ITGWU. But under ICTU rules they could not join another union, so they broke away and formed their own. In October 1963 the National Busmen's Union was born and soon grew to rival the ITGWU among busmen.

In fact the men had won. CIE was exhausted by its pyrrhic victory and never again took up a further extension of one-man bus operations with any vigour or determination. And by now other problems had been added to the débâcle of the one-man buses. The deficit for 1961-62 had jumped to £1.7 million, not far short of what it had been at the start of the five-year plan. This had been caused mainly by high wage settlements characteristic of those years; CIE was a labour-intensive company, and 60 per cent of all its expenditure went upon wages and salaries. These increases cost the company an extra £2.35 million,[8] which could be only partly offset by increased fares, and hardly at all by increased productivity, the scope for which was notoriously restricted in the transport industry. In 1962-63 the deficit rose again, although there was a marginal improvement in the final year of the plan.

By then the hopes for a self-financing CIE had finally been abandoned. By December 1963 Childers was acknowledging that the company had to serve social as well as commercial needs, a quite different emphasis from that of the heady days of 1961. The 1964 Transport Act bowed to the inevitable and built in a yearly grant of £2 million for the company. It is doubtful if it could ever have been made to run at a profit, a point Childers took up, rather belatedly, in May 1965 when he told the annual dinner of the Permanent Way Institution in Dublin that the attempt to make it break even had not been realisable. Despite the extraordinary achievements of the first two years of the Andrews regime, there were underlying problems which were always likely to tell against the company in the long run. Its rates of revenue tended to be lower than the rate of inflation, but were offset in the early years by a large increase in the volume of traffic, Equally, its increases in productivity per worker were less than half the national average. These were permanent features of the company's make-up, whereas the features that had stood to it in the late fifties and early sixties — the voluntary redundancies it secured on the railways, for example — could not be carried forward from year to year; and in the end it was always going to be vulnerable to a high wage round.

But it was the 1963 strike that broke CIE's spirit, for it closed off the one avenue that could have offset the effects of mounting costs. It also acted as a cold shower on that zealous spirit of innovation which had been a hallmark of the company since 1958: there was little point in pursuing new initiatives if the price to be paid for them was financial ruin, even if they did yield a paper victory in the end.

At the heart of the strike had lain an absence of trust between the ITGWU and the men. The parallels with the building workers' strike are suggestive:

The union recognised that CIE was a public undertaking, run in the public interest, on the board of which was a retired president of the union. Furthermore, its efficient and economic management was seen to be in the interests of all the workers. In these circumstances, the union took the view that CIE management was there to manage. The union did not wish to interfere with that right; they merely wished to ensure that when changes were made, their members would be protected. They therefore did not oppose one-man buses in principle, but instead sought certain guarantees regarding job security.... But the men saw the whole thing quite differently; it appears that to them job security was the principal concern and they were not impressed by the guarantees that they had received.[9]

If that last point is correct, then nothing could have satisfied the men, for the guarantees were as comprehensive as could possibly be expected. CIE's courageous if over-optimistic crusade had been about the transformation of a state of mind, as much as anything else. It effected that transformation among its own executives, and likewise among many of the union officials with whom it dealt. But it broke on the suspicious conservatism of the work-force. Once again, it was ordinary people — remote from positions of power and influence; not particularly well paid or materially comfortable; whose employments made nonsense of such vogue ideas as individual dynamism; and whose strong sense of communal tradition predisposed them to a defensive truculence — who remained mentally in traditional Ireland while the new Ireland was beating on their doors.

Chapter Seven

1965

A road block has been removed

No one who has lived in Ireland, or studied Irish conditions, in recent decades can have failed to realise that, at least until the political explosion of 1968-9 in Northern Ireland, the Republic had begun to turn its back upon the legacy of bitterness bequeathed to it by the partition of the country and the Civil War. So far as the first of these is concerned, the exchange of visits between the two Prime Ministers of north and south in 1965 — the first such exchange since the division of the island has become an accomplished fact — was widely seen at the time as an indication that old animosities were quietly being laid aside.   F. S. L. LYONS

> This is our fate: eight hundred years' disaster
> crazily tangled as the Book of Kells,
> the dream's distortion and the land's division,
> the midnight raiders and the prison cells.
> Yet like Lir's children banished to the waters
> our hearts still listen for the landward bells.
>   JOHN HEWITT

THE Second Vatican Council ended in Rome on 8 December 1965. Despite the soothing words of the more conservative bishops, it was clear that the Council had effected a transformation in the life and habits of the Church. Even the mass, the central mystery of Catholic life, had been revolutionised. The Latin mass had passed into history for the majority of Irish Catholics the previous March when the new vernacular rite had been adopted. No change was more keenly felt among conservative Catholics, for the seemingly immutable and universal form of the old mass had lain at the emotional heart of pre-Conciliar Catholicism. At Christmas 1965, for the first time, another ancient rule was set aside, and the faithful were permitted to receive Holy Communion at midnight mass and again on Christmas morning. Moreover, some members of the hierarchy were positively exhorting Catholics to think in new ways. In his televised Christmas message Cardinal Conway advised against the tendency to huddle inside the Church and disregard what was happening in the outside world.

Of course, not all prelates were as ready as the Cardinal in urging new ways upon their flocks. The Archbishop of Dublin had little enthusiasm for

117

the new style. In January 1965 he ordered the removal from the church at Dublin Airport of a crib with modernistic, non-representational carved wooden figures. The figures undoubtedly were a break with the Irish tradition of pious plaster. But Dr McQuaid's action was regarded by many as high-handed and insensitive, not least in view of the fact that the church in question had been built largely with funds contributed by airport workers and on land donated by the state. In another area, however, Dr McQuaid made a shrewd concession to modernity. In March he appointed the first-ever press officer for the country's largest diocese. Hitherto the Church had no need to concern itself with press relations. But in the changed climate of the mid-sixties press interest in the Church increased; the national newspapers all had correspondents at the Vatican Council and were conscious as never before of the different factions and tendencies within Catholicism. The Church was increasingly analysed in terms which might have been employed in the case of a large political party, representing a coalition of conflicting interests. The obedient deference of the fourth estate could no longer be presumed upon.

The regular June meeting of the hierarchy at Maynooth took this process much further. It was decided to establish a communications centre to train the clergy in modern mass communications methods. Henceforth the emphasis was to be on efficient exploitation of the media, rather than plaintive lamentations about the snares and perils thereof. A National Council for the Apostolate of the Laity was also created.

The last great monument to the old Church was dedicated in August. Galway cathedral, the 'Taj Meehawl', unrepentantly conservative in design as befitted the diocesan cathedral of Dr Michael Browne, was opened for worship. It is a very large, domed, cruciform structure whose internal mosaics — including tableaux of Patrick Pearse and John F. Kennedy — are among the most sublime examples of Irish Catholic *kitsch*.

In some respects, one might have thought that nothing had changed or would ever change. On 1 June the second novel of a young Irish school teacher, John McGahern, was banned by the Censorship Board. It was *The Dark*, a deeply unflattering account of the narrow claustrophobia of Irish provincial life. In a new age it seemed a woefully anachronistic decision. Even the *Irish Independent*, generally the most cautious and conservative national daily, deplored the ban. But worse followed. In September McGahern, who had been on a year's leave of absence from the Dublin primary school where he worked (in order to take up a Macaulay Fellowship), was not re-employed. His employer was the school manager, the local parish priest. Because of this, the Department of Education refused to interest itself in the case. The Irish National Teachers' Organisation, McGahern's trade union, asked the parish priest to explain his action. The priest replied that McGahern 'was quite well aware of the valid reason which would render his resumption of duties inadvisable'. However, he refused to elaborate, although he told the press that *The Dark* was not a factor in his decision and that he had not read it. It would be fair to say that this remark was greeted with scepticism.

The clamour against the absurd literary censorship in the Republic was growing and attracting some unaccustomed supporters. In February Father Peter Connolly, professor of English at Maynooth, told a Tuairim* meeting in Dublin that something had to be done to create a better system of book censorship. The voice of the creative writer was missing from the Censorship Board and should be added; failing that, a literary editor or critic should be co-opted. Within a week, however, the Archbishop of Dublin had issued a pointed restatement of the traditional view. Speaking to the National Film Institute, he said that a majority of Irish people wanted censorship 'because they accept the natural and Christian moral law'. He dismissed 'the fractional element in our society that chooses to exercise itself in acrid hostility towards censorship'.

Another pillar of traditional Ireland, the Gaelic Athletic Association, was in the throes of internal debate. The rules of the Association forbade membership to anyone who played or attended foreign games — defined as soccer, rugby, hockey and cricket — or attended foreign dances. Here was a piece of simon-pure tribalism if ever there was one. Under the standing orders of the GAA's annual congress, the ban could only be discussed once every three years, and 1965 was such a year. It was also the first time that the abolitionists mounted a concerted effort, which at least amplified the subject and made it an issue with implications far beyond the GAA. The move to change the rules failed by a large majority, as it did again in 1968.† Its defenders saw its retention as a matter of symbolic importance. They resented its very discussion: to discuss change was to contemplate change; change was heresy, therefore discussion was heresy. Their arguments tended to lack a sense of proportion. Mr M. Costigan told the Laois County Board that 'The ban should be retained. Men like Davis, Pearse, and Wolfe Tone died for its retention.' A more comprehensive case was made out by Mr L. McGovern, chairman of the Mayo County Board:

Our enemies are many, both inside and outside our Association. To those outside we must present a united front and show them that we here in Mayo are prepared to withstand their influence.

Mr F. Brennan added that on many occasions the Irish rugby team had played

---

*A discussion group, largely composed of liberal intellectuals and controversialists. It acted as a ginger group for many new ideas, in the first half of the decade in particular.
†The ban was finally removed in 1971.

in Belfast and stood to attention for 'God Save the Queen'; anyone who asked if these players were as good Irishmen as the next needed their heads examined.

The case for the abolition of the ban turned on its ignoring of reality. In Mayo Mr J. Garrett called it a farce: he knew that there was not a county in Ireland which could field fifteen men who did not attend foreign dances. In Kerry Mr M. Begley said he could not see any difference between watching a foreign game on television and crossing a fence to see one. But the most incisive point was made in *The Spotlight*, a Dominican monthly, in March:

> If Rome can change, why not the GAA? . . . The ban has the flavour of certain things ungreen on the far side of the border. . . . It is out of tune with the ecumenical note of the times.
>
> Does it not seem a little odd that when the Catholic Church is to allow its members to attend services of other faiths, the GAA still pronounces excommunication on its members who attend other games?

The debate about the GAA ban was interesting less for itself than for the way in which it epitomised the attitudes on both sides of a larger cultural debate in Ireland. Broadly speaking, the abolitionists represented those forces in Irish life which either welcomed the changes of the 1960s or acknowledged their inevitability. They tended to argue pragmatically from the empirical facts of Irish life. Their instincts were to oppose the kind of tribal laager represented by the ban. The defenders, on the other hand, were conservatives under siege. They saw enemies at the gates and conspirators within the walls. They appealed to symbols and to that idealised image of the people which lay at the heart of traditional Ireland's self-deception. When the behaviour of ordinary people departed from that demanded by the ideal, they simply averted their gaze in disgust. They comforted themselves with the thought that there were 'good' Irishmen and 'bad' Irishmen. Only the 'good' Irishmen really mattered; the rest were cultural quislings whose behaviour could be discounted.

But what possible hope was there for their kind of Ireland in the face of modern mass media? On 1 May the first fixed satellite television transmission between Europe and America was broadcast via the 'Early Bird' satellite. Pictures transmitted from nine countries were seen live in Ireland. A few months earlier a new international phenomenon, the Rolling Stones, staged their first-ever concert in Ireland; by an ironic coincidence, on that very day the death occurred of Jimmy O'Dea, Dublin's best-loved troubadour.

Life in the Republic began to manifest the strains of a transitional society. By the end of 1965 the hopes of industrial peace held out by the national wage agreement lay in ruins. The newly formed National Busmen's Union cut its teeth in June with a two-week national strike in support of a pay increase and a forty-hour week. Thereafter it seemed as if the dam had burst. In the second half of 1965 there was a plethora of strikes: the gravediggers (four weeks); printers (eight weeks); bakery workers (seven weeks), as well as less protracted disputes involving telephonists, electricians, maintenance craftsmen and drapery store workers. Once more there were conflicts of interpretation over a clause in the national agreement, this time the one dealing with anomaly claims. The unions claimed that it allowed reasonable latitude for such things as working hours and length-of-service claims; the employers thought them precluded by the agreement and resisted to the point where the unions had to capitulate or strike. Furthermore, prices were charging ahead. In the two years following the national agreement the rate of inflation almost doubled in comparison to the two years preceding it. In the autumn of 1965 the unions asked for a revision of the agreement; instead the employers suggested a totally new one. What they really wanted was an agreement which could be enforced like a contract. This was more than the unions could agree to, and talks were suspended in December without any money offer even being discussed. It was a dismal end to a troubled year.

Tourism and foreign travel alike had a good year, however. Aer Lingus introduced the BAC-111 short-haul jet, and British Rail the roll-on roll-off car ferry. The number of tourists' cars arriving in Ireland increased by 53 per cent. British Rail's competitor on the Irish Sea passenger trade, the B + I Line, was bought by the government. Tourist revenue went up to £77 million for the year, and the recent steep rise in the number of American tourists was maintained.

In Dublin the contract for the new housing scheme in Ballymun, the largest public housing enterprise in the history of the state, was signed. There were a few, very few, voices raised on the subject of planners' blight, but no attention was paid to them. Four miles away, at the city end of Ballymun Road in Phibsborough, a row of small single-storey cottages stood vacant and idle, awaiting demolition to make way for a skyscraper and supermarket complex. The cottages had been mostly inhabited by old people, and the Corporation was thoughtfully providing caravan accommodation for them nearby as the property developers were preparing to smash their way onto the site. It was a little thing, but a telling one. There was an increasing niggle of unease about the energetic young men who were doing well out of the boom and taking no prisoners on the way.

Two other developments towards the end of the year signalled the passing of old ways. In November it was announced that the Bank of Ireland, the National Bank and the Hibernian Bank were to merge completely in a new Bank of Ireland group. It was a decision which, in the view of one scholar,

In a country which loves
horses, no decade ever passes
without producing some Irish
champion. Arkle (above) was
the great champion of the
1960s, and in the opinion of
many the greatest of all
steeplechasers. Dundrum
(right), one of the smallest of
all show jumpers, was
nevertheless immensely
successful both in competition
and in the hearts of the
public.

'transformed the organisation of banking in Ireland'.[1] The other Irish banks hastened to merge as well, and Allied Irish Banks was formed in August 1966. These mergers brought some unthinkable consequences in their wake. Banks jazzed themselves up and began to advertise on television, which to some must have seemed like consultant surgeons employing sandwich-board men. The Royal Bank, which for years had assumed the characteristics of a home for distressed Protestants, was pitched into a promiscuous alliance with the rough-and-tumble Romans from the Munster and Leinster. The quaint and sleepy Irish banking system which had served the quaint and sleepy Irish economy was swept away, to be replaced by larger, modernised units geared to the needs of a free trade economy.

For that is what we now became. The Anglo-Irish Free Trade Area Agreement (AIFTAA) was signed in London by Harold Wilson and Seán Lemass on 14 December. It came into effect on 1 July 1966, when the United Kingdom abolished all import duties on Irish goods, with a few named exceptions. Ireland cut her import duties on goods from the UK by 10 per cent on the same date and undertook to make similar reductions in successive years until they disappeared in 1975. There was hardly a murmur of opposition to this announcement, which represented the fulfilment of one of Seán Lemass's greatest ambitions. Yet it was a historic turnaround, the absolute negation of traditional Sinn Féin economics. When the transitional period was completed,

the British Isles would once again become a free trade area; economically, the Act of Union would be restored.[2]

Only one voice was raised against the agreement on this count in the Dáil. On 5 January 1966 Seán Dunne of the Labour Party asked if we had forgotten that the British were ever referred to as oppressors? Speaking of Lemass, he said:

Did he mention anything at all to Harold about partition? I suppose that'd be in bad taste too — he might think you were a Fenian or something.

This may have caused a faint echo in the hearts of some government TDs. They said nothing. The AIFTAA was supported in the Dáil by the Fianna Fáil (the Republican party) majority in the first month of the year in which Ireland celebrated the golden anniversary of the Easter Rising.

At about ten o'clock on the morning of 14 January 1965 Seán Lemass left Dublin. An hour and a half later his car crossed the border into Northern Ireland, where an RUC escort met him and accompanied him to Stormont Castle.

Ever since he had become Taoiseach, Lemass had been seeking to break the ice with the North. While Brookeborough had been in power in Belfast this had been a hopeless business. But Terence O'Neill had been more encouraging. A few months after O'Neill had become Prime Minister, Lemass spoke in Tralee about the need to recognise the reality of the Unionist majority in Northern Ireland, albeit an artificially created majority. O'Neill responded in a reasonable way to this, and Lemass in turn suggested talks on economic matters. There followed a coolness, from the autumn of 1963 to the summer of 1964. Lemass made a couple of unnecessary speeches about the evils of partition — one to the National Press Club in Washington, DC, the other to a Fianna Fáil party meeting in Arklow — which caused O'Neill to back off angrily, telling an interviewer from the *Belfast Telegraph* that he was 'disillusioned' with the Taoiseach. But the overwhelming emphasis in Lemass's speeches on Northern Ireland since 1959 had been well removed from such traditional rhetoric, and eventually it was O'Neill who sent Lemass a discreet invitation to Belfast.

Lemass did not hesitate. O'Neill greeted him with the careful words 'Welcome to the North': he realised that to use the words 'Northern Ireland' would expose Lemass to the charge of having given formal recognition to the province's constitutional position. He was satisfied, as he indicated repeatedly afterwards when under pressure from the Unionist Party's right wing, that the fact of Lemass's presence transcended all verbal considerations. He emphasised the breakthrough involved in the Taoiseach of the Republic of Ireland driving 'through the gates of Stormont...the very...symbol of the separate existence of Northern Ireland'.

The discussion between Lemass and O'Neill did not touch on constitutional or political matters. Economic questions alone were discussed, as was appropriate for two men of their practical and modernising temperaments. Lemass summed up the meeting thus:

There is no question that this meeting was significant ... [but] its significance should not be exaggerated. I think I can say that a road block has been removed. How far the road may go is not yet known. It has been truly said, however, that it is better to travel hopefully than to arrive.

Reaction to the meeting on both sides of the border was good; in the South it was almost buoyant. The general feeling remained that partition was 'artificial' and could not last. In the meantime sensible relations and economic co-operation were to be welcomed. In fact some Southern opinion had moved very far indeed from traditional rhetoric. Mr J. F. Dempsey, general manager of Aer Lingus and president of the Irish Association for Cultural, Economic and Social Relations, had told a group of Dublin industrialists in February 1964 that the present constitutional position of Northern Ireland should be recognised and accepted if proper neighbourly relations were to be established.

The Lemass/O'Neill meeting had an immediate effect on Irish nationalist opinion. It emphasised the importance of friendship between hitherto divided communities and played down the territorial claim. A week after the meeting an Nationalist Party delegation under the party leader, Eddie McAteer, saw Lemass in Dublin, and his prompting led the Nationalists to take up the role of official opposition at Stormont. Thus, while maintaining their 'fidelity to the united Ireland ideal', the Nationalists became Her Majesty's loyal opposition. It was not very logical, but it was the stuff of political accommodation.

There followed a hectic few weeks. On 4 February Brian Faulkner, the Northern Minister of Commerce, met Jack Lynch, the Republic's Minister for Industry and Commerce, in Dublin. On the 9th O'Neill himself came to Dublin. On the 12th the two Agriculture ministers met: Charles Haughey displayed his customary sense of style by entertaining Harry West to dinner in his house at Raheny. O'Neill appeared on television and publicly praised the Taoiseach, the Cardinal Archbishop of Armagh and the Pope, three unlikely candidates for the approbation of a Northern Ireland Prime Minister. In early April a joint North/South committee on tourism was established, thus giving the first practical expression to the new mood.

The reaction among Unionists to this transformation was much less certain. There was widespread public approval in Northern Ireland for the new spirit of co-operation, and a feeling that the North would have to move with the times. But opinion in the Unionist Party had been disturbed by the fact that the original meeting had been arranged by O'Neill in total secrecy. Even his cabinet colleagues were kept in the dark until it was all over, and this combination of secrecy and lack of trust told against O'Neill in the long run. Faulkner, although hardly an impartial judge of a matter like this, claimed later that the circumstances of the first Lemass/O'Neill meeting marked the beginning of 'the slide away for support for O'Neill within the unionist community'.[3]

Moreover, Unionism showed little inclination to make the sort of historic compromise that the Nationalists had just made. On the very day that O'Neill was in Dublin the chairman of the Young Unionist Council, Edward Gibson, was forced to resign after failing to secure a vote of confidence from his colleagues. The previous October he had called on the Prime Minister to remedy the 'unhealthy situation' in the party:

It should have been stated clearly before now that the utterances of people like the Rev. Ian Paisley do not represent the opinions of the vast majority of our party.

125

His colleagues had made it plain to him that his views did not command the support of a majority in the branches. The temper of the Young Unionists — who might have been supposed to be the most liberal element in the party — can be gauged from the fact that, despite having debated the question twice, they were unable even to send O'Neill a telegram of congratulation on his meeting with Lemass.

The Grand Orange Lodge passed a vote of confidence in the Prime Minister at the end of February, but the anger of the Unionist right eventually surfaced in full at the start of April. Almost inevitably, it was Edmund Warnock who first took up the cudgels. Both he and Desmond Boal had criticised the Lemass/O'Neill meetings in Stormont. He now made a sweeping attack on O'Neill, saying that three months earlier

Constitutionally we were untroubled, and economically we were making gradual progress. . . .
Today the position has gravely deteriorated, due to the well-meaning but unwise action of one man, the Prime Minister of Northern Ireland.
He has succeeded single-handed in doing, within the last couple of months, what all our enemies failed to achieve in twenty-five years of ceaseless endeavour, for he has thrown the whole Ulster question back into the political arena with consequences already apparent and with worse to come.

He hinted, as others had done, that the arrival of Harold Wilson in Downing Street the previous October had lain behind O'Neill's *démarche*. He feared tripartite talks between Dublin, Belfast and London, from which Northern Ireland would have nothing to gain and in which she would inevitably be under severe pressure to make some unreciprocated concessions to the Republic. O'Neill had 'made haste' to throw away the 'perfect shield' of a position adopted by his three 'wise' predecessors: no talks in advance of a formal recognition of the Northern Ireland government:

I say 'made haste', for he acted in complete secrecy behind the back of his cabinet and ignoring the parliamentary party which maintained him in office.

It was a powerful speech, and it summed up the anti-O'Neill case most comprehensively. The next day Warnock's views were echoed by Dr Robert Nixon, the MP for North Down. Nixon actually called for O'Neill's resignation, and suggested Brian Faulkner to replace him.*

Despite these volleys from the right, O'Neill duly got what the chief whip described as an 'absolutely overwhelming vote of confidence' at a private parliamentary party meeting on 8 April.

In the meantime a number of material issues arose within Northern

---

*Nixon had originally supported the Lemass/O'Neill meetings, but subsequently claimed that O'Neill had been 'duped' by Dublin.

Ireland which gave O'Neill the opportunity to indicate to the Catholic minority that a new era was at hand. Sadly, he did not take it.

O'Neill's six and a half years as Minister of Finance had convinced him of the need for rapid economic modernisation. A number of committees had been established to examine various aspects of the economy, and their reports punctuated O'Neill's first two years as Prime Minister. The Benson Report on the railways recommended a severe pruning of the system, with the heaviest cuts falling on the western half of the province. The Mathew Report on the future development of the Belfast region recommended halting the growth of Belfast itself in favour of a new city which should be sited in the Lurgan/Portadown district; again the claims of the west of the province, with its extremely high rates of male unemployment, were ignored. The government acted on both these reports and could argue that the neglect of the mainly Catholic west was not sectarian, but merely the logic of economics. They could point to the fact that in both areas of policy they were merely following a pattern already visible in the Republic.

But the problem was that it was hard to discount sectarianism from any aspect of Northern life. One powerful and embarrassing voice had been raised against the decision to locate the new town at Lurgan/Portadown. In August 1964 Geoffrey Copcutt, the planner who had been appointed eighteen months before to design the new city, resigned and issued a damaging statement on the whole affair. The site chosen, he said, was a poor one. Derry had been the obvious choice, not only as the second city but as a centre for higher education. He flatly accused the government of sectarian political motives in choosing the Co. Armagh site ahead of Derry.

I have become disenchanted with the Stormont scene. Stormont, on my brief but deep acquaintance, has shown signs of a crisis-ridden regime — too busy looking over its shoulder to look outwards.

The decision, taken in July 1965, to call the new town Craigavon was a particularly insensitive one. Catholics could only regard it as an affront, and the town commissioners, who were appointed by the Minister of Development, William Craig, were very much in the old style. The chairman was a company director with strong Unionist Party connections; there were three other members of the Unionist Party on it and just one token Catholic, who was based in Derry, on the far side of the province.

The greatest controversy, however, centred on the Lockwood Committee on higher education, which made the astonishing recommendation that Northern Ireland's proposed second university should be sited, not in Derry, where there was already a well-established university college, but in the sedate, and overwhelmingly Protestant, market town of Coleraine, near the

The marked improvement in the Northern Ireland economy in the mid sixties owed much to the energy and drive of Brian Faulkner (above), the Minister of Commerce. But Northern prosperity tended to be concentrated in largely Protestant areas, and Catholic enclaves like Derry's Bogside (right below), seen here from the city walls with the Walker Memorial - later blown up by the IRA - still in position, still had very high levels of unemployment. Despite this, North/South relations remained excellent until 1968: the O'Neill/Lemass meetings were continued under Lemass's successor, Jack Lynch, seen here at Stormont in 1967.

mouth of the Bann. The Lockwood Committee's recommendation was published on 8 February 1965, three weeks after the first Lemass/O'Neill meeting and the day before O'Neill's return visit to Dublin. Here was a timely opportunity for the government to make a dramatic gesture to Catholics, and one, furthermore, that would have been politically feasible for O'Neill, since the committee's recommendation was regarded as scandalous by many members of his own party. Many Derry Unionists, in particular, were outraged.

Instead the government accepted and acted on the Lockwood Report. It was the worst decision of O'Neill's career, and the one that did most to earn him a reputation for bland verbalising. It is hard to say anything in extenuation of it.

It was not only an affront to Catholics, but a potent weapon for those Unionists unhappy with O'Neill since his meetings with Lemass. The danger of defeat by a backbench Unionist revolt grew so great that O'Neill actually had to threaten to resign if the Lockwood decision were defeated. The ubiquitous Edmund Warnock was once more in high dudgeon. In a long and bitter debate at Stormont Warnock attacked the government for announcing the decision without giving parliament, press or public any opportunity for discussion. Robert Nixon claimed that it was common knowledge that the Lockwood Committee had been influenced in its decision to site the university at Coleraine. He added pointedly that while the Prime Minister now talked of the decision being a collective cabinet one, there had been little sign of collective cabinet responsibility in the decision to invite Lemass to Belfast.

Nixon later went beyond anything that any Unionist had said before. Addressing a meeting of Derry Unionists, he elaborated on his hint in the Stormont debate. He claimed to have it on the authority of a cabinet minister — not Faulkner or Ivan Neill — that the government had actually instructed Lockwood to site the university at Coleraine. Moreover, O'Neill had acted thus because he had been lobbied by certain 'faceless men' from Derry, Protestants all, urging him not to site the university there under any circumstances because it was a 'papish city' and should therefore be starved of industry and prestige institutions. The Prime Minister afterwards denied this point-blank, adding that 'All my cabinet colleagues, without exception, categorically deny ever having made any such statement to Dr Nixon.'

Nixon, in fact, had overstepped the mark. He neither substantiated his allegations nor withdrew them, and his constituency party turned temporarily against him. In addition, he had the Unionist Party whip withdrawn from him at Stormont for 'impugning the integrity of the government'.

But in a society where conspiracy theories were as common as wet days, the legend of the 'faceless men' took hold in the popular imagination. People thought again about the implications of the Benson and Mathew Reports and wondered whether the influence of the 'faceless men' could be detected there too.

Despite this unpromising background, there was a widespread feeling that O'Neill represented a sea-change in the politics and life of Northern Ireland. He had cultivated a slightly liberal image, albeit in symbolic things. He was clearly ill at ease with the more obnoxiously sectarian forms of Unionism. He may have temporised with them in some matters, the university question in particular, but against all that was the fact of his dramatic breakthrough in relations with the Republic. He had taken his political life in his hands and shown a unique degree of courage and statesmanship. Moreover, his liberalism seemed to have captured the spirit of the times. The whole western world was swept to the left in the second half of the 1960s;* it seemed that the neanderthal forms of Ulster loyalism must inevitably perish in the face of new ideas, the international media, ecumenism, and so on. This kind of thing was infectious: the small number of liberals in Ulster really believed that their hour had come at last.

They had something else to sustain them. Traditional forms of loyalism and nationalism alike thrived on poverty and depression. Now, however, the Northern Ireland economy was expanding again. Brian Faulkner had been an outstanding success as Minister of Commerce and had injected the sense of purpose and energy into the job which had been so conspicuously absent before. A new package of incentives to industrial investors, based on those available in the Republic, produced similar results. Such multinational companies as Ford Motors, ICI, Goodyear, Du Pont and Courtaulds established plants in the province. Twenty-two American firms alone came to Northern Ireland in the first half of the 1960s. The annual unemployment figures for 1965 were the lowest of the decade, although once again the greatest improvements came east of the Bann. (In Derry and other western areas, by contrast, unemployment remained as intractable a problem as ever.) In February 1965 the government published the Wilson Report, which consolidated many existing plans into one master-plan. It proposed to create over 60,000 jobs and build a similar number of houses in a six-year period. Its strategy rested on the development of major growth centres, located mainly in the eastern half of the province — it endorsed Craigavon as the principal one — a high level of government expenditure, and an extensive programme for the retraining of the exceptionally high number of unskilled and semi-skilled persons among the Northern Ireland unemployed.

*Even in the Republic in 1965, the Anti-Apartheid Movement, a good bell-wether of this process, organised its first effective protests against a touring South African rugby team.

O'Neill's political gamble paid off in November. He called a snap general election, which resulted in an increase of 7 per cent in the Unionist vote and the recapture of two of the four Belfast seats which the NILP had held since 1958. Economic advance had allowed O'Neill to steal the NILP's clothes. Besides, there had been a split in the NILP at the end of 1964 because William Boyd, MP, and two colleagues on Belfast City Council refused to support party policy and vote for the Sunday opening of children's play centres. Boyd's sabbatarianism may have found its reward in heaven; it found none from the electorate. He was one of the two NILP victims at the general election.

By the end of 1965 Terence O'Neill had triumphed. He had opened up relations with the Republic, continued his tentative process of reconciliation between Protestants and Catholics within Northern Ireland, confounded his political enemies, both within Unionism and without, and swept to a crushing victory in a general election. Could it be that the tide really was flowing for liberalism?

It was an election year in the Republic as well. A lot had changed in the party system since the dull election of 1961. The generational change in Fianna Fáil continued, and the young men in mohair suits came more and more to dominate the party's public image. The dogmatism associated with the twin national aims of de Valera's time — reunification of the country and revival of the Irish language — had disappeared. Much of the party's idealism had gone with it, and most of its radicalism as well. Only the brief and tragic efflorescence of Donogh O'Malley's career remained to bear witness to what was best in Fianna Fáil. The capable, assertive men were moving in, pragmatic managerial types who liked power. Older republicans were uneasy:

[Lemass] came to office a poor man and was a poor man when he left it, but in his later years he accepted the ability to make money as a criterion of success in others. It is a standard which enables successful businessmen to buy their way into politics.[4]

The new men were a product of Fianna Fáil's extraordinary success in recent years. It had transformed the country and had become the party of dynamic capitalist development: the party of reality. Its sense of reality had been an overdue corrective to the fantasies that had sustained traditional Ireland, but it held its own dangers: pragmatism is a hollow philosophy which can easily shade into cyncism.

Fianna Fáil was still the party to beat. It enjoyed winning, and no victories had given it more satisfaction than those in the Cork and Kildare by-elections of February 1964. For a sitting government to achieve two such

132

victories after three years in office and within a year of the introduction of the turnover tax said as much about the opposition as anything else.

Those by-election defeats caused an upheaval in Fine Gael. The party leadership was as moribund as ever. General Seán MacEoin, for example, the defence spokesman, was on holiday in Spain during the campaigns, while Fianna Fáil's busy young men were canvassing hard. A few days after the by-elections 'Backbencher' in the *Irish Times* summed up Fine Gael:

This morning it stands discredited, in tatters and tears, a veritable shambles....
The Fine Gael party [is] a group of amateur and part-time gentlemen ... pitted against some of the best professionals in Europe.

The shock of the by-election defeats had one interesting consequence. On 3 March 1964, for the first time that year, there was a full attendance of the Fine Gael front bench in Dáil Éireann. This corrected, at least temporarily, one of the more ludicrous aspects of the party. It had been said that if you wanted to find the Fine Gael front bench, the place to look for it was not the Dáil but the Law Library.

The discontent in the party, especially among younger members, finally found a focus in May. Declan Costello, son of the former Taoiseach John A. Costello, presented the party with a draft eight-point programme which was very radical by Irish standards, and almost insanely so by those of Fine Gael. It called for full economic planning, not just programming; legislation to ensure that private sector targets were met; the creation of a Department of Economic Affairs; government control of the banks' credit policies; direct government investment in industry; an increase in social capital investment; an emphasis on direct taxation; and price controls.

The elders were not pleased. A few days later, addressing the party's Ard-Fheis, James Dillon denounced 'young men in a hurry'. Gerard Sweetman, the party's finance spokesman and the one really capable and energetic figure among the conservatives, was opposed to the Costello plan. Liam Cosgrave, on the other hand, inclined towards Costello, and his contribution to the Ard-Fheis proved decisive. The party agreed on a nine-point programme, comprising Costello's original eight points — with the proposals on taxation and price control watered down — plus a platitudinous declaration about improving the living standards of farmers.

The Fine Gael party now embarked on a schizophrenic existence. The 'Just Society' proposals, as they came to be known, were no sooner endorsed as official policy than conservative party spokesmen were making clear their dislike for them. Sweetman, for example, was careful to emphasise in June 1964 that Fine Gael was 'a middle-of-the-road party, suitable for the changing times in which we live'; Dillon, meanwhile, was emphasising the

Gerry Sweetman, the bête noir of the Young Tigers. Sweetman was a formidable conservative who, more than anybody else, was responsible for ensuring that Fine Gael did not reform itself from within in the 1960s.

party's devotion to private enterprise, in case anyone had missed the point. A committee appointed to draw up a comprehensive policy document based on the nine-point plan seemed in no hurry to discharge its task.

Fine Gael won two by-elections in the second half of 1964, both in traditionally Fianna Fáil constituencies, but in both cases their candidates secured a strong non-party sympathy vote, being the widow and eldest son of the deceased incumbents. One of them, John Donnellan, had the additional advantage of having just captained the Galway football team to the all-Ireland title; it was a useful bonus in the constituency of East Galway.

A further by-election, in Mid-Cork in March 1965, returned yet another widow, Mrs Eileen Desmond of the Labour Party. Lemass had threatened a general election if the Fianna Fáil candidate were defeated. He proved as good as his word. The Dáil was dissolved, and polling was announced for 8 April.

Fianna Fáil, as usual, issued no manifesto and simply ran on its record. The party glowed in the aftermath of the Lemass/O'Neill meetings and invited the electorate simply to 'Let Lemass Lead On'. Its newspaper advertisements were contemptuous of the opposition parties: 'Our plans are working — don't let them mess everything up again.' In the middle of the campaign the government was pleased to report that the national accounts showed the budget deficit to be so minute that no new heavy taxes would be needed. On the other hand, it did not announce an increase of ½d on the two-pound loaf of bread; that was delayed a few weeks until the election was safely won.

The Labour Party produced a document entitled *The Next Five Years* which declared that the party stood for public enterprise, economic planning, and an equitable distribution of the national wealth. It urged an end to the 'free-for-all' in price increases, more direct taxation, capital gains tax, and social welfare increases; but still it avoided using the word 'socialism'.

Since 1961 the Labour Party had been moving very cautiously to the left, but the emphasis was more on the caution than on the movement. The phrase 'Christian socialism' had been employed repeatedly by Corish in speeches and interviews in recent years, but Labour remained vulnerable to and nervous of the danger of a 'red smear' campaign. Nevertheless, the party had made some useful acquisitions during the lifetime of the Seventeenth Dáil. Noel Browne and Jack McQuillan wound up their National Progressive Democrat vehicle and joined Labour in 1963, and in the following year the Workers' Union of Ireland affiliated to the party.

The crucial Labour Party intervention in the 1965 campaign was its decision not to enter a coalition government. This effectively handed the election to Fianna Fáil.

The announcement of the election found Fine Gael in an embarrassing position. The committee which had been entrusted ten months before with the task of formulating a full policy document had still failed to do so. Clearly the party was deeply split on the Costello plan. The dissolution of the Dáil forced everyone's hand. Within a week a manifesto was produced. *Towards a Just Society* was a victory for the liberals in the party. It embodied most of Costello's original eight points and emphasised the party's concern 'with making a reality of two concepts: "freedom and equality"'. It stressed the need for a comprehensive social policy based on equality of opportunity. Its emphasis on social justice attacked Fianna Fáil where it was most vulnerable — so much so that Lemass was forced to disinter his 1963 pledge of a social policy in order to counter the 'Just Society'. But, as in 1963, it was just talk. Lemass believed in a rising tide lifting all boats: if you create wealth in sufficient abundance, social justice will automatically follow in its wake. The 'Just Society' challenged this idea directly. Introducing it to the press, however, James Dillon felt moved to stress that 'We shall rely on private enterprise. We are a private enterprise party, believing in the democratic institutions.' The political correspondent of the *Irish Times* summed up the position:

> The tragedy of the Costello plan is that it was launched by Fine Gael. . . . Its whole purpose was destroyed . . . when James Dillon declared that the party was still a 'party of private enterprise'.
> All who understand economic or political language know that there is no intention by Fine Gael of taking over the plan.

They never had to, because Fianna Fáil won exactly half the seats in the Dáil when the polls were declared. This gave them an effective overall majority, since the Ceann Comhairle was once again Patrick Hogan of the Labour Party. All the major parties improved their share of the vote; minor parties and independents were swamped. Labour did well in Dublin for a change, and Frank Cluskey, Dr John O'Connell and Michael O'Leary were all returned for the first time. Noel Browne, however, lost to Seán Moore of Fianna Fáil in Dublin South-East. Labour improved its representation in the Dáil to twenty-two, the best figure it has ever achieved. Fine Gael, despite a 2 per cent increase in its support, stayed put at forty-seven seats.

It was a triumph for Seán Lemass, and an encouraging performance by Brendan Corish. But for James Dillon it was the end. He resigned the leadership of Fine Gael on 21 April 1965 and was replaced by Liam Cosgrave. On 13 May Cosgrave made his first major speech in Dáil Éireann as leader of the opposition, on the budget debate. There were five other Fine Gael TDs in the chamber to hear him speak.

Cosgrave was considered a cautious liberal in 1965, at least by Fine Gael standards. He had swung the Ard-Fheis towards the Costello plan and had chaired the sub-committee that had eventually produced the 'Just Society'

136

document. It was generally felt that the main opposition party had at last acquired a man for the times and was about to engage in that root-and-branch reform of its structure which was so badly needed.

The 1965 general election was the first to have received widespread television coverage. One member in particular of the panel of experts had displayed indefatigable energy with an almost unbroken ten-hour performance. It stood him in good stead when he launched his own political career in the Senate election a few weeks later. In a cloud of statistics and high-velocity opinions, Garret FitzGerald had arrived in the political arena.

Chapter Eight

1966

Let Erin remember

— The memory of the dead, says the citizen taking up his
pintglass and glaring at Bloom.
— Ay, ay, says Joe.
— You don't grasp my point, says Bloom. What I mean is ...
— *Sinn Féin!* says the citizen. *Sinn féin amháin!* The friends
we love are by our side and the foes we hate before us.

                                                        JAMES JOYCE

The revivalists do not seek merely to revive a language, which task
would be an objective one, susceptible of scientific planning and
accomplishment. They seek to propagate the thesis that to be 'Irish'
(through and through) one must be a very low-grade peasant, with
peasant concepts of virtue, jollity, wealth, success, and 'art'. To be a
Gael, one has to change oneself, clothes, brogue and all, into the
simulacrum of a western farm labourer.   MYLES NA GOPALEEN

IT was a year for the backward glance. The Easter Rising of 1916 was duly
commemorated, and Eamon de Valera was re-elected President, although
his margin was embarrassingly slight considering the year that was in it.
Sectarian murder reappeared on the streets of Belfast; and in Dublin the IRA
blew up poor old Admiral Nelson, Pillar and all, for the greater glory of
Ireland. It was not the best of years.

In the first half of the year 'The Late Late Show' established a reputation
for scandal which has never wholly deserted it. A number of incidents in
quick succession were responsible for this. The first was a suggestion that a
bunny girl was going to appear on the programme on Saturday 29 January as
part of a campaign to attract Irish girls to work in the Playboy Club in
London. There had never been any intention of having a bunny girl on the
show. The whole thing had been a classic piece of mis-reporting by the newspapers, but so intense had been the wrath of the righteous that the eventual
non-appearance of a bunny girl was credited to the power of outraged public
opinion.

A fortnight later, however, there was a more tangible source of
controversy. One item on the show entailed a husband and wife being asked
the same questions out of earshot of each other, in order to compare — and

Poor old Admiral Nelson! This was the scene in O'Connell Street on the morning of 9 March 1966.

more important, contrast — their answers. The questions had to do with their lives together, but were harmless and banal, and were intended only as a vehicle for some innocent laughter over what was hoped would be the differing answers. One of the questions concerned the colour of the nightie worn by the wife on their wedding night. The lady herself was at a loss to remember what colour it was, and suggested that in fact she may have worn none at all. This moved one viewer, the Bishop of Clonfert, Dr Thomas Ryan, to protest vigorously 'In fairness to Christian morality'. He denounced the item as objectionable, saying that 'everybody who watched the programme will know what I'm talking about'. Within forty-eight hours the matter of 'the Bishop and the Nightie' was a *cause célèbre*. People all over the country who had no objection to the item on the Saturday night were in high moral dudgeon by Monday afternoon, having realised *ex post facto* that the bishop spoke for the affronted conscience of the country. Gunnar Rugheimer, the Swedish-born controller of programmes, who was a favourite whipping-boy of most traditionalists in Ireland,

was in rollicking good form about the whole saga. He thought it was all intensely funny and another indication of the quaintness of the Irish mind.[1]

Nevertheless, RTE was sufficiently shaken by the brouhaha to issue a rather craven apology for the incident.

The whole thing had served to crystallise the vague sense of resentment which was one strand in the web of public response to the television service. Provincial Ireland, in particular, could not help feeling that RTE's whole ethos was rather too slick and metropolitan, and that it took a condescending view of older and slower ways. RTE, and 'The Late Late Show' in particular, were perceived to be influential agents of change in Irish life.

Gay Byrne, the presenter and producer of 'The Late Late Show', seemed the very personification of the new Irishman: natty, metropolitan, and slightly liberal in some of his views. He was also very good at his job, which caused some people — especially men — to say they couldn't stand him. He was a Christian Brothers' boy who had got on by his own efforts and talent, but who retained little of the narrow dogmatism commonly associated with his teachers. He was, in many ways, a conventional self-made young bourgeois, but this alone was enough to mark him out as a man of the sixties, for the self-made young bourgeois was a species only newly introduced into Ireland.

The incident of the Bishop and the Nightie, for all its absurdity, demonstrated once again how easily conservative opinion could be mobilised among ordinary people against an exposed and prominent group. It was subsequently remembered as a farcical incident, and the consensus of opinion was that the bishop had lost his sense of proportion. But he was not the only one.

No sooner had that furore settled, however, than another one blew up. A young Trinity College student and part-time playwright, Brian Trevaskis, referred on the show to Galway cathedral as 'a ghastly monstrosity', and to the Bishop of Galway as 'a moron', and suggested obliquely that the Galway people were being forced to pay for the cost of building the cathedral. Firing from the hip, he managed to hit a few more targets: the Archbishop of Dublin, the Christian Brothers, the parish priest who would not re-employ John McGahern, the Irish language. He generated more heat than light. A couple of people in the studio audience made plain their hostility to Trevaskis and emphasised the ready willingness of ordinary Catholics to sub-scribe to the building and maintenance of churches. The *Irish Catholic* compared RTE to Cromwell, which is about as rough as you can get in Ireland. Once again, there was a chorus of motions from county councils deploring and denouncing. The most level-headed pronouncement on the whole business came from the bishop, not usually, in all truth, the most temperate man in Ireland. Noting that there were 'strange ideas about art and architecture' current, he declared himself not in the least surprised to have been called a moron by a student of Trinity College, but he also made it clear that he objected to being defamed on a publicly funded medium with-out right of redress. (Technically, one supposes, he could have sued Trevaskis, but in reality this avenue was closed to him.) He also pointed out that he had given a public account of the disposition of all funds in connection with the cathedral and 'was surprised and indignant at the accus-ation that I used coercion to obtain the funds required'.

Trevaskis offered to apologise publicly, and went on the following week's 'Late Late Show' for that purpose. He apologised for the use of the word 'moron', as being 'an obscene and indecent' word, but then launched off on another peroration, which ended with his doubting whether the bishop, to whom he had just apologised, knew the meaning of the word 'Christianity'! This time, however, there was a balanced panel of mature and intelligent people* in the studio, and the discussion which immediately erupted was structured and coherent, with Trevaskis being made to adduce evidence for his assertions.

It is unfair to 'The Late Late Show', in a sense, to recall only those programmes that touched on farce, although they are among the best-remembered television programmes of the 1960s. It has long since become a commonplace to say that the show itself has played an extraordinary part in

*Vincent Grogan, Seán Whelan and Conor Cruise O'Brien.

expanding the agenda of public discussion in Ireland. It made adult debate accessible to a mass audience, because its staple fare was a *pot-pourri* of light entertainment. It was not unusual for parts one and two of the show to be concerned with trivia, while the final part tackled a serious public issue seriously. At their best, its discussions combined the spontaneity of public-house arguments with the discipline of legal debates. It is hard to think of a major issue of public concern to which the show has not addressed itself over the years. In addition, it occasionally devoted a whole evening to one vocational or social group — priests or itinerants for instance, to take but two examples from the 1960s — and by presenting them in an informal setting did much to alter the stereotyped public images of them.

The most intriguing election of the decade occupied the early summer of 1966. The Presidency was the unlikely office to be the object of such a contest, but de Valera, running again in his eighty-fourth year, was challenged by T. F. O'Higgins, a Fine Gael lawyer from the 'Just Society' wing of the party. Fianna Fáil has always had an element which regards opposition to its wishes as barely this side of treason, and their numbers were swollen by this piece of political cheek. Opposing the patriarchal Chief on the golden anniversary of the Rising: sacrilege rather than treason, perhaps, in some minds! O'Higgins ran a splendid campaign, presenting himself as a man of a new generation, best suited to the changed times. The Presidency is not an office to attract political promises, but O'Higgins stumped the country, pressed the flesh, and conveyed the vague idea that he would somehow strip away the patina of remoteness and formality associated with Arus an Uachtaráin. For once in the decade, Fine Gael managed to look a younger, livelier party than Fianna Fáil.

O'Higgins built up a sufficient head of steam to worry Fianna Fáil into some old-style mud-slinging. President de Valera, of course, did not himself campaign, which was probably just as well, for the election produced some undignified exchanges. For example, Micheál Ó Moráin, Minister for Lands and the Gaeltacht, had this to say in Coachford, Co. Cork, in support of the President's candidacy:

> For a time it appeared that there would not be any candidate opposing the President. The *Irish Times* spoke, however, demanding that Fine Gael oppose the President.... We all know the *Irish Times* is the mistress of the Fine Gael party and mistresses can be both vicious and demanding.
>
> Now it may be necessary for the Fine Gael party to jump to the crack of the *Irish Times*'s whip and gather the relics of the old ascendancy around them. It would, however, be a sad day for our people if the outlook of the President of the Irish people was forged and shaped by the occupants of a back room in Westmoreland Street.

O'Higgins took himself to Swinford, in Ó Moráin's own county of Mayo, in order to reply:

I do not know that the *Irish Times* is the mistress of our party, and I certainly do not know anything about the vicious demands of mistresses. On these questions I bow to the superior knowledge of Mr Moran.

The best summary of Fianna Fáil attitudes came from the *Irish Independent*, which commented that 'To judge from ministerial speeches,[it] looks upon the Presidency as a kind of honorary doctorate.'

When the result was declared at the start of June, it became clear that Fianna Fáil had had every reason for anxiety. Out of a poll of 1,100,000, de Valera's winning margin was a mere 10,500 votes, compared with 120,000 in 1959. O'Higgins's performance had been a revelation, suggesting to Fine Gael that under its new leadership it was poised to make the breakthrough that would enable it to offer a serious challenge to Fianna Fáil in the next general election.

The Easter Rising was celebrated both North and South. At a time when the hard shell of Ulster politics had at last showed signs of cracking, the timing was unfortunate. The spirit of compromise and accommodation visible in parts of both sectarian camps in 1965 was severely tested. In early March, about a month before the anniversary, Captain O'Neill appealed for restraint, and Cardinal Conway made a pointed call for Catholics to play a greater role in the Northern Ireland community and 'to desert the paths of party self-interest'. In the event, the Northern celebrations passed off quietly; there was the usual declamatory violence, but nothing worse. The government practically sealed the border in a fit of nerves, a move that Dublin thought melodramatic. O'Neill felt obliged to reply to a speech which President de Valera had made in Dublin calling for Stormont to be made subordinate to the Dáil rather than Westminster, but the reply was really aimed at the Rev. Ian Paisley. Paisley and his Ulster Constitution Defence Committee organised their own celebration, to commemorate the defeat of the Rising, and at a service in the Ulster Hall Paisley 'declared war' on the Prime Minister as a 'Lundy who will sell the province down South unless he is removed from office'.

But at least Northern Ireland had been spared the sort of disgraceful rioting and disorder that had been seen in West Belfast during the Westminster general election campaign of 1964. Whatever old foolishness had been involved in the republican marches and the flourishing of the tricolour was at least part of a traditional pattern in the North, and the celebrations were confined to Catholic areas. Similarly, Protestant commemorations of the Battle of the Somme also assumed the characteristics of 'traditional

There were rival ceremonies North and South to celebrate golden anniversaries in 1966.
Rev. Ian Paisley (above) held a prayer service in the Ulster Hall to commemorate the
Ulstermen who died at the Battle of the Somme and to celebrate the 'defeat' of the Easter
Rising of 1916. In the South the Rising was commemorated with the full pomp of state
ceremony: this picture shows President de Valera arriving at the reviewing stand outside the GPO.

processions'. What happened next, however, as the summer came on, went beyond ordinary tradition.

It had been assumed that if there was serious trouble in Northern Ireland in 1966 it would come from the Catholic community, but in fact the republican movement was a spent force. Militant Protestantism, however, was rippling with life. Ian Paisley was elbowing his way towards the centre of the stage. He was the incarnation of reactionary Protestant bigotry. A loud-mouthed, ranting clergyman in a long and dismal Ulster tradition, his twin hatreds were the ecumenical movement and Irish nationalism, or, to use his own words, 'Romanism and Republicanism'. The first half of 1966, with so many minds turned to the past, gave him an ideal climate in which to flourish. And when he flourished, trouble followed. For two years he had been denouncing every move that could possibly serve to reconcile Catholic and Protestant in Northern Ireland, and the province itself with the Republic, as a sell-out to Rome or Dublin or both.

In early June he led a noisy march, which contained some offensively anti-Catholic banners, through the Cromac Square area of Belfast. It was a Catholic enclave, and rioting ensued. Paisley had been en route to the General Assembly of the Presbyterian Church in Ireland to protest against the Church's 'Romeward tendencies'. (In fact the Presbyterian General Assembly proved its own conservatism by its inability to endorse a report on religious discrimination in Ireland, although it did pass a resolution opposing 'all forms of unfair religious discrimination'.) Some of his followers got to their destination and harried and jeered Lord Erskine, the Governor of Northern Ireland, no less, and had to be restrained by the RUC from attacking him and his wife. O'Neill attacked Paisley's 'sordid techniques of gangsterism' in a Stormont debate, but, incredibly, the Unionist right could still find soft words for the Protestant extremists. Desmond Boal, R. B. Simpson and the inevitable Warnock all made equivocal speeches, and Boal's reward was to be dismissed as a junior counsel to the Northern Ireland Attorney-General.

At the end of June came the Malvern Street murder, when Peter Ward, a young Catholic barman, was shot dead. Three men were arrested and convicted of his murder, one of whom was reported as saying: 'I am terribly sorry I ever heard tell of that man Paisley or ever decided to follow him.' The men responsible for this and an earlier murder were members of a group calling itself the Ulster Volunteer Force*which had 'declare[d] war against the IRA'. The UVF was promptly outlawed; Paisley hastened to dissociate

*The relationship between Paisley, his associates, the UCDC and the two paramilitary groupings known as the Ulster Volunteer Force (UVF) and the Ulster Protestant Volunteers (UPV) is shadowy. The most authoritative examination of them appears in David Boulton, *The UVF*, chapters 4 and 5.

himself from it, although, as O'Neill told Stormont, he had hitherto received and welcomed its support. O'Neill also announced that one of Paisley's closest associates, Noel Doherty, was a member of the UVF. Paisley subsequently got three months in jail for his part in the riots at the Presbyterian General Assembly in May.

The Orange marching season followed hard on these unsavoury events. There were a number of vaguely anti-O'Neill motions at Orange demonstrations, and some government ministers were heckled and shouted down by extremists. In the autumn there was a brief right-wing push in the Unionist Party against O'Neill's leadership, but it faded as quickly as it had arisen. However, the most telling evidence for the survival of a particularly squalid kind of Orange bigotry came in a little-reported incident in Belfast in September.

Mrs Thomas Watson was a middle-aged member of the Association of Loyal Orangewomen. Her brother had fought in the war and had been wounded and captured by the Germans. His life had been saved by a German military surgeon, who was a Catholic. The two families had remained in contact with each other over the years, and the surgeon had written recently to say that his son was being ordained a priest in Rome. He invited Mrs Watson to the ceremony, and she accepted. However, when she informed her Orange lodge of her intention, she was invited to get out or be thrown out. She resigned.

It was this kind of quiet bigotry that made any kind of liberal advance so difficult in the North. In its name, enough people could always be mobilised to make modern politics or social relations impossible. It did not even require a majority of Protestants to adhere, either actively or passively, to the extreme right. It was enough to secure the support or the complaisance of such a sizeable minority within Unionism as would subvert the position of any progressive leader. Given the siege mentality at the heart of Unionism, there were always enough people to hand for this purpose.

In the Republic the 1916 commemoration ceremonies passed quietly in a country where the invocation of the spirit of the Rising seemed anachronistic. There were one or two local examples of nationalist bigotry, as when GAA men on the Drogheda commemoration committee wanted to exclude representatives of the local soccer and rugby clubs from the ceremonies. They were not, however, representative of feelings in general. The growing psychological gap between North and South was underlined by the reaction to the commemoration in either place. In the North old ghosts walked again briefly and served as a reminder of how thin was the veneer of modernisation. In the South there was much traditional speechifying, certainly, but also a considerable amount of reflection and self-criticism. For all its faults, this was a society whose present and future were not mortgaged to the past. The Republic of Ireland was learning to think on its feet, and influential men were not content with old shibboleths. For example, Mr Patrick Lynch, chairman of Aer Lingus, lecturer in economics in UCD, and one of the outstanding advocates of modernisation in Irish life, told a meeting in Trinity College in February:

We would best honour 1916 by being honest with ourselves and in our attitudes towards 1916. As a people we have deliberately chosen not to realise many of the ideals of 1916. Neither Pearse nor Connolly contemplated a predominantly middle-class society of the kind that we have created over the last fifty years. Socially, we have become a conservative, self-satisfied people. To judge from the pictures in the evening papers, our middle class, which sets standards for all of us, is more concerned to be seen publicly rejoicing in materialist affluence than with idealisms of any kind.

In its attempt to describe Ireland as it was rather than as the observer wished it to be, this kind of summary was typical of the sense of realism among the Irish modernising elite. However, a controversy was soon to explode in the Republic which would emphasise the depth of passion still invested in the ideals of traditional Ireland.

The position of the Irish language was, and is, one of the most sensitive subjects in Irish national life. Its place at the very heart of official nationalist ideology, combined with its ineluctable decline as a vernacular, have ensured its strategic importance in the never-ending Irish battle between illusion and reality.

The report of the Commission on the Restoration of the Irish Language, under the chairmanship of An tAthair Tomás Ó Fiaich, was published in January 1964. It made 288 recommendations designed to bring Irish into regular use in public bodies, to resuscitate the Gaeltacht, and to improve the standard of Irish in all branches of education. It urged the government to publish a national plan for Irish with annual targets, to establish a language fund and a state-sponsored publications board, and to encourage more Irish in the press. It also advised that the policy of 'essential' Irish — the report avoided the word 'compulsory' — be retained, but suggested that Leaving Certificate candidates who failed the examination simply through failing Irish should be given a second chance in the subject. It called for a massive propaganda campaign, and for Irish to be made a compulsory matriculation subject for Trinity College students normally resident in the state. Its recommendations for the Gaeltacht included the setting up of single-language communities on the edge of big cities and turning Galway into an Irish-speaking city.

These recommendations were made in a context which freely acknowledged the spiral of decline, and proposed to arrest it by a mixture of compulsion and heavy persuasion. What the commission did not acknowledge was that the decline was due to the apathy and lack of interest of ordinary English-speaking Irish people. There had been numerous compulsions and inducements over the years, and practically every school-child in the country for forty years had been obliged to study the language; yet public support for Irish went no farther than a general desire for its survival. In some quarters compulsion had actually increased public hostility to the language. The Irish language was dying for two reasons: the places where it still clung on as a vernacular were the most impoverished and marginal areas in a severely under-developed region; and, more disturbing still, the majority of the Irish people were not going to discomfort themselves or make sacrifices in order to revive it. English had been accepted as the language of commerce, law, administration (despite some comically ritual forms of address in civil service correspondence since 1922) and public affairs since Tudor times and had been the majority vernacular since the middle of the nineteenth century. To this inheritance was now added the effect of modern systems of mass communication, the new international youth culture centred on the pop music industry, and the reorientation of the country towards the outside world in general. In the face of this cultural juggernaut, and the people's ready acceptance of it, or at least acquiesence in it, no programme could have effected the revival of Irish without, as Lemass noted in January 1965, sacrificing 'democratic freedom and even some fundamental human rights'.

All this was cold comfort to lovers of the Irish language, whose passionate and despairing hopes for their beloved tongue seemed to recede with every decade. They could not believe that it was simply public neglect that had brought the language to the pass it had reached by the mid-sixties. For them, Irish was the very soul of the nation — and how could a free nation blithely allow its soul to be purchased by another? So they took refuge in conspiracy theories: government was lazy about the language; big business was contemptuous of it; RTE was positively hostile to it. Micheál Ó Domhnaill, head of the successful Coláiste na Rinne in Co. Waterford, speaking early in 1966, identified the two main obstacles to the revival of Irish as the attitude of parents who would not help their children at home, and of 'many in high places, well versed in the language, who disdain to speak it in their jobs and in public'.

A national petition was organised from the summer of 1964 onward aimed at mobilising and expressing public support for the revival of Irish. It was very successful; it was easy enough to sign a petition.

The government's white paper on Irish was published at the start of 1965. Broadly speaking, it accepted the recommendations of the commission's report and proposed a ten-year plan, under the control of the Minister for Finance, aimed at securing the restoration of Irish 'as a general medium of communication' in a bilingual Ireland. It agreed to implement the recommendation concerning the Leaving Certificate,* but rejected one of the commission's more controversial proposals: that increments due to public servants whose Irish was deficient be deferred. In general, neither the commission's report nor the government's white paper pointed to anything new.

For years governments had been endorsing plans for revival; language groups had been upbraiding them for their insufficient commitment; the public had signed petitions and indicated their goodwill, but no more than that. It was the familiar pattern of national self-deception. In the autumn of 1965, however, a group was formed whose object was to remove the element of compulsion in the revival policy. To do so would be to torpedo the whole policy, for all the revivalists were agreed on the necessity for some compulsion. They claimed it to be an earnest of the government's will in the business, but in fact they could not trust the Irish people to see to the revival of the language themselves, unless prodded by an official goad. For Irish-language groups, the Language Freedom Movement was a sinister development.

The LFM had a quiet first year. The public had a low boredom threshold as far as the perennial subject of Irish was concerned. What shot the LFM into the limelight was the policy-making of the Fine Gael party. As far back as the 1961 general election the party had declared against compulsory Irish. Now, in 1966, they fleshed out their attitude. In March their candidate for the Presidency, T. F. O'Higgins, told the Cork branch of Tuairim that many young people were wondering if the restoration of a Gaelic Ireland in the traditional sense was relevant in the modern world, and he called for a re-assessment of aims in the whole area of language revival. Then the party produced a policy document which pledged Fine Gael to abolish completely the mandatory pass in Irish in the Intermediate and Leaving Certificates and the proficiency tests necessary to secure appointments to public and state bodies.

Fine Gael was careful to stress that it was committed to the revival of Irish, but that any government policy must rest on popular support. Such support, it believed, was being alienated by the element of compulsion. It reiterated its

---

*In 1965, the first year of this dispensation, 301 candidates failed the Leaving Certificate through failing Irish; 91 of these passed on the second attempt.

Images of Ireland fifty years after the Rising. Ireland's first shopping centre, at Stillorgan,
Co. Dublin (above). Brendan Bowyer and the Royal Showband (below): showbands were still
a little old-fashioned in comparison to what was happening in the rest of the pop music
world, but they were hugely popular, especially in the provinces. A large new public
housing scheme at Ballymun, on the northern outskirts of Dublin (opposite).

commitment to ensuring that all Irish people got a chance to learn the language and had access to effective teaching methods.

If Fine Gael thought that that would assuage the *gaelgoirí*, they were wrong. Every Irish-language body in the country united in opposition to their proposals. The LFM, on the other hand, declared their support.

The temperature began to rise. It was, as we have already seen, a year when the idealism of the past was constantly being recalled to mind, and the timing of this revisionist campaign on the language was provocative in the eyes of some. Already, during Easter Week, a radical group called Misneach, which comprised a number of well-known writers in Irish, had gone on a seven-day public hunger-strike in an attempt to focus the national conscience on the plight of the language.

Just how bad the plight was was made plain at the end of August, when the preliminary report of the 1966 census was published. In an inter-censal period in which the total population had risen for the first time in the history of the state, the number of native speakers had fallen to less than 70,000 compared with nearly 400,000 only forty years before. It seemed to many Irish enthusiasts that for a group like the LFM to agitate in these circumstances was tantamount to kicking the language when it was down and dying. Language revivalists had always been a somewhat intemperate element in the population; now they became possessed by the sort of heart-wringing devotion peculiar to the adherents of every beautiful losing cause. And that soon developed into an unpleasant zealotry.

There had, up to this point, been one or two minor incidents involving language groups and the LFM. Protestors had burst into an LFM meeting in a Dublin hotel at the start of August, overturned a table, and delivered an ironic rendering of 'God Save the Queen'. A rumour had been circulated that LFM members were making a point of attending Irish-language masses and studiously bawling the responses of the faithful in English; the LFM denied this indignantly.

This was merely a prelude to the main action. On 21 September 1966 the LFM held a meeting in the Mansion House, Dublin. About 2,000 people turned up and jammed into every available space in the room. It was clear that the overwhelming majority of them were unfriendly to the organisers of the meeting. There was enough shouting, jeering, heckling, booing and chanting to drown the chairman's opening remarks. Union Jacks were waved derisively at the platform. On the platform itself was an Irish tricolour, which a member of the audience made haste to seize at the outset, shouting that the national flag should not be displayed at a meeting of this kind. As he was hustled away a shower of papers was flung at the stage and a stink bomb was let off.

Immediately after this a fight broke out, involving about ten men. It was evident that there was going to be serious trouble unless something was done to lower the temperature. Dónall Ó Moráin, the chief executive of Gael-Linn, mounted the platform at this moment and, pleading for calm, said:

We must have a discussion here with all points of view represented. I don't care how anti-Irish any speaker on this platform is, I will defend his right to speak as long as the other spokesmen for those who represent my viewpoint are allowed to express an opinion.

It was a courageous move by Mr Ó Moráin, and in the view of the chairman of the meeting, it probably averted a riot. In the circumstances, it may well have done, but it provided a very queer notion of the right to free speech. Such a right, it seemed, was not absolute, but was contingent upon the organisers of the meeting, who had made all arrangements and paid for the hall in the expectation of being able to propagate their cause, suffering their sworn opponents to have equal right of reply. It was as if a Fianna Fáil Ard-Fheis could only proceed in good order if every second speaker from the rostrum articulated the Fine Gael point of view.

The president of the LFM, Christopher Morris, agreed to Ó Moráin's proposal, and something like a debate ensued. LFM speakers had to struggle to make themselves heard, while the audience clearly indicated its preference for the anti-LFM group. The points made on both sides were familiar. For the LFM, Mr John B. Keane stressed the regrettable fact that the majority vernacular was English, and that an attempt to revive Irish through compulsion was futile; Mrs Maureen Ahern was concerned about the illiberal provisions in the commission's report and in the white paper; Mr Roderick Buckley attacked the unfairness of the system whereby children could fail examinations merely through failing Irish, and emphasised that the place of the language in the educational system had not produced an increase in general fluency; Morris asked rhetorically what were the technical, political, or cultural advantages of supplanting English, and appealed for a more liberal attitude to the language in keeping with the spirit of the times. On the other side, Mr Seán Ó hÉigeartaigh claimed that it was the duty of the people to hand on their heritage to their successors; and An tAthair Colmán Ó hUallacháin, who was the language-teaching specialist responsible for the 'Buntús Cainte' programme on RTE, suggested that modern educational theory would tend to support the view that the revival programme in the educational system should be improved rather than abandoned; Mr Risteárd Ó Glaisne accused the LFM of being untrue to its name because of its lack of concern for the discrimination which he alleged was suffered by native speakers in the Gaeltacht; and An tAthair Tomás Ó Fiaich said that, as a

Northener, he was a product of a non-compulsory system of a type favoured by the LFM, and if he had to choose between ignorance — which was what the Northern system was inclined to produce — and compulsory knowledge, he would have no hesitation in choosing the latter.

The Irish language was notoriously a subject on which tempers were easily lost, but the circumstances of this meeting went beyond anything anyone might have expected. It demonstrated that the forces of traditionalism in the South could be as unsavoury in their methods as their mirror-images in the North. But it would be wrong to exaggerate this parallel: the Republic in the 1960s was a society where the open contention of ideas was part of the social fabric. For all its inherited authoritarianism, it had a national self-confidence, born of its remarkable social homogeneity, which could contain and resolve the conflict of opposites without recourse to violence. The LFM meeting in the Mansion House was remarkable because it happened, once.

Nothing changed. A few weeks after the meeting the consultative council on the language, which had been set up after the white paper, was complaining that the 'white paper policy is not being put into effect, apart from some disconnected sections of it'. The contending parties settled into their familiar positions, and after the drama of pitched battle the monotony of trench warfare was resumed. The decline of the Irish language was neither arrested nor accelerated by the events of 1966. But a new orientation had been given to a cultural debate which had been growing more urgent since the saturation of the country by those cosmopolitan influences which had followed in the wake of material prosperity. In particular, all those who dissented from the traditional orthodoxies concerning the Irish language now had a focus for their views and a voice within the political system.

The population of the Republic of Ireland stood at 2,884,002 on census night 1966. This represented an increase of 66,000 over 1961 and was in marked contrast to a fall of almost 80,000 in the previous inter-censal period. The number of people in the 15-29 age group increased by over 10 per cent. The overall rise was confined to Leinster and Munster, whose populations increased by 6 per cent and 1.1 per cent respectively. In Connacht and the three Ulster counties in the Republic the population loss was over 4 per cent, although the rate of decline had slowed considerably compared with the years between 1956 and 1961. Even within the western region there were signs of hope. Towns and cities were expanding, especially Galway, which was launched on a spectacular period of population growth. Most significantly, the population of Co. Clare had stabilised, with a fall of only 163 persons; and indeed, one rural area west of the Shannon — the

Seán Lemass pictured in London prior to the signing of the Anglo-Irish Free Trade Area Agreement, one of the corner-stones of his new economic policy.

Ennis Rural District, containing the Shannon Industrial Estate — actually experienced a population increase.

The growth in population was concentrated most heavily in towns and cities. In almost every case — Waterford was the only major exception to this rule — the rate of increase in cities and large towns was significantly higher than that for the region of which they were a part. The move to the suburbs was made clear: in Dublin, excluding the Corporation area and Dún Laoghaire, the number of people increased by a staggering 30 per cent. The growth in the number of urban dwellers was remarkable. Eleven towns with 5,000 people or more grew by amounts varying from 8 to 12 per cent, and these included not just the big cities but places like Cóbh, Arklow, Tramore and Newbridge. The flight from the land was continuing, as it had for years, and as it was doing everywhere else in Europe. What had changed was that those who were leaving the land were going, not to England or America, but to the expanding towns and cities of Ireland.

This was reflected in the heartening drop in the rate of emigration. The average rate per thousand of the population had fallen from 14.8 to 5.9. Garret FitzGerald commented:

A net emigration rate of 17,000 is equivalent to a quarter of the number of people born in Ireland eighteen or twenty years earlier. This is the age group from which most emigrants are drawn. It would appear therefore that we have reached the stage of being able to provide employment in Ireland for about three-quarters of our young people. This contrasts sharply with the position between 1954 and 1961 when net emigration averaged over 45,000 a year, or the equivalent of 80 per cent of those born eighteen or twenty years earlier.[2]

No recitation of statistics can do justice to the generation of national leaders and policy-makers who were responsible for the staggering metamorphosis in the Irish population in the single decade from 1956 to 1966. In the former year the country seemed drained and exhausted. Its finances were depleted, its people emigrating in droves, its industry complacent and feather-bedded, its agriculture backward, its confidence in the future ebbing away. Yet in a mere ten years it had swept aside problems that had previously threatened to overwhelm it, and had staunched the debilitating flow of emigration to the point where demographers could predict the beginning of a population explosion.

By 1966 Ireland was a country whose physical fabric was changing and whose material expectations were increasing. It was the year when the huge new Cornelscourt shopping complex was opened in south Dublin, when the first families moved into the Ballymun high-rise flats, and when there was a 15 per cent increase in the numbers of people taking continental holidays. Some of its new difficulties were those classically associated with sudden material success: a hard edge of opportunism and an assertive vulgarity cutting into national life, and so much vestigial squalor cheek-by-jowl with Mammon. But it was a country animated by a sense of urgency. The energy and creative abilities of Irishmen now had a future in Ireland, and to this extent at least, the exigent problems of a decade before had been banished.

Many men and women had joined their abilities to accomplish this revolution in Irish expectations. But it is with the name of Seán Lemass that it will always be associated, and that is as it should be. His passionate commitment to the policies which saved his country from ruin was the crucial element in their success. The best plans will wither on the vine for want of political purpose. His personal qualities were not those one usually associates with the Irish: he was quiet, phlegmatic, punctual, efficient and unsentimental. He remained true to those characteristics in his public life, and was never tempted to play the fool and flatter the country with bombastic phrases about its superiority to all others. As Taoiseach, his principal concern was to make Ireland face the reality of its position in the world.

He retired in November 1966, and with him went the fountainhead of energetic idealism that had galvanised his party. He was succeeded by Jack Lynch, a quiet Corkman of indeterminate views, who had emerged as a compromise candidate when an open split threatened between the supporters of Charles Haughey and those of George Colley.

In recent years there has been a tendency to canonise Lemass, and in one sense this is appropriate. In a country where achievement is often denigrated by the small-minded, cynical sneer, it is right that Lemass, whose accomplishments stand as a rebuke to the begrudgers, should be remembered with honour.

Chapter Nine

1967

Cherishing all the children equally

And the blessings of the Most Reverend Dr Michael Browne be upon you and all yours but there's nothing like the wallop of a crozier to give Ireland a touch of the democracy.   JOHN HEALY

I think it is agreed by all parties that this prodigious number of children, in the arms, or on the backs, or at the heels of their mothers, and frequently of their fathers, is in the present deplorable state of the kingdom a very great additional grievance; and therefore whoever could find out a fair, cheap, and easy method of making these children sound useful members of the commonwealth would deserve so well of the public as to have his statue set up for a preserver of the nation.   JONATHAN SWIFT

A N explosion of energy had revolutionised Irish life in the first half of the 1960s, dispelling the inertia of the post-war years. But Ireland was thereby transformed into a frontier society, for the old Irish-Ireland cultural portmanteau had become a sentimental anachronism, and the ability of the Catholic Church to control the secular behaviour of its flock had been severely weakened. The disappearance of these old anchor-points of communal aspiration and, personal conduct, combined with the fact that there were fortunes to be made in a booming economy, ensured the emergence of a self-serving and unscrupulous class of *arrivistes*, wedded to money and power. Theirs was a world of the shallowest pragmatism, in which values, beliefs and standards of conduct became provisional and arbitrary. They gravitated naturally enough towards the Fianna Fáil party, for it was pre-eminently the party of industry and enterprise. In one area in particular, construction and property development, the connection between money and the party began to emerge as a focus of discontent.

Fianna Fáil had always been a no-nonsense party, but one with a severe republican conscience, epitomised by the austere figure of Eamon de Valera. Its conscience made it take seriously those twin national aims which it always declared were its *raison d'être*, the reunification of Ireland and the restoration of the Irish language, even though this idealism was in such sharp contrast to the pragmatism of its quotidian politics. But by the end of

Lemass's career the twin national aims were being quietly ignored, and there was nothing with which to replace them. Fianna Fáil was now merely 'the party of reality', and a prey to those cynical, realistic men who knew how the world worked, and that you could put a price on everything. As they became more prominently identified with the party, it was not only the old republicans who felt a sense of unease. In February 1967, within a few weeks of one another, two members of the cabinet made plain their disquiet. First, Kevin Boland, the Minister for Local Government, who had never been totally happy with new order and still hankered for the conservative Sinn Féin economics of de Valera's day,[1] made a pointed attack on property speculation. He particularly deplored the construction industry's preference for commercial rather than domestic building, and the kind of speculation in land that forced up the price of houses. The Minister for Industry and Commerce, George Colley, later amplified Boland's remarks, when he replied to a Dáil speech by the Labour Party's Michael O'Leary. He would not, he said, 'disagree entirely' with O'Leary's description of land speculators as 'crooks' engaged in 'highway robbery'.

Land speculators were, of course, easy and popular targets for politicians' abuse. But the point of such attacks as these derived from the growing anxiety within Fianna Fáil that the party was becoming identified in the public eye with an unsavoury, get-rich-quick cabal. Fianna Fáil had traditionally represented itself as the party of the small man, but had now, in the space of a few years, become identified with men of considerable property who were uninhibited in the way they flaunted their wealth. There were bound to be many in the party unhappy with this changed image: the sleek Mercedes; the mohair suits; the expensive monthly fund-raising lunches in the Russell Hotel.

It was the fund-raising arm of the party, Taca, which became the focus of all this unease. It symbolised the transfiguration of Fianna Fáil, because it was an organisation for the wealthy, and they were made to buy their way in. Clearly the party profited from this injection of funds, but in a world where you get nothing for nothing it was too much to suppose that the political allegiance of Taca members was entirely idealistic. Moreover, in a little country that loved rumour and gossip the possibilities presented by Taca were almost limitless. Stories of corruption flew everywhere. In the course of time the party realised the folly of exposing itself to this kind of thing, and Taca was allowed to fade away, at least as a formal, open organisation.

The division of opinion in the party on the question of Taca was symptomatic of another new development. Fianna Fáil had always been famed for its public unity. The occasional dissenter, like Paddy Smith in

159

The young political prince. Charles J. Haughey held the important portfolios of Justice, Agriculture and Finance in the course of the 1960s. He was once described as the 'very epitome of the men in mohair suits'.

1964, was dispatched without ceremony, and open conflicts and splits were unknown. But in 1966 there had been a leadership contest for the first time ever; now, on the question of Taca, dissent was again made public. The habit was to grow over the next two years, first on the question of the referendum to abolish proportional representation, and later, and most decisively, on the North.

The increasing moral aimlessness of the Fianna Fáil establishment prompted much of the dissent and self-analysis, especially among the young and the educated, which was a feature of Irish life in the closing years of the sixties. Moreover, Irish life had been opened up to external influences at a moment when radical protest was sweeping the western world. The Labour Party's swing to the left; the emergence of radical voices within the Catholic Church in Ireland and their widespread exposure in the media; the increasing independence of RTE's current affairs broadcasting; the growing practice of taking politics to the streets, especially where social issues were concerned: all were symptoms of a diminished confidence in the nostrums of the new economic establishment. There was, furthermore, refreshing evidence of an internal opposition emerging among intellectuals and opinion-makers, who, on the whole, had accepted the changes of the first half of the decade without demur. However, there had been a kind of heroic simplicity about events in the early sixties: the country had had to modernise or die. Precisely because of the success of the modernisers, Ireland had now become a vastly more complicated social organism, in which the urgent question no longer related to the mere creation of prosperity, but to what the country was to do with it and how it was to extend it. At that point the sort of debate and dialogue characteristic of a modern society became possible in Ireland. The new establishment became a victim of its own success by calling into being a critical opposition. And it was no coincidence that this opposition started to make its voice heard most consistently at the time when the political arm of the new establishment appeared to be in rather too cosy a relationship with a powerful moneyed interest, threatening the country with rule by businessmen at one remove.

One reform on which there was, however, almost unanimous public agreement by 1967 related to the literary censorship. At last the legislation came which amended the extraordinary regulations by which Ireland had contrived to ban nearly all works of literary excellence by her native sons and daughters, and many of foreign provenance as well. The censorship had been under increasing pressure, not only from the more liberal climate of public opinion, but also from the fact that the paperback revolution in publishing had made restrictive laws much harder to enforce consistently. The new legislation for books abolished the permanent ban, replacing it with a twelve-year ban which could be appealed at any time. It automatically released all books which had been banned before 1955, the total number of which amounted to no less than 5,000 titles![2] Later in the year the film censorship was also liberalised. It is worth noting the important part played in the movement for reform of the censorship by a small number of Catholic priests and intellectuals, in particular Father Peter Connolly, professor of English at St Patrick's College, Maynooth, and Father John C. Kelly, SJ, of Belvedere College, Dublin. In a succession of articles and reviews in such periodicals and journals as *Hibernia, Doctrine and Life, The Furrow* and *Christus Rex* they had treated and discussed works of art on their merits, refusing to be drawn into the hurly-burly of the censorship debate on either side. They obviously wrote as sincere and committed Catholics, but demonstrated that within that tradition it was possible to react lucidly and sympathetically to twentieth-century sensibility without compromising Catholic morality.

By a nice coincidence, only a week before the Minister for Justice announced his intentions regarding censorship a contretemps occurred in Tralee, Co. Kerry, which was reminiscent of somewhat older attitudes. Tralee was a prosperous county town, and the home of the Festival of Kerry, the daddy of all the festivals that provincial Ireland concocted during the 1960s on any happy pretext whatsoever: in Tralee's case it was the fact that the town had been immortalised in a sentimental ballad, 'The Rose of Tralee'; this prompted the central event of the Festival of Kerry, the annual sanitised beauty contest to discover the female who would hold that title for the coming year. In the spring of 1967 the management of the Mount Brandon Hotel, a large building on the town's outskirts which stood as a symbol of new and better times, announced that the film actress Jayne Mansfield would perform her cabaret act in the hotel in late April. Miss Mansfield was distinguished by a shock of blond hair, a minimal talent, and a titanic pair of breasts. Since the death of Marilyn Monroe male America had been searching for the sex-object of its dreams, and Miss Mansfield was gamely trying to fill the bill.

This ambition was never likely to excite the approval of the ecclesiastical authorities in the diocese of Kerry. Both the bishop and the dean of the diocese issued a call to the faithful not to attend 'the entertainment'. 'This woman boasts', they fulminated, 'that her New York critics said of her that she sold sex better than any other performer in the world.' Her presence, they declared, was a slur on the good name of Tralee. The hotel management knew when it was beaten. Jayne Mansfield's cabaret act was cancelled a few hours before it was due to begin. Miss Mansfield was dismayed. She told the press that she was a good Catholic and that she had been misquoted regarding her comments on the New York critics. Moreover, said she, when the car bringing her to Tralee had got a flat tyre at Castleisland, she had gone into the church there to light a candle for herself and her young son: 'I felt great peace, satisfaction, and happiness for this.'

If all this was farce, there was a more bitter irony to the relaxation of censorship. As noted earlier, the middle years of the decade brought the deaths of a whole generation of Irish writers. Frank O'Connor and Flann O'Brien (otherwise Myles na Gopaleen) died within weeks of each other in the spring of 1966. (Incidentally, not one government minister could be found to attend O'Connor's funeral.) A lesser figure, Walter Macken, died a year later. But the greatest loss was that of Patrick Kavanagh in November 1967, for he had written about rural Ireland both in prose and verse, especially verse, with a fidelity and lack of humbug born of intimate and affectionate knowledge. In a generation when so many voices were raised in praise of a chimerical rural arcadia, Kavanagh held fast to the truth. And little thanks he got for it. The generation of writers who had suffered most at the hands of the censorship did not live to enjoy the kinder climate for creative artists which was about to develop in Ireland, symbolised by the imaginative provision in the 1969 budget that earnings from creative work would no longer be liable to income tax.

The last six weeks of 1967 brought the first ROSC exhibition of modern art to Dublin. It was a major European art event, and its presence in Dublin symbolised the city's — and the country's — gradual integration into a wider cultural milieu after generations of insularity. At the same time Dublin's monumental sculpture was enhanced by the addition of two new items, one by an acknowledged modern master. Henry Moore's Yeats memorial was unveiled in a regrettably obscure part of St Stephen's Green, and Edward Delaney's Wolfe Tone memorial appeared, also in St Stephen's Green, but on a far better site, at the north-east corner, opposite the Shelbourne Hotel.

At the very end of the year, a couple of days before Christmas, the report of the Committee on the Constitution was published. It had been established by Lemass under the chairmanship of George Colley, the Minister for Industry and Commerce. Lemass had suggested that the constitution should be reviewed in a routine way every quarter of a century or so. The implication was that reform and revision should follow: Lemass had little time for committees and commissions whose reports led to nothing.

This committee's report was a workmanlike document, which contained three potentially controversial recommendations. It proposed that the names of religions should be deleted from the constitution; that provisions for civil divorce be made available to those who wished to have recourse to them; and that article 3 of the existing constitution — which claims the legal

The more liberal climate of opinion that developed in the course of the 1960s encouraged a renaissance in the arts in Ireland. Traditional Ireland had been hostile territory for artists and intellectuals. Now came a revival: Seamus Heaney **(left)** published his first volume of poetry, Death of a Naturalist, in 1966. The artist Louis Le Brocquy **(below)** confirmed his reputation as the finest Irish painter of his generation and began to receive a recognition at home commensurate with his international reputation. The Carrolls building in Dundalk **(right below)** designed by Ronald Tallon in the style of Mies van der Rohe, was one of the most successful pieces of modern Irish architecture. Brian Friel emerged in the course of the decade as the outstanding playwright of his generation: 'Philadelphia, Here I Come', first produced in the Abbey in 1964, made his reputation. The photograph **(right above)** is from the 1972 production.

right of the Oireachtas to legislate for Northern Ireland — be modified. Of particular significance was the fact that the phraseology which the committee suggested for the amended article 3 was much more conciliatory than that in the existing article.

The committee, which comprised members of all three parties in Leinster House, had indicated in an odd preamble that 'It was agreed between the political parties that participation in this committee would involve no obligation to support any recommendation . . . even if made unanimously.' This detracted from the weight of the report and gave politicians the opportunity to shy away from acting on it. To be fair, there was no public demand for constitutional reform, and the referenda necessary to secure amendments could have led to the most unexpected political complications. Furthermore, the idea that the Republic might amend its constitution to induce the Northern Unionists towards Irish unity had not yet occurred to many Southerners, and would not do so until pressure of events in the North caused them to rethink some comfortable traditional assumptions.

Nothing was done. The committee's report was placed carefully on a shelf in the bowels of Government Buildings, where, presumably, it still lies. There have been seven attempts to amend the constitution since 1967. Only one, the successful proposal to delete the reference under article 44 to the 'special position' of the Catholic Church, reflected the spirit of the report. More recent constitutional developments have done little to suggest that its spirit will eventually prevail.

In the autumn of 1967 the last great measure of reform to come from Fianna Fáil in the 1960s, and the most far-reaching in its effects, was implemented. 'Free education' was introduced, giving every child in the state access to post-primary schooling. The scheme entailed a direct payment from the Department of Education to all secondary schools below the highest fee bracket to cover tuition, book and transport costs. It resulted in over 90 per cent of Irish schoolchildren being educated in schools which were part of the 'free' system, while the remaining 10 per cent enjoyed the expensive *cachet* that continued to attach to private schooling. It ended the scandalous situation whereby poverty could deny a child the opportunity for a full education; the extent of this deprivation was highlighted by the rapid increase in secondary school enrolments in the closing years of the decade, as the effects of the new scheme began to be felt.

At the start of the 1960s Ireland had been almost alone among Western European countries in its disregard for equal educational opportunity. In this, as in so much else, the country had ignored external developments. Whereas in West Germany almost four children in five received some sort of secondary education, in Ireland the figure was barely one in three. The economic under-development of Ireland had ensured that pressure for educational reform was not strong. The stagnant Ireland of the 1950s was content with its inequitable and classically orientated secondary education system, which was well suited to the production of a small professional elite and a somewhat larger (but not too large) class of clerkly scriveners who could look forward to a lifetime of placid security behind a desk in a bank or a government department. Economic expansion and growth of manufacturing industry put an end to this cosy arrangement. An industrial nation aiming at full employment would have few places for the uneducated and would demand higher, broader and universal standards of education from its youth.

Until it actually happened, the idea of a free education scheme for all was considered utopian. Even advocates of radical change in the educational system, while acknowledging its desirability as an ideal, were inclined to concentrate on more 'realistic' objectives. Nearly all such schemes from the early sixties onwards involved an expansion of the inadequate scholarship system. The other principal point of attack on the old educational structure was the curriculum. As early as March 1960 the dean of the science faculty at UCD, Professor T. S. Wheeler, told an OEEC seminar on chemistry teaching that less than one secondary school in six in the Republic taught chemistry to Leaving Certificate level. Moreover, the problem fed on itself owing to the tendency among university science graduates to avoid a teaching career in favour of industry, thus creating a shortage of science teachers in the secondary school system. Not until 1962 was an association of Irish science teachers formed; they cannot have been cheered at their first annual general meeting to hear from Professor Wheeler that the standard of chemistry teaching in Ireland had been so stagnant until recent times that a student trained in 1880 or thereabouts would have had a good chance of passing the science papers in the matriculation examination in the mid-twentieth century.

This catalogue of complaints about the inadequacy of science teaching in Ireland was given official confirmation in the OECD report policy review on Ireland in early 1963. It noted the very strong classical bias in the Irish secondary curriculum. It stated plainly that the Irish standard in second-level science and mathematics was inadequate as a preparation for advanced study, and that the Leaving Certificate did not prepare the student sufficiently to enable him (or, less likely, her) to progress to the study of advanced technology.

The prejudice against the sciences ran deep among Irish educators. For example, Father James Finnucane, the president of Rockwell College, told the college's union dinner in 1961 that a liberal education was the best foundation for life which a secondary school could give: 'The aim of a secondary school ought to be to train men, not to be doctors or engineers or scientists or accountants, but to be men.' He was of the opinion that occupational training and 'practical knowledge' could be acquired later by men who had first been taught to think. Not that this humane prescription should be taken at face value: in a system overwhelmingly controlled by a deeply conservative and anti-intellectual Catholicism, there were very severe limits indeed to what might be encouraged in the way of original thought.

In such a system 'intellectual development' was code for 'spiritual development'. The first major government-sponsored report on education in the 1960s bore this out. The Council of Education's report on secondary education appeared in April 1962 and was a model of complacent conservatism. The Council's thirty-one members came largely from within the existing system, and only two of them had science degrees. One critical observer has summarised the report in these terms:

> The principal objective of education was stated to be the religious, moral and cultural development of the child. It was pretty clear that the social and economic aspects of this development — that is the relation of socio-economic background to educational attainment and the relation between education and subsequent opportunities — were largely ignored. Indeed there was an implicit hostility to such considerations, as in the statement that 'in general the aim of science teaching in the secondary school is cultural rather than practical'.
>
> The council went on to recommend *against* the state-financing or ownership of new secondary school buildings, publicly financed vocational guidance schemes and the abolition of fees. Secondary education for all was seen as utopian on both financial and educational grounds.... Any fundamental changes were dismissed and the reasons given were almost invariably not based on empirical evidence.... In its deductivist approach to analysing problems, its deference to the status quo, and its isolation of educational issues from their wider social context, it is an almost perfect reflection of much contemporary educational thinking.[3]

In the time when the Council was preparing its report, however, an important change was occurring in the administration of Irish education. Traditionally the post of Minister for Education had been a political dead-end, or a way-station for an ageing mediocrity on his journey towards retirement. But in forming his last government in 1957 de Valera chose Jack Lynch for the job and began a practice which Lemass continued enthusiastically. Henceforth Education was to go to young men with a political career to build and the incentive to reform and innovate. Lynch's successors were Patrick Hillery, George Colley, Donogh O'Malley and Brian Lenihan.

168

By the time the latter took over, after the tragic death of O'Malley in 1968, the job had so grown in importance that he moved from Justice to take it on, something that would have been considered a serious demotion only a decade earlier.

Barely two months after the report of the Council of Education was made public, another, and very different, team was appointed to investigate the state of Irish education. Unlike the Council, it was a small body, comprising only three people under the chairmanship of Professor Patrick Lynch. It was established jointly under the auspices of the Irish government and the OECD. Its report, published just before Christmas 1965 under the title *Investment in Education*, is one of the most important documents in the history of modern Ireland. It was severely utilitarian in its assumptions and approach. It defined the central problem facing an educational system which wished to promote economic development as the need to increase and broaden participation in post-primary education, irrespective of social background. It made only one specific recommendation, but its real value lay in its analysis of the existing system and its identification of those areas where change was required if the social and economic objectives of education were to be achieved. Unlike the Council of Education's report three years earlier, which had declined to compare Irish and foreign educational systems (on the lazy basis that since the Irish one was so different to the others, points of comparison were hard to find), *Investment in Education* implicitly accepted the standards current in other western countries. In this it was every inch a document of the sixties.

The existing educational system was substantially that inherited from the British. Nevertheless, it was thought of as distinctively Irish, and in one sense this was so. In the early years of the century British administrations had attempted to reform it in order to introduce a greater measure of state control and direction. These efforts had been bitterly and successfully resisted by the Catholic Church and by nationalist parties of every kidney, so that when the British left the twenty-six counties in 1922, the educational system they bequeathed to the new state was already an anachronism. For forty years Irish governments left it more or less as they had found it. It was, like much else in traditional Ireland, 'national' less because of its native provenance than of its backwardness and under-development. It is no surprise, therefore, that when it was challenged at last, it was tested according to the standards of modern and developed industrial societies and found wanting.

What *Investment in Education* discovered about the state of Irish education was truly shocking. Of national school leavers in 1962-63, only 28 per cent had passed the Primary Certificate; 18 per cent had failed or been absent; and no less than 54 per cent simply could not be traced. In other words, over half the population of the Irish primary school system could not be located on any examination list for the years 1961, 1962 or 1963. In some cases even the school list itself was lost! Therefore, out of a total of 17,459 pupils in the system, about 8,000 had dropped out altogether without even reaching or completing sixth standard in primary school. Nearly 70 per cent of one- and two-teacher schools had no supply of drinking water available; the number without flush toilets was even larger. In the secondary system nearly one teacher in five was teaching a subject he had not taken in his degree course. While about half the time in secondary schools was devoted to languages, only 5 per cent in the case of boys and 12 per cent in that of girls went on modern continental languages. Only 10 per cent of boys took science; predictably, the number of girls was even smaller. The provision of facilities for the teaching of science was more usual in schools where the fees were above average. About a quarter of all pupils who entered secondary education left without sitting the Intermediate Certificate, and of these about two in three left education altogether.

The whole thrust of *Investment in Education* was that the existing system needed a radical overhaul to end the scandalous inequality of educational opportunity, to increase the amount of science and technical subjects in the curriculum, and to employ existing resources more efficiently by phasing out small, old-fashioned schools which could never afford to offer a satisfactory range of facilities to their pupils. It was directed towards the development of an educational system geared to the needs of an expanding industrial economy.

Reform did not have to await the publication of *Investment in Education*, however. In May 1963 Dr Hillery, the Minister for Education, had introduced an extremely radical new principle into the system when he announced the establishment of the country's first comprehensive schools, aimed at the large number of children who received no post-primary education at all. It was also proposed that the state should involve itself directly in the provision of post-primary school buildings, hitherto the sole preserve of the churches. In February 1964 the government announced a new plan to subsidise directly school buildings, subject to the school having a minimum of 150 pupils.* This departure from tradition was considered sufficiently bold for the entire Labour Party parliamentary representation to enter the government lobby in the Dáil in support of it.

On the principle that he who pays the piper calls the tune, all this activity raised the prospect of creeping government control. It was on this question

---

*Interestingly, this qualification excluded more than half the country's schools from the scheme.

that the next phase of the educational story was focused. Lemass fired the opening shot at the Fianna Fáil Ard-Fheis at the end of 1964 when he dwelt on

the problems of planning and co-ordination in a system which, for historical reasons, had a minimum of centrally placed authority. The Minister for Education now has to take initiatives formerly left to hazard. If we are to obtain ... the best value for expenditure, all who are concerned in our education ... must agree that the Minister should be given sufficient authority to carry out his responsibilities.

This was potentially troublesome territory. The Catholic Church had, since the time of Cardinal Cullen, fought relentlessly for control of its own schools, and never consented to the principle of central direction under British rule. Not until the British had left did the Church permit the establishment of a Department of Education, safe in the knowledge that it would be staffed and run by Irish Catholics rather than English Anglicans or Scots Calvinists; even then, its powers were minimal. What Lemass was hinting at, therefore, threatened to disturb an arrangement that had been a central feature of the Irish state.

Against this background, what was surprising was the ease with which the reforms of the next few years were accomplished. The Church did not abdicate its pre-eminent position in Irish education, but it recognised the need for some prudent concessions to the demands of the state. Only the Bishop of Galway, Dr Browne, stood out against any change. He had long been the leading traditionalist in the hierarchy on the issue. He was particularly protective of the existing national school system. As far back as 1960 he was attacking the 'small but noisy group' in Dublin who were opposed to the system of clerical management simply because it ensured that the teaching of religion was given an assured and honoured place in the curriculum. He regarded them as the agents of 'the most violent and vicious campaign against religion that history has yet seen': the resources of the atheistic powers were organised against religion; they had traitors placed everywhere, and nowhere was too remote for their machinations. The bishop felt that the best tribute that could be paid to the country's national schools was the number of people they had turned out since the Famine to build up the Catholic Church in England, America and Australia.

Even allowing for the colour with which the Bishop of Galway was habitually wont to embellish his observations, this was clearly not a set of arguments on which the Irish Catholic Church could stand and fight in the middle of the 1960s. Besides, the particular issue on which the reformers were concentrating by then, the closure of small and remote rural schools, was as much a social and secular one as a religious one. Nothing daunted, Dr

Browne became embroiled in a running public controversy with the new minister, George Colley, on this very issue in the autumn of 1965 and the early spring of 1966. Colley was moved to deplore the 'distressingly inaccurate and intemperate' attacks which the bishop launched on his policy. The bishop made plain his fears of larger schools: they would merely be production lines for children (*Investment in Education* disagreed totally with this view) and they would involve increased state control.

The matter came to a head on the evening of 5 February 1966. Mr Colley was in Galway to address the annual dinner of the western branch of the Irish Graduates' Association. Dr Browne was present, and after the minister's speech he rose and attacked the government's policy on one- and two-teacher schools. He then left the building before the minister had an opportunity to reply, explaining afterwards that he had to be early to bed on a Saturday night in view of his busy schedule on the sabbath!*

It was clear, however, that Colley was not contemplating any fundamental structural reforms of Irish education. The principle of clerical management, in particular, was not under assault, as the minister had made clear only a month before. He defended the policy regarding one- and two-teacher schools on the basis that resources needed to be pooled efficiently, but added pointedly that he saw a similar development taking place between the facilities of secondary and vocational schools, thus obviating the necessity for a major expansion of the comprehensives. No vital Church interest was threatened by all this. The existing system was to be modified and reformed, but it was still the existing system. Indeed, it appears that the hierarchy actually encouraged and welcomed most of the reforms of the mid-sixties, including the provision of new comprehensive schools, although this was a subject on which they were to take a far less conciliatory line in the seventies.[4]

By now, however, the bit players were preparing to depart and the central character was about to swagger on stage. In July 1966 a new Department of Labour was established, and a small cabinet reshuffle ensued. Colley moved up to the Department of Industry and Commerce. His replacement in Education was the Minister for Health, Donogh O'Malley.

O'Malley was a tempestuous and energetic character, long recognised as a man of signal ability and intellect, but about whose discipline and capacity to work within a team doubts were expressed from time to time. His style can be gathered from a remark he made in the Dáil in 1960: 'What we need is an industrial, agricultural, and intellectual revolution in the next five years.'

---

*This remark caused some amusement a week later when the incident of 'the Bishop and the Nightie' occurred (see page 140). What, the wits asked, was the Bishop of Clonfert doing up watching television after the proper episcopal Saturday-night bedtime?

Donogh O'Malley, the man who revolutionised Irish education and gave all Irish children, irrespective of their families' means, access to second-level education.

O'Malley was a revolutionary by temperament: he was, at least, in open revolt against the complacency of traditional Ireland. But withal he possessed the political skills. He worked his constituency as carefully as any ward-heeler; he knew the value of good press relations; he never missed a chance to attend to the interests of his native Limerick, and to make sure that he was seen to get the credit for it; he had a theatrical touch, revelling in 'strokes' and coups.

He barely had time to warm the ministerial seat in Education before he pulled off his greatest 'stroke'. On the evening of 10 September 1966 he announced that he would be introducing a free post-primary education scheme the following year. Typically, the announcement was made at a weekend school run by the National Union of Journalists. He said that he proposed to introduce a detailed plan in the Dáil before the end of the year, and that formal discussions with the Church and other interested parties could be expected soon. Significantly, he had not felt it necessary to consult the Church in advance. Less happily, he had also neglected to mention anything to the Minister for Finance, who was going to have to find the cash for the scheme. This placed Mr Lynch in an awkward spot, since there was no retreating from the commitment once it was made, so great was the public enthusiasm for it. Lynch was actually out of the country when O'Malley made his speech, and complained subsequently in cabinet about the Minister for Education's penchant for administrative short-cuts, of which this was merely the latest and most spectacular example. But O'Malley had Lemass's protection, and that was that. As Lemass's biographer observes,

> There is evidence to indicate that Lemass had seen and even amended the text in advance; more precisely, five members of that cabinet have separately told the present author that they believed Lemass had seen the speech before delivery.[5]

The opening up of free post-primary education to all the children of the state, together with the introduction of a comprehensive free school bus service in the rural areas and maintenance grants for families who might suffer financially from the mere fact of having a child at school at all, was a magnificent achievement, beyond the hopes of the most ardent educational reformers until it was announced. There was some opposition, in addition to the complaints from the Department of Finance. The religious orders, who owned the majority of the schools affected, were unhappy at first,[6] but by the summer of 1967, three months before the scheme began, the hierarchy had signalled its approval.

O'Malley did not rest on his laurels. When he realised that the government subsidy for school transport was going to prove inadequate, he had it increased by 60 per cent. Three-quarters of all those eligible for school transport were being catered for by the start of October, within three weeks of the introduction of the scheme. CIE was building an extra 238 buses and was also hiring from Ulsterbus to meet short-term demand.

A week later the minister was cutting more corners. He announced a crash assault on inadequate national school buildings, writing to all national school managers to arrange for 'adequate sanitation and heating'. They were told to put the work in hands immediately and that the Department would meet two-thirds of the cost. Managers were further encouraged to undertake the work directly through local contractors rather than through the Board of Works as before.

The day after this proposal was made public the minister announced the abolition of the Primary Certificate. A week after that the Department of Education was startled to learn that it was going to have to remove to Athlone. Just before Christmas the minister was positively jaunty when he announced plans for three new comprehensive schools, two of them in Dublin, at a cost of £1.4 million over two years: 'I would like to pay a particular tribute to the present Minister for Finance. I don't know where he's getting the money. I must have him robbed.' A few days after Christmas he was announcing reforms in the structure of the Leaving Certificate.

It is tempting to see in all this frenetic activity a man unconsciously racing against time. For on Sunday 10 March 1968 Donogh O'Malley collapsed and died in Sixmilebridge, Co. Clare, eighteen months to the day since his 'free education' announcement. He was only forty-seven years old. *Si monumentum requiris, circumspice.*

The innate superiority of rural life had been an article of faith in traditional Ireland. When the boom came, however, rural Ireland was left behind. The prosperity of the 1960s was overwhelmingly concentrated in towns and in the east of the country. The flight from the land continued, and a growing number of people in the towns resigned themselves to the thought that it was simply one of the facts of life in the modern world. The economic modernisers and the eastern establishment were frequently accused by those devoted to the interests of rural Ireland of simply writing off the surplus population of the countryside as a demographic embarrassment.

Farmers are a notoriously cranky lot. In addition to their day-to-day complaints, their anger was fuelled in the 1960s by their exclusion from the feast. The National Farmers' Association, the principal farming organisation, had organised a series of campaigns from early in the decade aimed at bringing farming incomes into line with those of industrial workers. They all came to nothing. Then, in the middle sixties, farmers watched with real fury as trade unionists and industrial workers leaped ahead, with high national wage settlements being augmented by special claims backed up by what often seemed like strong-arm industrial action. All the talk about farmers and rural dwellers being the real soul of the nation was beginning to sound hollow.

In the spring of 1966 the NFA threatened a series of commodity strikes in protest against agricultural prices. The other farming body, the Irish Creamery Milk Suppliers' Association, picketed the Dáil in protest against milk prices; twenty-eight of them were jailed for their pains. To make matters worse, the NFA and the ICMSA, in the best Irish manner, did not get along with each other: the NFA represented mainly large farmers, and the ICMSA small farmers. The ICMSA protest dragged on in one form or another for about a month and eventually resulted in an increase of 2d on a gallon of milk to the producer. Its real significance, however, was to raise the temperature for what followed.

At the end of August the NFA threatened 'less orthodox but speedier' methods of protest if talks failed on cattle prices. They deplored the absence of a coherent beef policy, especially the failure to establish a meat marketing board as first mooted in 1964. The president, Mr Rickard Deasy, attacked the Minister for Agriculture in a speech to his organisation's annual meeting in Dublin. The minister, Charles Haughey, responded by cancelling a meeting which had been previously arranged with the NFA. The contact, once broken, stayed broken.

By early October Deasy was obliged to act on his threat. He organised and led a protest march of farmers from Bantry, in south-west Co. Cork, to the Department of Agriculture in Dublin, a distance of over 200 miles. Deasy was not what one would expect in an Irish farmers' leader. The low levels of educational attainment among Irish farmers were notorious, but Deasy was exceptionally well educated — Oxford and Louvain, no less. He had been an army officer, and his military bearing stood him in good stead on the way from Bantry to Dublin. He was not a reticent man; indeed, he was given to the odd colourful flourish, which in the circumstances that were developing in the autumn of 1966 was of no particular help.

The marchers had their numbers swollen as they went along, and by the time they arrived outside the Department of Agriculture in Merrion Street they were estimated at anywhere between 10,000 and 30,000 souls. After a rally nine leaders of the NFA went to the Department, to be told that the minister was not available to see them. Deasy thereupon vowed to wait 'a bloody month' if necessary, and the nine of them camped outside the Department's front door and waited.

176

Farmers from all over Ireland marched to Dublin in the autumn of 1967 to join with the main body of marchers coming from the south, led by the President of the NFA, Rickard Deasy (right). The photograph above is of a group of Co. Cavan farmers making their way through Drogheda en route for Dublin.

This was something new in Irish public life, and Lemass made the government's dislike of it very plain in the Dáil, referring to the protesters as 'a small group of ambitious men' attempting to dictate policy to the government of the state. There was, however, considerable public sympathy for the farmers, who had trudged 200 miles only to get the back of the minister's hand. Mr Haughey became intensely unpopular with farmers and was the object of a number of nasty incidents, including one occasion when his car was attacked in Athlone. The whole business came at a bad time for the minister, for Lemass was about to announce his retirement, and Haughey's chances of the succession were bound to suffer in the circumstances.

A patched-up compromise was worked out in early November. The nine protesters withdrew from the steps of Government Buildings and met Lemass and Haughey, who had agreed to a meeting if the pickets were first removed. Lemass's last act as Taoiseach was to propose to the incoming Taoiseach and Minister for Agriculture that they meet the NFA for comprehensive talks.

The new Minister for Agriculture in Jack Lynch's government was Neil Blaney, a stubborn, lantern-jawed Donegal republican. He was barely a fortnight in office before he had his first meeting with the NFA, which after two and a half hours of talks they described as totally unsatisfactory. By 1 December NFA men were camped once more outside the Department, 'because of the marked deterioration in the attitude of the government'. By now the original NFA aim of an improvement in cattle prices and the establishment of a meat marketing board had been augmented by a series of eleven generalised demands, set out in a farmers' charter of rights, which covered such areas as an incomes policy to close the gap between farmers and urban dwellers, the implementation of the NFA's small farms plan, the right to full consultation in the determination of agricultural policy, and so on. It was more a statement of aims than a negotiating document, but its mere existence had raised the stakes for farmers; and that, combined with the breakdown of the talks with Blaney and the renewed protest in Merrion Street, ensured that, as 1966 passed into 1967, a solution was more remote than ever, and that bitterness was increasing among the farmers.

Nineteen sixty-seven was a dismal year for Irish agriculture, consumed in a running battle between the government and the NFA. In January the farmers caused chaos by blocking roads all over the country with farm machinery, after the example of their continental brethren. Prosecutions followed, and when sixty-five farmers refused to pay their fines, they were jailed. There was a brief commodity strike and various illegal incidents, as when an NFA group waylaid a cattle truck in Co. Louth, threatened the driver and his mate, and scattered the cattle. In the midst of all this, Mr Blaney attempted to set up a National Agricultural Council, which the NFA boycotted from the start because they were not consulted in its formation. It spluttered along for a while, but then NFA nominees won control of the Beet Growers' Association, which had previously co-operated with the NAC, and that finished it as a representative body. Farmers threatened to withhold rates; the government threatened in return to withhold grants and to send sheriffs in to seize defaulters' property. More farmers were jailed for their participation in the January incidents. The Department of Agriculture, in a petty move typical of the whole dispute, withdrew all advertising from the *Farmers' Journal,* the NFA paper.

By the second half of the year activity on both sides had slowed down, out of exhaustion as much as anything else. But still nothing was solved. Deasy was succeeded as president of the NFA by T. J. Maher in August, but Maher did not meet Blaney until the summer of 1968, and then their meeting was fruitless. The hostility between the two sides lingered on into 1969, but gradually the ice melted as Jack Lynch intervened more directly with an offer 'to wipe the slate clean'.

The farmers' protest was made particularly difficult to solve by three factors. The traditional pre-eminence of the Department of Agriculture in the determination of policy was something it was reluctant to forfeit in a more corporate arrangement which would embrace the farmers. Secondly, the farmers' demands were of such a generalised nature — claiming equal 'rights' with the rest of the community, whom they judged to be doing much better than themselves — that it was difficult to find specific points on which to negotiate. Thirdly, and most importantly, the farmers themselves were badly split. The NFA and the ICMSA pulled so hard against one another that Blaney was able to dismiss the whole NFA agitation as a smokescreen to cover the disunity of the farming organisations.

Peace returned gradually, in the sense of peace being the absence of war. By the end of the decade government and farmers were talking again. The farmers' demands were not met — could not be met — until Ireland joined the EEC in 1973. Their resentment was not assuaged, but they learned the limits of street politics, and re-learned the techniques of political lobbying which they had been developing in the early sixties. The protests were an emotional spasm, which served to carry away their frustrations in the years when everyone in Ireland seemed to be prospering except them. But when it was all over, and they came in from the streets to the negotiating table, they set themselves to master those skills of persuasion and argument which were to stand them in good stead in the seventies. For the farmers, it was to prove a surprisingly short journey from the steps of Government Buildings to the corridors of the Berlaymont.

Chapter Ten

1968

Croppies, stand up!

The justice and fruitlessness of my complaints left a seed of indignation in my heart against our absurd civil institutions, whereby the real welfare of the public and true justice are always sacrificed to some kind of apparent order, which is in reality detrimental to all order, and which merely gives the sanction of public authority to the oppression of the weak and the iniquity of the strong.   JEAN-JACQUES ROUSSEAU

A state without the means of some change is without the means of its conservation.   EDMUND BURKE

THIS was the convulsive year in which were focused all the radical passions of the sixties. From Prague to Paris to Chicago the streets were filled with a new generation weary of the cynical conventions of established politics. In Czechoslovakia the stranglehold of the Soviet empire was broken for a few brave months; in France the Fifth Republic came within an ace of collapse; in Chicago at the Democratic Party convention Mayor Richard Daley's city police ran amok among student protesters. Martin Luther King and Robert Kennedy were assassinated, and Richard Nixon was elected, in the words of one American commentator, 'President of every place in this country which does not have a bookstore'.[1]

The radical fury touched Ireland too: a small Maoist group called the Internationalists grabbed the headlines by staging a noisy demonstration when King Baudoin and Queen Fabiola of Belgium visited TCD; in the autumn there was a brief surge of student unrest in UCD, followed in the spring of 1969 by the celebrated 'gentle revolution', when a protest against the manner in which the move to Belfield was being handled escalated into Ireland's first full-scale campus revolt. The administration offices were occupied, and lectures were boycotted in favour of a continuous teach-in in the Aula Max. The students drew considerable support from younger members of the academic staff, and the 'gentle revolution' was an important step towards liberalising the notoriously authoritarian power structure in the college. In Northern Ireland, however, street politics and the vocabulary of popular liberation and civil rights were borrowed from abroad to deadlier effect.

The lurch to the left in Ireland seemed nothing less than the second phase of modernisation. The first phase had been accomplished by businessmen and administrators, normally thought of as men of the right, who had at least shaken the country out of its immemorial torpor and opened it up to the wider world. But by the standards of that world, they had made a society which was grossly unequal, in which no thought was given to the redistribution of material wealth, and which was wholly lacking a coherent social policy. They had carried through a revolution; but now, it seemed, they had no more to give. While they would become complacent and smug with their own success, it would fall to a new breed of moderniser to complete the task which they had begun. Left and right were terms that only made sense in a modern society; since the right had created and consolidated a modern society in Ireland, it had *ipso facto* called the Irish left into being as well, and now its hour had struck. So the theory went.

It was a plausible theory. The new left, like the new right, drew its ideas and inspiration from abroad and seemed to have little time for the introspective nostrums of the old Sinn Féin ideal. The Labour Party had declared boldly for socialism and was at last admitted to the ranks of the Socialist International — not a wildly revolutionary body, to be sure, but this was at least a step forward. The student radicals had absorbed both the ideas and the vocabulary of a worldwide movement of dissent. Everyone in Ireland who was left of centre, from the most tentative suburban liberal to the most deranged Maoist, was at least agreed that the bell was about to toll for 'Civil War politics' and that there would be a political shake-up, commensurate with the shake-up in other areas of Irish life in the sixties, which would produce 'normal' politics, in which, of course, they expected the left to emerge triumphant.

The material for the creation of an Irish left was to hand. The uneven spread of sudden prosperity in a hitherto impoverished society inevitably left large pools of poverty and deprivation which were now all the more of an affront to the conscience of the nation. In no area was this more the case than in public housing.

Dublin had been a decaying city for generations. Its sordid tenements had, at the start of the century, been unique in Europe in the extent and depth of their destitution. The very worst of them had been cleared from the 1920s onwards, but by the 1960s much remained yet to be done. The building boom of that decade was concentrated overwhelmingly in commercial property and private housing. In public housing, demand continued to exceed supply, and the numbers on the waiting list for Corporation houses grew with the years. Indeed, the building boom actually contributed to the problem by offering unskilled labouring work to young men who might otherwise have emigrated to the English building sites, but who now were in a position to marry at home. As the pressure built up, so did the anger of those on the housing lists. What was needed was an organisation to orchestrate their protests.

The Dublin Housing Action Committee provided just that. A series of incidents in early 1968 made it clear that they would not content themselves with polite submissions to the city fathers. A group of DHAC activists were ejected from City Hall in early January after they staged a noisy protest at a meeting of Dublin City Council. A week later over twenty people were injured in scuffles at Islandbridge as Corporation bailiffs were evicting tenants for non-payment of rent; the DHAC had attended in support of the tenants and had become embroiled with the Gardaí. In the course of the year there were numerous other confrontations and frequent accusations of Garda brutality from the DHAC.

The origins of the committee were interesting. Far from being a spontaneous organisation of the conventional left, it had been formed in May 1967 out of the Sinn Féin Citizens' Advice Bureau. This in itself was remarkable, for traditionally Sinn Féin had been a one-issue party of re-actionary deadbeats, who disdained any truck with social issues. There had been a brief period of socialist ascendancy within the republican movement in the 1930s, but the right had soon reasserted itself.

The republican right had, however, been so discredited by the fiasco of the 1956-62 border campaign that when the movement's rump re-formed in the mid-sixties, it looked for a new direction. It found it in socialism. Under the influence of Roy Johnston and Cathal Goulding, it involved itself actively in the politics of radical protest and attracted many hitherto dormant left-wingers who had had no political home to go to in a country traditionally hostile to socialism. The DHAC was one of the products of Sinn Féin's new radicalism.

In the spring of 1968 Father Austin Flannery, OP, one of a new breed of liberal post-Conciliar Irish priests, presented a series of 'Outlook' programmes on RTE which dealt with the housing crisis. 'Outlook' was a five-minute religious programme at the fag-end of the evening's television schedule, usually devoted to a soporific homily. Father Flannery, however, had other ideas than to lull his viewers to sleep with nocturnal platitudes. On one programme in particular he produced a panel of four persons, who were all agreed on the necessity to declare a 'housing emergency', followed by a crash programme to tackle the crisis head-on. The problem was that, of the four, two were members of Sinn Féin, another was the general secretary of the Irish Workers' Party (otherwise the official Irish communist party, as recognised by Moscow), and the last was a Jesuit, Father Michael Sweetman, who had spoken on a number of occasions from DHAC platforms.

Eyebrows were raised. The idea of the general secretary of the Irish communists turning up on the late-night religious television show was particularly disorientating for the conventionally pious. The whole series of programmes drew the wrath of the Minister for Local Government, Kevin Boland, on the head of Father Flannery, to whom he referred as 'a so-called priest'. He said that the programmes were maliciously conceived with the intention of giving a grossly distorted picture of the housing situation, and he charged that 'no one, clerical or lay, could by any stretch of the imagination have selected this group as experts with the intention of giving a true and realistic view' of the problem. Father Flannery might well have responded that bearing Christian witness as he saw it in the face of a public scandal left little room for notional impartiality. The radicalism of the late sixties was impatient with the whole idea of impartiality.

The 'Outlook' controversy had a deeper significance. For over a year relations between RTE and the Fianna Fáil government had been steadily deteriorating. In October 1966, as the dispute between the Department of Agriculture and the NFA was developing, the Minister for Agriculture, Charles Haughey, issued a statement saying that farmers should hold on to cattle which they had at the time; the NFA immediately disagreed, and the two statements were presented together on the early evening news. Haughey rang RTE to protest that his advice, given with the authority of his office, had been carried immediately alongside a statement which contradicted it. Just at that time the air was thick with rumours of Lemass's impending resignation, and Haughey was one of the fancied runners in the succession stakes. He was known to be ambitious and not a little arrogant; but this was an extraordinary action, as petty as it was unnecessary.

The NFA statement was removed from later bulletins on instructions from the 'highest news division level', according to RTE's director-general. He added that 'an error of editoral judgment had been made and had been corrected'. The National Union of Journalists took exception to this and counter-charged that the only error of judgment involved was the head of news's decision not to run the NFA statement on the later bulletins.

The head of news resigned shortly thereafter. Lemass, meanwhile, had responded to the storm with one of his most quoted dicta: RTE had been 'set up by legislation as an instrument of public policy'. This was the opening shot in a running battle between broadcasters and politicians that lasted for the remainder of the decade.

There followed the decision by RTE management to discontinue the consumer affairs programme, 'Home Truths', which had adopted an openly sceptical attitude to the claims of advertisers. Inevitably there was a suspicion that RTE was allowing itself to be pressurised by its own advertisers, on whose money the station relied. Then a decision to send a 'Seven Days' team to North Vietnam was rescinded by the RTE Authority following strong government pressure. This was particularly disappointing for RTE, because the North Vietnamese were deeply suspicious of most Western television, and their invitation was a real scoop for RTE. Hard on the heels of that incident came another, when a 'Seven Days' team was dispatched to cover the Nigerian civil war without the knowledge of either the controller of programmes or the director-general; moreover, the trip was organised by the Biafran publicity agency. They had reached Lisbon *en route* to Biafra before word of their mission broke. The then chairman of RTE, C. S. Andrews, who was a lifelong Fianna Fáil stalwart and who 'believed strongly that it was the duty of the television authority to support official policy', tells what happened next:

[The director-general] told me over lunch about the situation. On my strong advice and his judgment he decided to recall the team.... As far as I knew, the government were completely unaware of the incident.... To have done otherwise [than recall the team] would have been irresponsible considering the delicacy of the situation. In the eyes of the Nigerian government, with whom Ireland had diplomatic relations, the Biafran secession was an act of rebellion and, whatever the rights or wrongs of the case, the position of Irish missionaries in Nigeria were [*sic*] such as to warrant caution in circumstances where the national TV authority might be accused of hob-nobbing with rebels.[2]

Although there was no direct government pressure in this case, the decision was inevitably construed as a capitulation to supposed government preferences. It further lowered morale among the current affairs broadcasters in RTE by emphasising that whenever a conflict arose between the principle of editorial independence in RTE and the station's role as 'an instrument of public policy', the latter would always triumph over the former.

There had been, in addition to the controversies already mentioned, a series of investigative programmes done by 'Seven Days' in 1967 and early 1968 which had displeased the mighty. Shortly after the Nigerian contretemps 'Seven Days' was transferred from the hands of the controller of programmes and put under the head of news, for what were explained as 'organisational reasons'. Nobody in RTE thought it was for any reason other than to silence the troublesome programme by placing it in a department where straight reporting without comment was all that was permitted. The director-general, Kevin McCourt, effectively confirmed this view in an explanatory statement a few days after the decision: he had, he said, been frequently concerned about the lack of impartiality on 'Seven Days' in view of the fact that the Authority 'is not allowed to have an editorial view of its own in what it broadcasts'. It has to be said, however, that 'Seven Days' did not help its own cause by the clear breach of internal discipline involved in its secret trip to Biafra.

There was little doubt that many RTE current affairs journalists and production staff identified with that wider stream of dissent which was a feature of the second half of the 1960s, especially among intellectuals who were close to, but excluded from, the corridors of power. The Irish political and business worlds — which, as we have already seen, were tending to become one around this time — were notoriously close and secretive. Nobody wrote memoirs; nobody spilled the beans; personal contact and the soft word in the right ear got things done. In such a society there was plenty to arouse the curiosity of a journalist, and there was a legitimate professional pride among 'Seven Days' personnel and their supporters concerning their achievements. Jim Fitzgerald, a television and theatre producer, praised the contribution of 'leftist Catholics' to 'progress in television' in a speech to a conference of Christian socialists late in 1968, and deplored the 'colossal' political interference in Irish television. C. S. Andrews confirms that there were at least attempts at such interference, citing a demand by Erskine Childers, the Minister for Posts and Telegraphs, to be shown the names of the applicants for the director-general's job when McCourt resigned. (It was refused.) Andrews, who can be taken to stand for the establishment in this argument, was, however, less than impressed by the 'creative people' in RTE:

Many of them were convinced that they were living and working in a society which was rotten to the core; they believed that they had a mission to change it through the use of television. ... It was difficult to see how they expected so rotten a society to provide them with the expensive and complicated facilities of a television network and pay them while they rushed into the fray to establish the new Jerusalem.[3]

It was not to be wondered at that the disputes between RTE and the government should have come at a time when Fianna Fáil was widely believed to have grown cynical and immoral in its exercise of power. The limits of Fianna Fáil's modernising tendencies were now clearly seen. It had created the economic conditions which could transform Irish society, but its politics were still those of a primitive mafia: secretive, exclusive, and demanding loyalty in return for patronage. It could hardly complain if journalists and others expected a degree of open accountability more in keeping with an advanced, developed industrial country.

But there was yet a further dimension to the antagonism between Fianna Fáil and the 'Seven Days' team. In 1959 the party had tried to secure a constitutional change to abolish proportional representation and replace it by the straight vote. It was defeated. Incredibly, the idea was revived in 1967, and a referendum on the subject took place in 1968. The country was cynical, for the proposal was a piece of gross opportunism aimed at securing Fianna Fáil in power forever, despite all the party's pious rhetoric about the instability created by PR and the need for strong government. There could be no better testimony to the hubris and lack of proportion in Fianna Fáil after Lemass had retired than its revival of this issue within a decade of its previous defeat. It seemed a lost cause from the start, but any chance it had was effectively torpedoed by a 'Seven Days' programme in January 1968 which showed that, if the proposal were carried, Fianna Fáil could expect to win nearly 100 seats in a parliament of less than 150. From that moment on, the proposal was doomed. Fianna Fáil rejected an escape route when Patrick Norton, TD, proposed a compromise — the single transferable vote in single-member constituencies — and the party blundered on like a big, wounded animal to a crushing defeat. It was widely believed that the decision to place 'Seven Days' under the head of news in the spring of 1968 was due to government determination to avoid any repetition of the '100 seats' programme at a time when the referendum campaign was just beginning in earnest.

For sheer confusion, however, nothing in 1968 could match the controversy that surrounded the government's proposal to merge University College, Dublin, and Trinity College, Dublin, in a single university. This bold initiative was first announced in April 1967 by Donogh O'Malley in an attempt, as he put it, 'to end an insidious form of partition on our own doorstep'. Negotiators from the two colleges began discussions on ways and means of realising this highly idealistic ambition. Right from the start there was opposition to the very idea in both institutions: in TCD liberals like Owen Sheehy-Skeffington feared the loss of Trinity's independent, secular voice in a merged institution where the influence of the Catholic hierarchy could not be kept wholly at bay; in UCD the deeply conservative element represented by the ex-president, Dr Michael Tierney, was inclined to regard Trinity as an alien excrescence which should be left to rot quietly by itself. However, the broad body of academic opinion was prepared to give the outline scheme a chance. But by early March 1968 negotiations between the two sides had run into difficulties, and the optimistic euphoria which had greeted O'Malley's original announcement was fast dissipating. At this crucial moment, just when O'Malley's infectious powers of persuasion and decision were needed to propel the antagonists towards an agreement, he died. It might be said that the merger, the last great liberal initiative of the 1960s, died with him.

Thereafter the fur flew as only it can in an academic brawl, and the air was thick with the venomous, introspective logic-chopping that makes these spectacles so amusing to the outsider. The UCD negotiators had presented proposals which would have effectively ensured the supremacy of their college in any new arrangement. The TCD staff association was quick to attack its own negotiators for not taking a harder line in the face of the UCD proposals; indeed, it published proposals of its own which were as uncompromising, in their own way, as those emanating from the UCD negotiators. The new minister, Brian Lenihan, gamely tried to intimidate the savants by threatening legislation over their heads if they could not agree among themselves.

By now everyone was in on the act. The UCD staff association declared for a softer line than the college's official negotiators, and the Irish Federation of University Teachers agreed. Then the TCD staff association rejected the idea of a merger altogether, preferring the recommendation of the Commission on Higher Education that UCD, UCC and UCG be reconstituted as three independent universities, with TCD's status remaining unchanged. In July 1968 Lenihan acted on his threat and announced his own legislative proposals, which would have dissolved the National University of Ireland, would have created a new University of Dublin with two constituent colleges, TCD and UCD, and made UCC and UCG independent universities.

The original O'Malley outline scheme had provided for a comprehensive range of subjects to be retained in both the Dublin colleges, and this stipulation had been regarded as the *sine qua non* for any progress, because to strip either college of a range of important faculties in the name of economy and rationalisation would be to destroy its existence as a university. But there would be complementarity between the two colleges: neither would do what the other did, and yet each would have a sufficient spread of disciplines to maintain its standing as a university. The Lenihan proposals, however, departed from this principle by providing for the duplication of arts and science faculties in both colleges, as well as the consolidation of some of the smaller professional faculties in one college or the other. The net effect of the minister's proposals was to unite all the warring factions against him, and the merger eventually expired in a babble of recrimination.

It had been a noble, if somewhat ingenuous, proposal. The free secondary education scheme was bound to produce a greater demand for university places, and the merger was intended in part as a search for the most rational way of accommodating this extra pressure. But the existing interests of the two colleges proved stronger than the goodwill needed to effect the merger. UCD, in particular, had expended vast amounts of money, time and energy in arranging for its transfer to Belfield, only to have the whole basis of its plans threatened by the Lenihan proposals. It feared that it would become the junior partner in the arrangement and that it could easily end up as a kind of glorified polytechnic.

But for all that, the death of the merger was widely regarded at the time as an opportunity lost, for it would have had the immediate effect of circumventing the episcopal ban on Catholics attending Trinity, and would therefore have ensured the full integration of that college into the life of the nation. Happily, the problem has since been solved, thanks neither to the government nor to the universities, but to a change of heart in the Catholic hierarchy.

Another set of hopes were frustrated in July when Potez Aerospace Ltd of Baldonnel, Co. Dublin, collapsed with the loss of 150 jobs. It had been supported by public money to the tune of more than £1.5 million, and was the most spectacular failure of the decade among grant-aided industries. The French parent company had originally hoped to employ 1,800 people in the construction of private turbo-prop planes, but none was ever built.

The year drew to a close with Dublin being introduced for the first time to the delights of traffic wardens and parking meters; with the Galway suburb of Rahoon disgracing itself by thwarting the attempts of the county manager to establish an itinerant settlement site there; and with Limerick welcoming a native son, Seán Bourke, home from Moscow after helping George Blake, the spy, to escape from Wormwood Scrubs two years before.

Earlier in the year, one of Ireland's few world record-holders had been welcomed home in the neighbouring county of Tipperary. Mike Meaney, a barman, had permitted himself to be buried alive in a coffin eleven feet underneath Butty Sugrue's pub in London for sixty-one days. The record having been thus attained, the coffin was hoisted into Butty's bar, opened, and Mr Meaney issued forth, full of the joys of spring. His achievement generated more mirth than pride among his countrymen, who were churlish enough to spend their time speculating on his toilet arrangements in the coffin. These were, it seems, adequate to the world champion's demands.

In December 1968 An tAthair Tomás Ó Fiaich of St Patrick's College, Maynooth, pointed out that the signs of a weakening of faith among Irish Catholics were too obvious to be ignored. He attributed this to the gradual erosion of native culture, and remarked on the number of people, including priests, who had previously been disinclined to believe that the two processes could be linked together. He was himself in little doubt that the decline in both areas was being eagerly encouraged in some quarters: 'It is remarkable ... that the two institutions most under fire in Ireland in recent years are the Church and the Irish language.'

The Catholic Church had been the most conspicuous pillar of traditional Ireland. It was inevitable that, once that static society had been jerked into life, the Church would feel the strain. But in addition to this internal pressure, there was the tremendous influence of the Vatican Council bearing simultaneously upon it. The Church had to bend or break. In choosing to bend, it undoubtedly resigned itself to a 'weakening of faith', in the sense that its spiritual and moral influence was no longer absolute, but this was the price of survival. Changes in the secular world had themselves ensured that the Church's voice was now but one among many in the area of moral authority. But though no longer alone, the Church ended the sixties as still the most important moral arbiter in Ireland, and for this it can thank in particular those members of the hierarchy whose judicious conservatism allowed it to absorb change in moderation. In boxing parlance, it rolled with the punch.

On Tuesday 18 January 1966 Monsignor Arthur Ryan, the former reader in scholastic philosophy at Queen's University, Belfast, delivered a lecture in the Mansion House, Dublin, on the Vatican Council's decree on ecumenism. It was attended by both the Catholic and the Church of Ireland Archbishops of Dublin, the first occasion on which they had ever attended a public meeting together. After the meeting Dr McQuaid and Dr Simms recited the Lord's Prayer together. It was a notable landmark in the progress of the ecumenical movement in Ireland: the contrast with the exclusion of Protestants from the Patrician Congress celebrations five years before could hardly be more complete.

The new spirit touched other deeply conservative Catholic prelates as well as Dr McQuaid. A few weeks after the Mansion House meeting the Bishop of Cork, Dr Lucey, positively applauded the new ecumenism. For too long, he said, Catholics and Protestants alike in Ireland had brooded on their differences and on the wrongs of the past. While still believing the Catholic Church to be the one true church, he presumed that 'those outside it [were] in good faith rather than in bad faith. I respect them for the witness, limited though I think it to be, which they bear to Christ.' Dr Lucey, a strong supporter of sterner laws on censorship, may have been a bit put out a few weeks later when one of the Vatican's own post-Conciliar reforms abolished the Index of Prohibited Books.

Later in 1966 the Catholic Church in Ireland relaxed some of its more offensive ordinances restraining contact between Catholic and Protestant. Catholics were now permitted to attend Protestant church services and act as witnesses at Protestant weddings. Moreover, there was a modification in the laws pertaining to mixed marriages. Hitherto, these had been hole-and-corner affairs, celebrated furtively in the sacristy; the Church made no secret of its disapproval. Now it would be possible for mixed marriages to be celebrated in the same way as ordinary Catholic marriages, before the high altar and with the full rite and blessings. A Church of Ireland statement, while welcoming these ceremonial concessions, was careful to observe that the full ferocity of the *Ne temere* decree still obtained. But on this question there was no yielding.

Nevertheless, the broad thrust of the ecumenical movement was maintained, although progress was inclined to be extremely slow. The burden of history as well as theology fell on inter-church relations in Ireland. But the central feature of ecumenism, dialogue, was present, if only in a polite, formal sense. It would be naïve to imagine that prelates who had spent a lifetime anathematising heretics could be expected to turn around and embrace them in their old age. But even politeness and courtesy marked an advance in Ireland. The theologians, on the other hand, were positively enthusiastic for ecumenism — and indeed for other new departures in ecclesiastical life — but like all Irish intellectuals they counted for little with the men who exercised power.

The sudden emergence of priests and theologians who were on the left of the Irish political spectrum was one of the most remarkable developments in the second half of the decade. Father Fergal O'Connor, OP, an academic social scientist, became a national figure for his outspoken views on political and social affairs on 'The Late Late Show'. Father Austin Flannery, as already mentioned, was another Dominican of generally anti-establishment views. Father Michael O'Neill appeared on the platform at an anti-Vietnam war meeting in the Mansion House, Dublin, at the beginning of 1968, an action that would have been regarded as almost heretical in the neurotically anti-communist Ireland of the fifties. Father Michael Sweetman, SJ, was one of the most prominent and passionate supporters of the Dublin Housing Action Committee. Another Jesuit, Father Patrick Simpson, professor of scripture at Milltown Park, Dublin, commenting on the report of the Committee on the Constitution in early 1968, argued that until a formal pronouncement on the matter of a possible constitutional change to allow divorce was issued by the Catholic hierarchy, nothing but good could come from moderate public discussion of the subject. Father Myles Rearden, professor of philosophy at All Hallows, Dublin, spoke the language of liberation theology later that year:

The Church is coming to a new age in its history, a period of intense commitment to the relief of human misery.

An increasing number of clerics of all views, liberal and conservative alike, were learning the importance of clever exploitation of the media. The

Communications Centre in Booterstown, Co. Dublin, established in April 1967 under the auspices of the Catholic Truth Society of Ireland, played a crucial role in teaching a whole generation of priests the skills of successful media projection. In addition to persuasive intellectuals, the clergy also began to throw up hearty lads like Father Michael Cleary, the 'singing priest', a populist who managed to combine conservative views with an appeal to a younger generation. Training in television techniques had a deep influence on the preaching methods of younger priests. Indignant denunciations of the evil ways of the world were not the thing for 'Outlook'. The ingratiating gesture, the word of brotherly advice, the projection of self as a fellow-sinner rather than a stainless judge: the priests of Ireland were getting on with the new style.

On the very farthest shore of the post-Conciliar Irish Church stood the Catholic Marxists. They were, it is true, few in number, but the fact that they existed at all was a wonder in itself. They even managed to produce a paper, *Grille*, by which name they were commonly known. In August 1968 they organised a Sunday afternoon prayer-meeting in St Andrew's Church, Westland Row, Dublin, where they were physically set upon by a crowd of hostile local parishioners, who were unsophisticated enough to suppose that a gang of communist blow-ins were profaning their church. The *Grille* people, about twenty in number, were forced to abandon their meeting to cries of 'Are you a Catholic?', 'Are you Irish?', 'Are you from this parish?', 'Are you a communist?' and so on. They retreated to University Church in St Stephen's Green, in which sedately bourgeois setting Catholic Marxism was suffered to flourish undisturbed.

The symbol and agent of renewal in the Irish Catholic Church was William Cardinal Conway, Archbishop of Armagh. He was, by the standards of the Vatican Council, a conservative although by no means a reactionary. But in Irish terms he represented a substantial break with the past. Most of all, he brought to the Irish Church a new tone of voice and an acceptance of the changed realities of secular life. He was good on television, avuncular but not patronising, and he never seemed to preach at people. He took a very soft line on Church/State relations, at least by the standards traditional among Irish bishops. There was never any danger that Armagh would precipitate a repeat of the Mother and Child affair. On the contrary, despite major state initiatives especially in the sensitive area of education, Cardinal Conway stood aside from any legislative controversy and even seemed to encourage reform. His commitment to the ideal of a socially involved Church was plain: he played a notable part in the foundation of Trocaire, the Irish Catholic Church's third-world relief agency. His Christmas address on RTE in 1968 testified to the effect which his own encounters with world poverty had had on him:

191

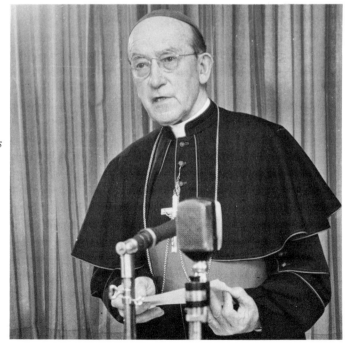

The Catholic bishops of Ireland, photographed at Maynooth prior to their annual summer meeting in 1968. It was the first year in which they had admitted photographers. For the more conservative bishops such as Dr McQuaid of Dublin (right), the publication of the papal encyclical 'Humanae Vitae' was a welcome reiteration of traditional values. This photograph shows him at a press conference at which the Irish bishops' response to the encyclical was made public.

I remember one morning standing on a foothill on the Andes outside Lima and looking down on a vast dark-brown plain, stretching for miles and covered as far as the eye could see with poor shacks in which over 700,000 people were living in dire poverty. It was like one enormous itinerant camp. One of the priests who was with me asked: 'Is it as bad as Bombay?' and I said: 'No, Bombay was worse.' I remember how after my journey from the airport to where I was staying in Bombay I sat down on the edge of the bed and I could have cried. . . .

This broadcast is not an appeal for funds. It is an appeal for a Christian mentality towards the poor, the poor of our community and the poor of the world. This is not a problem which could be solved by private charity; it requires massive assistance by governments backed up by public opinion.

He attempted to shift the emphasis of Irish Catholic practice away from its traditional private formalism to a more active witness in the world at large. Had he succeeded, he might have closed the gap, so often observed in Irish Catholics, between private piety and equivocal moral standards in secular life: he had little time for the ostentatious crawthumper who paid sweat-rates to his employees, or for whom mendacity and cheating were mere peccadillos. In his own personality he helped to dispel the assertive, puritanical image of the traditional Irish Church, and he seemed relaxed about the growing material affluence of Irish society and confident about the Church's capacity to maintain its position in it.

He summed up his attitudes in a couple of speeches to newly ordained priests in the summers of 1966 and 1967. In the first he observed that the old paternalistic relationship between priests and people was not suited to the temper of changed times. Likewise, coldness between Catholic and Protestant was anachronistic. Priests now had to deal with a more educated and sophisticated laity, no less devoted to their faith, but intellectually more developed, and they would have to adapt, as the Church itself had adapted in the Vatican Council, to the demands of a new world, 'rich and exciting in its possibilities'. He returned to this theme the following year:

It is only by a positive approach, recognising all that is healthy and good and wonderful in the modern world, that you can hope to penetrate the minds of those over whom it exercises such a fascination and effectively preach the gospel to them.

There was something approaching a revolution in seminary life in Ireland during the 1960s. In the old Church the seminary had been a place apart from the world, a spiritual cocoon for the formation of men who would themselves be apart from the world. Discipline was ferocious; books were discouraged, and knowledge was dispensed by authoritarian and scrupulously orthodox professors, who expected to get back in the examination papers what they had given out in the lecture halls. Within a few years this whole seminary regime had been swept away. Discipline was relaxed, as much in response to a new generation of seminarians bred in the ways of a more informal secular world as to the new spirit of liberalism abroad in the Church generally. Libraries were expanded, and books became as much a part of the seminarian's life as they were of any other undergraduate's. The work of 'advanced' continental theologians like Küng and Rahner became accessible through paperbacks, making the uniform orthodoxy of the past impossible to maintain. But it would be wrong to imply that these changes occurred wholly against the wishes of the clerical establishment. Catholic intellectuals had for over a decade been seriously concerned at the closed nature of the Irish Church, and in a number of journals and other periodicals — of which *Doctrine and Life* and *The Furrow* were the best known — they opened Irish eyes to developments in Catholic thought and practice in the wider world. These periodicals produced some of the most penetrating and incisive critiques of the Irish Church, and of Irish society in general, in the late fifties and early sixties. Within the Church they made smooth the path of the new thinking, and the ease with which the revolution in seminary life was accomplished testified to their influence.

From 1963 — the first full year of the Vatican Council and the year of Cardinal Conway's accession to Armagh — until 1968 there had been a welter of change in the Irish Catholic Church. Then, at the end of July 1968, Pope Paul VI issued *Humanae vitae*, restating traditional Church teaching on the immorality of artificial birth control, and thereby caused a convulsion in the Catholic world. In spirit it seemed to go against everything that had been happening since the pontificate of John XXIII, and it immediately provided a rallying-point for Catholic conservatives who felt that the engine of liberalism had got out of control.

It alienated the theologians, who tended to be overwhelmingly in the 'liberal' camp, not to mention millions of Catholics all over the world who were using artificial contraceptives in the expectation that the papacy was going to give them its moral endorsement. The Irish bishops hastened to affirm their loyalty to the Pope on the issue and declared their confidence in the Irish people's 'wholehearted assent'. For the older bishops, in particular, it was a happy return to an episcopal climate in which they felt at home: an unambiguous denunciation in the area of sexual morality, resting on a pledge of obedience to Rome. After five years during which all they ever seemed to hear was the squabbling of fractious theologians about ecumenism, or the third world, or the need to adapt the Church to modern life, this was the real thing, the old-time religion!

But it wasn't really. The most obvious feature of the old-time religion had been its unanimity, whereas *Humanae vitae* produced a storm of debate and conflicting opinions. In Ireland, not surprisingly, this was far less intense than in countries like the United States; but it happened all the same. One of the country's leading theologians, Father James Good, professor of theology at University College, Cork, described the encyclical as 'a major tragedy'. His bishop, Dr Lucey, immediately barred him from preaching. He followed this with a lecture ban, although lecturing to students on theology and philosophy in UCC was an integral part of Father Good's work.

Such an assertion of episcopal authority was a gesture to the past. The genuine opposition to *Humanae vitae* within the Church could neither be wished away nor banned away. Just as the Church was no longer the single voice of authority in Irish life which it had been, neither was it any longer an institution whose own members spoke with a single voice. Even bishops were no longer immune from criticism. Almost a year before the *Humanae vitae* controversy Father Patrick Brophy of St Patrick's College, Carlow, one of the most effective of the new clerical television performers, addressed a weekend seminar of the Knights of Columbanus in Sligo. He expressed regret that most of the official statements of Irish bishops about the media, particularly since the Vatican Council, had been critical in one way or another. He acknowledged the vital contribution of the media to the formation of public opinion on religious matters and praised it for communicating almost all that the people had learned about the Council. He continued:

While respecting the rights of bishops to criticise what they feel does less than justice to the religious situation, one would wish to hear from them some words of encouragement for the genuinely apostolic achievements of Irish radio, television, and press.

Such remarks would have been regarded as *lèse-majesté* ten years earlier. That they were made by Father Brophy, a measured man who was in no sense a radical firebrand, demonstrated how pervasive the habit of internal dialogue had become in the Irish Catholic Church. *Humanae vitae* did not change that. In the short run it undoubtedly discouraged the liberals. But in the long run, because of its own contentious nature, it probably accelerated the pace of debate. Moreover, the social and demographic changes which began in the sixties gathered pace in the seventies; and that alone ensured that the Church had to remain flexible, open to debate and ideas, and self-critical. There simply was no going back.

In December 1967 an opinion poll conducted in Northern Ireland suggested that the bulk of people in the province supported the politics of moderation. The policies of Terence O'Neill and Eddie McAteer alike were endorsed by their respective communities. The firm lines of the old sectarian divisions seemed to have softened. There was wide support for better relations between North and South, for O'Neill's meeting with Lemass nearly three years before, and for the continued series of meetings between O'Neill and Jack Lynch which followed.

The biggest shift in traditional beliefs came from the Catholics. Although less than 20 per cent of them were satisfied with the existing constitutional position, only 40 per cent supported the concept of a united Ireland; significantly, 47 per cent were willing to accept some kind of link with Britain if the border were removed. While there was also a movement of opinion on the Protestant side, the poll threw up one sinister statistic. A large minority of Unionists, between one-third and one-quarter, were still resolutely opposed to any meeting between the Taoiseach and the Prime Minister of Northern Ireland, and consequently to any new contacts between the two parts of Ireland.

There had been, in the course of 1967, a number of suggestions that the Unionist Party should open its doors to Catholics as a move to convert the party into a vehicle for communal unity. Even Brian Faulkner made such a suggestion, albeit in a typically qualified way, in a speech to the East Down Unionist Association in Downpatrick Orange Hall, not a venue accustomed to hearing such sentiments. In February 1968 O'Neill declared that he welcomed 'the support of anyone who finds in [Unionist] politics the right ... course for our province'. But even guarded suggestions of this kind were too much for the Unionist ultras. In March Mr Norman Porter, the director of the Evangelical Protestant Society of Belfast, laid down the law:

> The Unionist Party can be easily split from top to bottom if more Roman Catholics enter it. Once the Unionist Party's link with the Orange Order is broken — and many 'moderates' would love to see this happen — Ulster Protestants will no longer be able to depend on the Unionist Party....
>
> Every peace-loving person in Ulster rejoices in the tranquillity which is at present being enjoyed in Northern Ireland, and one wonders how long it will last and what will be the ultimate end of this campaign and plea for moderation.
>
> ... Let us seriously remember to make a distinction between moderation without compromise and moderation with compromise. One is Christian and the other is betrayal.

And what of the Orange Order itself? In the summer of 1968 it finally adjudicated in the case of two of its members who had broken the rules. One was none other than Phelim O'Neill, MP, the Prime Minister's liberal cousin, and he had done a truly awful thing. In 1966 a civic week was held in Ballymoney, Co. Antrim, a predominantly Catholic town in his constituency. Fired with enthusiasm for the new sense of moderation en-

196

couraged by Cousin Terence, he actually attended a Catholic service held in celebration of the event. For this act he and his fellow-malefactor, Colonel Crammie, the Deputy Lieutenant of Co. Antrim, were arraigned before an Orange Order disciplinary tribunal. Neither man, to his credit, bothered to turn up before this tinpot inquisition, which took two years to make up its mind on the issue.* The eventual decision to expel was actually taken by the Grand Orange Lodge of Ireland after what was described as an 'acrimonious' meeting. So it may be assumed that the Grand Lodge at least had the decency to argue about it.

It was rumoured that the real offence committed by the two was their failure to turn up for their 'trial'. A similar case involving Nat Minford, MP, who had attended the opening and blessing of a Catholic school in his constituency, resulted in a caution. But in that case the 'accused' had consented to stand in the Orange dock. The Phelim O'Neill case, however, led to a neat question in the House of Commons at Stormont from Eddie McAteer, who enquired whether 'dictation by the Orange and Black Orders to Unionist MPs infringed the privilege of the House?' The Speaker, Sir Norman Stronge, ruled in the negative. Sir Norman Stronge, in addition to his taxing duties as Speaker, was also the sovereign grand master of the Royal Black Institution.

The Prime Minister was a member of the Orange Order. To have left would have exposed him to yet another leadership crisis precipitated by the ultras. They were already angry at the dismissal of Harry West from the Ministry of Agriculture for an allegedly improper land deal, a charge West denied indignantly, claiming that O'Neill had misrepresented an innocent transaction in order to pay off an old political score (West had been one of those behind the last push against O'Neill in the autumn of 1966). But by staying in the Orange Order — clearly an organisation committed to the frustration of all the things O'Neill said he wanted — the Prime Minister weakened his credibility with Catholics. In February 1968 he refused to dissociate himself from the Order, in reply to a specific question at a meeting of the Irish Association for Cultural, Economic and Social Relations. He had just delivered a major speech on the subject of community relations. It was the speech of a decent, civilised, humane man wrestling with problems beyond his — or anyone's — capacity to resolve:

Do not believe for one moment that when I took office I faced irresistible pressures to try to unite the community or develop a friendly relationship with the South. Do not imagine that I sought a course likely to make my life simpler and

---

*There was much to-ing and fro-ing between the 'judges', the Grand Orange Lodge of Ireland, and the central committee, in the course of which counsel's opinion was sought as to whether or not the two men had broken any rule of the Order. They had not.

more pleasant with my party either in parliament or in the country.

I have been picketed, denounced and traduced as no previous Prime Minister in Northern Ireland's history. . . . People ought to accept that these matters are not just plain sailing; that the opinions and, yes, the prejudices of past generations cannot be abolished at the stroke of a pen or the dictates of a private member's bill; and that in trying to produce a more united community you must try to carry with you the majority of your supporters so that you will not simply substitute one division for another.

He looked to a gradual improvement in relations between Protestants and Catholics at individual and community level as the best hope for the future. As a consequence of this process, he saw 'an occupation of a broad area of middle ground by reasonable men and its steady widening in the course of time'. But time was the one thing Terence O'Neill did not have on his side.

In early 1968, however, it seemed otherwise. It was clear from the opinion poll that, when one discounted the ultra minority, there had been a significant move towards the moderate centre among Unionists. Nationalists, too, had softened their traditional demand for a united Ireland, partly in response to the promising developments of recent years, and partly to the destruction of traditional republicanism in the border campaign. A breach had been made in the walls of Ulster's prejudice. It hardly seemed over-optimistic to suppose that there was no turning back now from the task of widening that breach until the walls fell. The idea that history moves forward inexorably — does not crab sideways or double back on itself — is so thoroughly ingrained in the western mind that it cannot easily comprehend a society whose very rules ordain that the past can always hold the future to ransom.

The complacent optimism about the future of Northern Ireland was at its height in the summer of 1968. But the powder-trail was already alight. In Caledon, Co. Tyrone, the local Republican Club — otherwise Sinn Féin — organised a squat by homeless Catholics in new council houses. The Dungannon Rural District Council, in the time-honoured tradition of Unionist local government, had refused to allocate houses to the Catholics. While large families were left on the housing list, a young unmarried Protestant girl, who was secretary to a local Unionist bigwig, was given one of the new houses in Caledon. This shameless act of discrimination led a young Nationalist MP, Austin Currie, to occupy the house briefly; he was evicted in June and fined.

In August two groups combined in a protest march against discrimination in local government. The body called the Campaign for Social Justice had been formed in January 1964 and had expended considerable energy in propaganda work, especially among British Labour MPs, highlighting the blatant sectarian discrimination in Ulster life, particularly in local government. The CSJ organised the march on 24 August from Coalisland to Dungannon. They were joined by the Northern Ireland Civil Rights Association.

The NICRA was a broadly-based body which had been founded in January 1967 with the aim of establishing normal British standards in the public life of this peculiar and anachronistic corner of the United Kingdom. It wanted 'one man one vote' in local elections; an end to the gerrymandering of constituency boundaries; anti-discrimination legislation, especially in the area of local housing; repeal of the ferocious Special Powers' Act and disbandment of the B Specials. It had a mildly left-wing emphasis: its first executive was balanced between republicans and socialists on the one hand and liberals of various hues on the other. In ignoring, or at least suspending, the 'national' issue and concentrating instead on full British rights, it raised awkward questions for the Unionist Party, especially since there was a Labour government in power at Westminster. It also bore evidence of Catholics' willingness to soften their traditional demands in a way that seemed to many to offer a chance for a new kind of politics in Northern Ireland. The NICRA implicitly accepted Northern Ireland's constitutional position within the United Kingdom, although there can be no doubt that for some of its supporters, at least, this was a purely tactical and temporary compromise. While theoretically non-sectarian, it attracted very few Protestants.

The march from Coalisland to Dungannon was a success and prompted the left-wing Derry Housing Action Committee to organise one of their own. Once again, NICRA joined with local activists. Derry was the most blatant and exquisite example of Unionist gerrymandering, as a result of which a Protestant minority of nearly 40 per cent managed to return twelve Unionist candidates to the Londonderry City Council out of a total of twenty members, probably the most crooked and mischievous piece of electoral malpractice in Europe. Moreover, Derry was an economic slum, with one of the highest rates of male unemployment in the United Kingdom. The Derry march was fixed for 5 October, and the route would take the marchers into the very centre of the high-walled city, the bastion of Protestant power which overlooked the Catholic Bogside below. Local Protestants were outraged and called upon the Minister of Home Affairs to ban the march. The Minister of Home Affairs at this sensitive moment was Mr William Craig.

Bill Craig had been Unionist MP for Larne since 1960. He had first come to public notice in 1963, as the chief whip who had reconciled backbench opinion to the succession of Terence O'Neill to the party leadership. Whatever reputation he may have acquired for delicacy in discharging that task was steadily dissipated in the following five years. Bill Craig's feet were

199

as often in his mouth as on the ground. In 1963, at a time when O'Neill was trying to mend fences with the trade unions, Craig launched an attack on them. They were guilty, he said, of not giving a proper service to their members and of not moving with the times. He continued: 'It seems to me that the unemployed would rather be out of work than adjust themselves to modern requirements.' Naturally this raised a storm of protest and the trade unions demanded an apology. Undaunted, Craig replied:

Far from apologising, I would offer them this piece of advice: grow up, or failing that, for the good of all, take a running jump off a great height.

In September 1965, after the new British Labour government had introduced its economic plan, Craig made an extraordinary verbal assault on it, describing it as 'theoretical nonsense' and calling on the Unionist MPs at Westminster to help force the resignation of the British government. To make matters worse, Craig was at this time the minister responsible for implementing the Northern Ireland sections of the plan. O'Neill was sufficiently embarrassed to issue a public rebuke to Craig.

In the following April Craig was at pains to make clear his support for the rebel Rhodesian leader, Ian Smith, saying that there was no one else in Rhodesia whom he would support. In November he had to apologise 'unreservedly' for remarks in the House of Commons at Stormont when he said that there were 'social and educational' reasons to explain the fact that the ratio of Protestants to Catholics in the senior bar in Northern Ireland was greater than that in the junior bar.

Then, in July 1967, he managed to outrage the trade unions again. A Twelfth of July Orange march in Belfast stopped outside the gates of Crumlin Road jail and sent in 'fraternal greetings' to the Malvern Street murderers, no less. When Gerry Fitt protested at this disgraceful gesture, Craig replied blandly that he could not see what all the fuss was about, since it was common practice for trade union branches and other such organisations to have messages conveyed to prisoners. The unions naturally objected to this unhappy analogy.

On the issue of civil rights, Craig's views were, as ever, unambiguous. In July 1968, in the last calm summer before the NICRA marches began, he declared that if Roman Catholics did not accept the Northern Ireland government, they could not expect much sympathy from those who did. This was the man to whom, nine weeks later, Derry Unionists had recourse. He did not let them down. The march proposed for Derry on 5 October was banned by order of the Minister of Home Affairs.

The organisers, after much heart-searching, decided to defy the ban. They went ahead; the police blocked their way and warned that women and children should depart. They then batoned Gerry Fitt and Eddie McAteer, who were at the head of the crowd. What followed was a brutal police riot; while the RUC were undoubtedly provoked, they had been sent in large numbers by the Minister of Home Affairs to discharge the sort of tricky task for which they had almost no training at all. Instead they did what came naturally, which was to beat the tar out of the Teagues.

The trouble for Stormont was that there were television news cameras at the Derry march, and the pictures went around the globe. The Irish problem was back on the world's agenda. There certainly was nothing like riot and disturbance to capture international attention. Within a week of the Derry march, for example, David Frost presented a live forty-five-minute television debate from Belfast to try to explain to British viewers what was at issue in Northern Ireland. It was the first of many such attempts over the years, and it ended, as most of the others were to do, in rowdy disagreement.

Events now raced forward. The Nationalists withdrew from their role of official opposition at Stormont 'until such time as the government gives further concrete evidence of a sincere desire to remedy the situation'. The civil rights movement, with its rhetoric and songs borrowed from other such movements abroad, especially in the United States, embraced new and more radical groups. The People's Democracy, a body of left-wing students heavily influenced by the revolutionary *zeitgeist* of much contemporary student life, was formed at Queen's University, Belfast, within days of the Derry march. Civil rights marches were held across the province, and loyalist counter-demonstrations followed, usually organised by the Rev. Ian Paisley and an outfit called the Loyal Citizens of Ulster under the direction of an eccentric mathematics lecturer named Major Ronald Bunting. At the end of November loyalists successfully blocked the path of a civil rights march in Armagh, an action which resulted in jail sentences for Paisley and Bunting.

A week earlier Captain O'Neill had announced a package of reforms. There would be a points system for the allocation of local authority houses; an ombudsman would be appointed; the 'company vote' in local elections would be abolished; the Special Powers Act would be reviewed; and London-derry Corporation would be replaced by a development commission. But the provision of 'one man one vote' was not included among the concessions, and this was a fatal omission as far as the civil rights activists were concerned. It was the old story with O'Neill: he could not adequately meet Catholic demands without compromising his own political position within Unionism. Already he was under pressure from the West Ulster Unionist Council, a collection of ultras from the backwoods, to stand firm against all demands and to impose 'law and order'.

Naturally the turmoil in the North had an effect on the South. On 31

Images of Ulster, 1968.
Above, the famous civil
rights march in Derry on 5
October 1968, just before
the trouble began. Right,
young Orange bandmen.
Opposite, the Prime
Minister, Terence O'Neill,
about to deliver his famous
'crossroads' speech.

October Jack Lynch went to London to see Harold Wilson and said afterwards that partition was the root of the problem, which moved O'Neill to an angry retort. Lynch then made a more conciliatory speech in the Dáil, but his Minister for Agriculture, Neil Blaney, an old-style right-wing republican from Donegal, weighed in with a very hawkish speech in Letterkenny, ostensibly aimed at O'Neill but in reality a warning to his own leader not to hedge on the national issue. It was a foretaste of things to come.

O'Neill, like Lynch, was pressurised by a right-wing cabinet speechifier. Almost inevitably, it was Craig. On 28 November, two days before the potentially explosive confrontation in Armagh between civil rights marchers and loyalists, he addressed Unionists in the Ulster Hall, Belfast. There was, said the Minister of Home Affairs, a lot of nonsense talked about civil rights; in fact, behind the campaign stood the old traditional enemy: 'We face a reality. Where you have a Roman Catholic majority you have lower standards of democracy.' He denied that Catholics in Northern Ireland were the victims of discrimination and said that the only reforms needed were those made appropriate by growing prosperity. Although he was a member of a cabinet that had recently announced the appointment of an ombudsman, he said that he could see no great merit in such an office, except that it would expose those who made reckless and unfounded allegations. And although he supported the idea of a housing points scheme, he was quick to remark that the way some politicians talked, one would think the only people entitled to a house were those who had failed in their social obligations and had a family to look after! Was it any wonder that Mr Craig had a soft spot for the Rhodesian Front?

Phelim O'Neill called for Craig's resignation over this speech, but the Prime Minister made an excuse for Craig by saying he had been tired and under strain. The Minister of Home Affairs gave a curt answer to this by going to Clogher, Co Tyrone, and repeating the speech, speaking from a transcribed tape-recording of it! This action drew the applause of Ian Paisley. But still O'Neill desisted from sacking Craig.

On the same night that Craig was speaking in Clogher, an announcement in nearby Dungannon indicated the depth of bitterness that was being plumbed in Northern Ireland. Jack Hassard, a Protestant, and the lone Northern Ireland Labour Party member of the urban district council, resigned. He had become a figure of hatred to his fellow-Protestants because of the non-sectarian nature of his politics. As he tried to drive his car through the town he had been stopped by a mob of about 400 people, and his rear window was smashed with an axe. Threatening letters had been sent to his family.

In early December O'Neill went on television to make his famous 'crossroads' speech. It was an appeal for a breathing space, for time, for a chance to draw back from the brink. He reminded viewers of his attempts to foster communal harmony, and he promised further substantial reforms. He stressed the economic dependence of Northern Ireland on Great Britain and pointed out that Harold Wilson had made it perfectly clear to him that Westminster was prepared to act over Stormont's head, if need be, in the matter of reform. He ended with a direct plea for support to all the people of the province.

The effect of this, the best speech of Terence O'Neill's career, was tremendous. The Derry Citizens' Action Committee, a more moderate group who had ousted the left-wing Derry Housing Action Committee from the leadership of the local Catholics, announced a one-month moratorium on all marches. Gerry Fitt declared that he would make no more attacks on the Unionist Party until he saw the effects of the recently announced reforms. A great swell of support built up for the Prime Minister across the province. In Dublin he romped away with the *Sunday Independent*'s 'Man of the Year' award, which is decided by a poll of the paper's readers. He even managed to get rid of Craig at last. The Minister of Home Affairs had dissented publicly from the 'crossroads' speech, saying that he would 'resist any effort' by a London government to impose changes on Northern Ireland over the head of Stormont. O'Neill dismissed him.

For a few weeks it seemed that O'Neill had done it — had halted the slide to disaster with an almost Gaullist appeal to the whole community. The year ended, incredibly, with a feeling of nervous optimism: the Protestant right was isolated; the NICRA marches were suspended; O'Neill had gained a degree of confidence from the Catholics which was unprecedented for a Unionist politician, let alone a Prime Minister. Only the reckless student fringe of the civil rights movement, the People's Democracy, refused to observe the one-month ban on marches: they were planning a march from Belfast to Derry at the beginning of the new year.

Chapter Eleven

1969

The fire this time

My wife, shortly after this time, heard a priest in Dingle, Co. Kerry,
deliver a sermon on 'communism and socialism'. The priest gave
communism the expected treatment. Then he went on to socialism.
'Socialism', he said, 'is worse than communism. Socialism is a heresy
of communism. Socialists are a Protestant variety of communists.'
Not merely communists, but *Protestant* communists! Not many
votes for Labour in Dingle.   CONOR CRUISE O'BRIEN

Turning and turning in the widening gyre
The falcon cannot hear the falconer;
Things fall apart; the centre cannot hold;
Mere anarchy is loosed upon the world,
The blood-dimmed tide is loosed, and everywhere
The ceremony of innocence is drowned;
The best lack all conviction, while the worst
Are full of passionate intensity.
                                            W. B. YEATS

THE decade that had begun so buoyantly ended in flames. As recently as
1965 a distinguished British historian had argued that Lloyd George
had solved the Irish question, having 'conjured it out of existence with a
solution that was accepted by all except the rigorous extremists in the IRA'.[1]
This was the conventional view in the mid-1960s, and not just among
Englishmen. Few Irishmen, especially in the South — where ignorance of the
North is at least as great as it is in Britain, but is often worse for being an
opinionated ignorance — really believed that the old Irish sectarian quarrel
would ever again burst forth in prolonged violence. For Southerners there
was, of course, the vexation of the border, but, like the state in Marxist
theory, it was assumed that it would fade away in time, since it was 'un-
natural'. It was not the only complacent Southern illusion shattered in this
climactic year.

The wholesale insurrection of Catholics in Northern Ireland against the
Unionist regime overshadowed everything else that happened North and
South — and in Britain too — in 1969. Of necessity, much of this chapter
will be concerned with these events. But it is perhaps better to look first of all
at the year in the Republic, which was, even discounting the tumultuous
Northern revolt, one of disappointment and bitterness.

The second half of the 1960s was peppered with labour unrest. There was a bewildering series of strikes in the Electricity Supply Board, with a settlement in one category or grade having a domino effect on relativities in others. In 1966 the government was forced to rush through emergency legislation making it illegal for ESB personnel to strike in some circumstances. The National Busmen's Union led a number of Dublin bus strikes. The IRA even made a brief appearance on the industrial scene in a particularly bitter and contentious dispute between the EI Company at Shannon and the ITGWU over recognition of the union by the company. The staff were divided on whether or not they wanted to join a union; a referendum was agreed on by management and union, but the union later withdrew, claiming that the management had tried unfairly to influence the outcome. The vote showed only about 30 per cent in favour of union membership. EI then refused the union the right to organise this minority. The union placed pickets; the company got a court injunction restraining them; the union had this overturned on appeal. The Labour Court recommended that the company recognise the union. Still the company would not budge. At the end of May 1968 a fleet of buses used to carry EI workers from Limerick to Shannon was burnt out, and the IRA claimed responsibility. This was the period in which Sinn Féin was swinging to the left, and the action could be represented as a blow against pitiless capitalism; however, EI was also an American company, so xenophobia is as likely an explanation, and one more in keeping with the traditions of the IRA. The dispute was settled a month later, roughly along the lines of the Labour Court recommendation, after officials from the Department of Labour had visited the EI head office in the United States.

In the dreary opening months of 1969 the most infamous and destructive strike of the entire decade occurred. The maintenance workers' dispute, which was prosecuted with single-minded and inflexible purpose, ended with the total capitulation of the employers and a 20 per cent increase for the men. But it also humiliated the official trade union movement in Ireland and did much to create the climate which produced the national wage agreements of the 1970s.

The maintenance dispute had its origins in an agreement concluded in 1966 between the Federated Union of Employers and eighteen craft unions, all of which had members engaged in maintenance work of some sort or other. The men's skills varied widely, which meant that their negotiating coalition had less in common than might at first seem the case. The pressure for the agreement came not from them, but from the employers, still in search of the sort of comprehensive, hard-and-fast national deal — if only in a specific sector — that had eluded them in the national agreement of 1964. The employers got their deal with the maintenance workers in 1966, setting rates of pay which were to last until the end of 1968.

In the autumn of 1968 the representatives of the eighteen unions met to draw up a new claim.[2] There was a doubt, however, as to whether or not they met as equals, because a majority of the men represented were maintenance craftsmen in the engineering industry and were all members of just two of the unions, the AEF and the NEETU. Of the others, only the electricians' union, the ETU(I), and the woodworkers' union, the ASW, had any real influence; even at that, the electricians were only half in and half out of the overall group, because they were tied into a mesh of separate and highly complex agreements with the ESB. The group never settled the crucial question of whether, in a crisis, they would act on the basis of one vote for each of the eighteen unions or in proportion to the numbers each represented.

To make matters worse, they never sorted out the details regarding the basic rates of pay. The flat rate agreed in 1966 had effectively been improved in many cases by reductions in working hours, but no allowance was made for this variable in the claim which the group submitted to the FUE. The claim was for about 35 per cent; the FUE offered about 12 per cent. In the meantime, however, electricians in the ESB and Aer Lingus had received increases which, if applied to the maintenance men, would have given them about 22 per cent. This was the figure on which the unions now focused, while the FUE, with the tacit approval of the government, prepared to dig in in defence of the 12 per cent. The case went to the Labour Court, but the unions refused to attend, and in January 1969 they served strike notice instead. This was a clear breach of the 1966 agreement, which ruled out strikes until all normal procedures of negotiation and arbitration had been exhausted.

In accordance with established union procedure, the maintenance workers' group gave ICTU notice of their intention to strike. But they did not append a list of those companies where pickets would be placed; yet this was the whole point of notifying ICTU, so that other unions who might be affected by the strike could be consulted. When this information was eventually dragged out of the group, it was to prove misleading and inaccurate.

The strike began, despite frantic last-minute efforts by ICTU to stop it, on 24 January. A total of 193 employers were involved, and very soon it became clear that a policy of selective picketing had been decided on by the maintenance unions' group. First, companies who had representatives on the FUE maintenance committee were singled out; secondly, and more cynically, there was a clear tendency to picket firms where there were relatively few members employed belonging to any of the eighteen unions in the group, but where there might be large numbers of general workers. In other words, the eighteen unions were threatening the livelihoods of large numbers of their fellow trade unionists, while minimising their own inconvenience. This extraordinary departure from the spirit of union solidarity seemed all the nastier in the light of the group's inaccurate information to ICTU about the firms that would be hit. The bitterness it engendered went so far as to move general unions to mount counter-pickets in retaliation.

Before things got to that pass, however, an attempt at settlement had been made in the Labour Court, again largely at the urging of ICTU. An agreement of sorts was hammered out and accepted by the FUE. The group agreed that the strike should end immediately, pending reference to the various union executives, but with a recommendation from the group to accept. This was the point at which the ineptitude and confusion on the union side became clear. A majority of the eighteen unions had agreed to accept; but the three key groups, the electricians and the two engineering unions, were not in a position to do so, as they were bound by a previous decision they had them-selves made that there would be no return to work without the approval of their executive committees.

The FUE were livid when the settlement, which they thought to be firm, collapsed almost immediately. The shambles also split the engineering unions and the electricians off from the other fifteen unions, who effectively disappear from the story at this point. A strike committee from the two engineering unions was formed, and for nearly five weeks they pursued their objective with a Cromwellian intensity. These two unions had barely a thousand men in dispute, but their action threw over 30,000 people out of work. The arbitrary nature of the picketing left some, admittedly a minority, of the 193 firms in the dispute unaffected, although ten companies who were not parties to the dispute at all were closed.

By now all discipline and authority had disappeared from the trade union side. Labour Court proposals at the end of February were actually endorsed by the executives of the two engineering unions, but not by the joint strike committee. This was enough to ensure their defeat by a three-to-one majority of the men. The joint strike committee had everyone by the hasp. Now all they had to do was wait.

The employers caved in at the beginning of March and conceded the full claim. They had no choice. There was nobody on the union side with whom they could any longer negotiate with confidence. Bad as the result was for them, for the official trade union movement, and ICTU in particular, it was a disaster. Every precept of orderly union conduct, not to mention the ancient instinct for mutual support and solidarity in industrial disputes, had been flouted, and the malefactors had managed to bring their cause to a triumphant conclusion.

The trade unions had started the 1960s as outsiders, but the national

209

leadership of the movement had been integrated into the decision-making process by Seán Lemass. The ordinary member had remained suspicious and easily alienated, and his conservatism had ensured that there would be no major structural reforms in the movement such as might be appropriate to its new position in national life. This alienation between men and leadership was visible in nearly all the major industrial disputes of the 1960s, together with that extraordinary respect for the presence of a picket — almost *any* picket — which is a feature of Irish trade unionism. But in the case of the maintenance men's strike there was a sinister added factor. The strike was prosecuted with an unprecedented cynicism and selfishness. Is it too much to suggest that this was symptomatic of a wider social problem in Ireland in the late 1960s, and that the self-serving manipulators in Taca were not the only people in Ireland who were morally bankrupt? The maintenance men's strike did not happen in a vacuum. Charles McCarthy, writing about the sixties in general, makes the point eloquently:

And then in the sixties, the growing affluence, the new technologies, the great shift in personal relations which television produced, and above all the revolution in the Catholic Church which made provisional much that had appeared timeless and changeless — all this produced something of a state of *anomie:* that lonely anxious state where men no longer look to the warmth of fellowship, but seek all the time to acquire goods, to compete for success, to appear dominant since they have no other means of winning the regard of others and consequently of achieving self-regard; and because they must ruthlessly seek these things, they seem to be caught up by a greed that is never satisfied, and an envy that is so naked as to be disreputable.[3]

The view that Ireland had embraced some of the least attractive features of developing capitalist countries also lay behind the climax to the running battle between programme-makers and management in RTE. In May 1969 three producers, Jack Dowling, Bob Quinn, and Lelia Doolan, resigned within two weeks of each other. Dowling had been the producer of 'Home Truths', and he claimed — at one of a number of staff teach-ins (the vocabulary and practice of student radicals had reached RTE) — that the suppression of his programme was the origin of the whole problem. He had been responsible for fourteen transmissions of 'Home Truths', and 'I had eleven threats of civil action from advertisers.' Not one of them, however, pressed the matter, because 'everything we said on the programme was true'. On one occasion, Dowling claimed, a leading cosmetics firm rang the director-general and threatened to cancel £30,000 worth of advertising if a programme on cosmetics, aimed at working-class women and comparing value between different products, were not dropped. RTE management put pressure on Dowling to do precisely that, according to his own account, but he refused; it was then suggested to him that he might not be permitted to hold his job. He claimed that a reference to Charles Haughey had been deleted from another programme because management considered it in-appropriate that a cabinet minister should be spoken of disrespectfully. Lelia Doolan, the head of light entertainment and the most senior of the trio, charged that on five occasions in a year items prepared by Gay Byrne for 'The Late Late Show' were suppressed by order of the management. Jack Dowling summed up the case of the programme-makers thus: 'If a producer is not allowed to present what he knows is true, how can he continue working?'

The director-general, T. P. Hardiman, issued a statement which attempted to answer this volley of accusations. Like his predecessor, he was at pains to stress the fact that RTE was not permitted the luxury of an editorial policy. While denying that either advertisers or RTE's advertising sales department had had any influence on programme content, he noted RTE's obligation, under the Broadcasting Act (1960), to pay its way; this could only be done if an adequate level of advertising revenue were maintained. Moreover, the expansion in the number of home-produced programmes had only been possible because of the steady flow of advertising revenue. He denied any knowledge of the eleven threatened writs mentioned by Jack Dowling. He also suggested that the producers' protest was part of a wider movement of opinion and not just to do with circumstances in RTE. The producers them-selves concurred with this. Hardiman summed up by saying:

Broadcasting must be seen as a public service and it cannot therefore be legiti-mate that individuals in RTE should seek to use it arbitrarily. This is not to say that broadcasting must simply reflect the status quo. It inevitably had a leader-ship function.... How it should be performed in individual instances is the difficult area of policy decisions.

In other words, the business of management was managing, and RTE management did not propose to devolve its broad powers in this area to the programme-makers. This was regarded by the protesters as an excessive use of management power, which denied producers and others concerned in the making of programmes any real responsibility or discretion. For them, as for many other alienated intellectuals in the 1960s, they were parties to a conflict

between technologically trained minds who devise our structures and control their use and creatively formed minds who try to make programmes. The former control resources: the latter are controlled by them.

So saying, they went on their way. Within four months they had written and published *Sit Down and Be Counted*, part apologia, part broadside, part cultural inquiry. It was one of the most stimulating books written in Ireland in the 1960s, an impassioned plea for the principles of quality public-service broadcasting and against the debilitating pap — most of it imported — which choked the airwaves in circumstances where commercial criteria were permitted an excessive influence in the determination of programme content.

Running through all the crises and storms in RTE in the late sixties had been a very fair degree of government paranoia. They were at times almost neurotically suspicious of what was afoot in Montrose. In November 1969 they excelled themselves. 'Seven Days' produced a programme on money-lending which drew an extraordinary attack from the Minister for Justice, Micheál Ó Moráin, in the Dáil. He accused the programme of gross exaggeration, of paying interviewees to say sensational and untrue things, and of plying others with drink for the same purpose. The RTE Authority, wondering no doubt what they had to do to keep 'Seven Days' out of trouble, stood behind the programme. The government, with that lack of proportion that attended so many of their actions in the late sixties, ordered nothing less than a sworn public inquiry into the programme. This was a stupid piece of bullying, which, if intended to demoralise RTE, certainly succeeded in its object. David Thornley, a former 'Seven Days' presenter and now a Labour TD, told the Dáil, when opposing the legislation to set up the inquiry, that 'the government was launching a major assault on the whole principle of journalistic freedom', because the inquiry would be empowered to make people appear, and produce notes, tapes and documents. Some ministers were doubtless of the view that Thornley's presence on the Labour benches merely confirmed their suspicion that RTE was a nest of socialists and other undesirables hostile to Fianna Fáil. Television was the most conspicuous novelty in an age of novelties, and traditionalists were prone to exaggerate its impact and blame it for all the woes of the world.

The continuous harassing of RTE by the government, beginning with Haughey's cavalier demand of 1966 and ending with the 'Seven Days' inquiry — which, incidentally, found a number of unsatisfactory features in the money-lending programme — did much to generate something like a siege mentality among programme-makers. This in turn was acted upon by the dissenting spirit of the sixties, with its anti-authoritarian pull, which set them against not only the politicians but their own management as well.

But the 'creative people' had embarked on a battle that could not be won. They might influence public opinion, especially among the more liberal bour-geoisie, but within RTE itself the organisation men held all the cards. By the end of the decade the genie of television had not exactly been put back in the bottle, but it was at least the property of safe men. The politicians were happy to settle for that.

212

The seventies will be socialist! The general election of June 1969 rang to the battle hymn of the Labour Party. Nowhere did that swing to the left, already mentioned in other contexts, have such an effect. As late as 1966 it was possible for one observer to write of the Labour Party:

The Labour Party in this three-quarters-of-a-nation has been dominated for years by dismal poltroons, on the lines of O'Casey's Uncle Payther.[4]

By the end of 1968 the same observer was himself a member of the party, which was so pleased to have him that they organised a special meeting in Liberty Hall, at which he was the main speaker, to launch his political career. By the time the general election was over, six months later, he was Conor Cruise O'Brien, TD, having been returned to Dáil Éireann by the electors of Dublin North-East. Clearly, strange and wonderful things had been happening to the dismal poltroons.

Labour's swing to the left dated from the annual party conference of 1967. Brendan Corish made a ringing speech, in which he nailed the party's colours firmly to the socialist mast. Speaker after speaker reiterated the fact of Labour's socialism, as though after years of its being a taboo word, it was a relief simply to shout it aloud in public. The pressure to move left had been building up for a few years: the party had greatly expanded its membership, especially in Dublin, and the new people had no patience with the apologetic demeanour of the older stalwarts. Of course, the time was propitious, for, as the new general secretary of the party, Brendan Halligan, remarked in May 1967, 'It is almost respectable now to be a socialist.' In the same month the party received the moral, financial and organisational boost of the ITGWU's affiliation. Everything seemed to be coming round for Labour.

The 1967 conference threw the party into a ferment of euphoric activity. Bliss indeed it was to be alive in that dawn. The party acted in the sincere conviction that it was the agent of a peaceful political revolution which would sweep away the old Civil War issues forever. Corish told them that they could win fifty seats in the next Dáil and form a government, and few doubted him. For twenty months the Labour Party stormed through the Irish political world believing that hitherto unimaginable prizes were now within its grasp.

Even at this remove, the sheer exuberance of the Labour revival is so infectious that it seems almost ungenerous to point to some of the less auspicious signs. There was the expulsion of a former vice-chairman, Proinsias Mac Aonghusa. He had been a vigorous left-winger before the party as a whole swung left, and he had wounded a great many 'do-nothing backwoodsmen', as he once referred to them, by his eloquent attacks. He was expelled in early 1967 on a trivial and, it seemed to many, trumped-up offence against

The 1969 general election was
dominated by these men. The
photograph above shows the
Taoiseach, Jack Lynch, and the
Minister for Local Government,
Kevin Boland, at the last Fianna
Fáil Ard Fheis before the split over
the Arms Trial. Lynch's American-
style electioneering and Boland's
exquisitely sensitive constituency
carve-up were largely responsible for
Fianna Fáil's victory. The Labour
Party was led by Brendan Corish
(right), under whose leadership the
party had at last forged an opening
to the left.

party discipline. He appealed in person to the 1967 annual conference, where the temper of the delegates might be supposed to have favoured his cause, but the expulsion was not rescinded. The whole episode had a very nasty ring to it. In December 1967 Patrick Norton, son of the former leader, resigned from the party. The swing to the left had proved too much for him: indeed, his place in the party owed more to filial piety than to ideological conviction. In the spring of 1968 there was what amounted to another expulsion, this time of the near-veteran Senator Jack McQuillan, who had become general secretary of a breakaway, non-ICTU union, thus incurring the wrath of the official trade union establishment. They put pressure on the party, which, knowing the side its bread was buttered on, leaned hard on McQuillan. He resigned, but the party's image suffered. Finally, there were the local elections of June 1967, where Labour made gains in Dublin but fell back in rural areas. The gains were attributed to the party's more assertive brand of socialism; the losses were not. It was an omen.

But expulsions, resignations and local elections alike were swamped by the tidal wave of fervour and optimism which gripped Labour from the autumn of 1967. The party broadened its base and attracted some national figures to its ranks. Conor Cruise O'Brien has already been noted; David Thornley and Justin Keating, both academics in TCD and well known for their television appearances, also joined. Keating, in particular, was considered a happy acquisition because his television programmes were aimed almost exclusively at farmers, with whom he was very popular. Even better from the party's point of view, Rickard Deasy, the former president of the NFA, joined and was adopted as a candidate in North Tipperary, where there was a traditional Labour seat. It was hoped that his presence in the Labour camp would help the party's image with farmers, who had traditionally regarded it as no more than a lobbying vehicle for trade unionists, whom most Irish farmers regarded as the scum of the earth, or worse.

As the 1969 general election approached, Labour was supremely confident. They were going it alone, all the way for socialism. The Fine Gael party, which they now professed to despise even more than Fianna Fáil, had made a few tentative enquiries about the possibility of a coalition arrangement, but Labour was in no mood to entertain suitors, and Fine Gael was sent packing.

Herein lay a snag. Shrewd observers outside the Labour Party realised it at the time, but there was no acknowledgment of it within the party. Under proportional representation, it requires not just massive swings to make an electoral breakthrough, but the disciplined transfer of lower preferences. In the absence of an arrangement with Fine Gael, Labour could not get the benefit of enough anti-Fianna Fáil transfers: as in 1961 and 1965, the decision to go it alone handed the election to Fianna Fáil in advance.

When the election came, Fianna Fáil had the advantage of its peerless machine, together with the fact that Kevin Boland's recent revision of the constituencies — which became necessary once the straight-vote referendum was lost in 1968 — was a consummate gerrymander in the party's favour: Boland's revenge. On the other hand, Fianna Fáil had been twelve years in power, had obviously lost its way on a number of important questions in recent years, was associated in the public mind with greasy speculators and other Taca types, and had a leader who was untried and not in the mould of commanding figures with which the party was familiar.

Fine Gael, despite the promise of the 'Just Society' years, was the same as ever. There was no new broom under Cosgrave. He had not, as had seemed likely at the beginning of his leadership, made common cause with Declan Costello and the liberal wing of the party. He cleaved instead to Gerry Sweetman. Costello retired from public life in the spring of 1967, and although he made a brief return in the 1970s, this gifted and energetic man never held high cabinet office. Fine Gael made no lasting impression on Fianna Fáil's support between 1965 and 1969.

The general election of 1969 was all about the Labour Party. And it was dirty. Fianna Fáil went for the jugular by representing Labour's new policies as 'communist'. They were helped by Labour's agriculture policy document, which was extremely radical and contained the proposal that inefficient and neglectful farmers be removed and the land placed in the hands of younger and more energetic men. Fianna Fáil transformed this into expropriation, collectivisation, and anything else that would serve to scare the daylights out of the farmers. The Minister for Agriculture, Neil Blaney, was in the van of this *jihad* to rescue rural Ireland from Stalinism. He told the people of Drumoghill, Co. Donegal:

[The Marxists] have arisen suddenly among us in this election mouthing the glib jargon of atheistic socialism, preaching the message of class warfare. But it is a sugared pill. It is the same dialectic, the same false doctrine that preceded the downfall of democracy in Russia, in Cuba, in North Korea, in North Vietnam, and elsewhere.
They follow the classic Marxist path of infiltration followed by takeover. They have already successfully infiltrated the Irish Labour Party, and there are many decent men and women in the Labour Party who have become very uneasy, but as yet they are afraid to speak out.

This was by no means the most hysterical speech made in the course of the 'red smear' campaign, but it was reasonably typical of the tactics Fianna Fáil adopted. There were few wholesale denunciations, least of all in rural areas where there was a local Labour man whom people had known for years.

Instead the suggestion was put about that the 'old' Labour Party had been swamped by sinister intellectuals and fellow-travellers, and that, decent as the poor local slob might be, the truth of it was that a vote for him was as good as a vote for the Comintern (God between us and all harm).

What was more, this campaign of insinuation was not left to rough-house political brawlers like Blaney. Nice Mr Lynch, his face the very picture of seraphic innocence, made an extensive nationwide tour, introducing American-style presidential politics to Ireland in the process. 'Honest Jack' made a particular point of ingratiating himself with the nuns, and many was the convent parlour where the Taoiseach took tea and murmured about the dangers that could befall the poor country if the wrong people got their hands on the levers of power. The nuns, who controlled the girls' schools, told their pupils, and the pupils told their parents, the sovereign electors.

It worked. Against most predictions, Fianna Fáil won a handsome overall majority. Fine Gael, symbolically, stayed as they were. But Labour, after all the euphoria, lost three seats. For the devotees of the new republic, it was a very cold shower indeed. Labour did well in Dublin, where most of the glamour candidates were running and where full-blooded socialism was more likely to have electoral appeal. David Thornley became the first Labour candidate ever to top the poll in a Dublin constituency. In rural Ireland, however, it was a different story. Seats were lost, and even where they were held, it was with unwonted difficulty. Everywhere outside Dublin the Labour vote was down. In North Tipperary, Rickard Deasy, one of the party's brightest hopes, crashed to a humiliating defeat, pulling only 517 first pre-ferences and losing his deposit.

There had been no breakthrough, no smashing of the Civil War parties, no triumph of class politics. The Irish political imperative remained the same: Fianna Fáil against the Rest. For the moment the Labour Party was in a daze, not quite able to believe that history had failed to keep its appointment. Irish politics ended the sixties, not with a revolution, but with the old consensus renewed and strengthened, one of the great conservative and stable in-stitutions of Irish life.

Millions of words have been written about what happened in Northern Ireland in 1969, and there is little that can usefully be done here except to summarise the main events of that dreadful year. To do so is to bring the narrative of the 1960s to a melancholy end.

The march planned by People's Democracy from Belfast to Derry in defiance of the one-month ban accepted by NICRA began as scheduled on New Year's Day. The calm that had followed O'Neill's 'crossroads' speech was rudely broken. On 4 January a well-prepared loyalist mob made a vicious attack on the marchers at Burntollet Bridge, about five miles from Derry. In the opinion of the marchers, the RUC stood by and made no attempt to prevent the onslaught; although this was disputed by the Cameron Report, there was at least no doubt that a large proportion of the attackers were off-duty B Specials.

On the preceding night the Rev. Ian Paisley had held a religious meeting in Derry, and as so often happened when the Bible-thumping Doctor preached Christ crucified, there was trouble. It was, however, nothing to the trouble that ensued the next night. The battered PD marchers struggled into the city, pursued by furious policemen, who ran amok in the Bogside, terrorising the inhabitants.

The fragile breathing space was gone. The PD march was an act of irresponsible bravado, the work of naïve and doctrinaire militants, bent on provoking the wrath of Protestant extremists. In this it succeeded admirably; from here on, the events of 1969 have a sense of tragic inevitability about them. It should be said, however, that if it had not been Burntollet that shattered the calm, it would have been something else. If the sequence of events in Northern Ireland in the 1960s establishes anything, it is the utterly irreconcilable nature of the hardline Protestant right, and its willingness to countenance violence and criminal assault in pursuit of its goals. In the end the actions of the loyalist *freikorps* ensured that descent into barbarism and anarchy which swept away the very system they were pledged to defend.

After Burntollet and the police riot in Derry the temperature rose alarmingly. In mid-January another PD march, in Newry, Co. Down, ended in rioting, although this time at least the police behaved themselves. Stormont announced that a commission of inquiry (the Cameron Commission) was being established to investigate the cause and nature of all the trouble since the previous October. This announcement precipitated the resignation from the cabinet of its most able political craftsman, Brian Faulkner. He and O'Neill had coexisted uneasily for nearly six years; Faulkner had always remained bitter over the circumstances of O'Neill's succession to the leadership and had a poor opinion of the Prime Minister's abilities as a party manager. He was also considerably to the right of O'Neill. Faulkner was followed to the backbenches by William Morgan, the Minister of Health and Social Services, another able right-winger. A dozen other hardline Unionist MPs then forgathered in a hotel in Portadown, Co. Armagh, and this 'Portadown Parliament' called for the Prime Minister's resignation.

O'Neill responded by announcing a general election. The Unionist Party, that extraordinary monolith as it had seemed to its opponents, was split between pro- and anti-O'Neill factions, while on the Catholic side the young civil rights leaders were offering a challenge to the old 'green Tories' in the Nationalist Party. For the first and last time in his political life, Terence O'Neill faced an electoral contest in his Bannside constituency. None other than Ian Paisley himself offered the main challenge, while Michael Farrell of People's Democracy also entered the lists.

The election was a paper victory for O'Neill. His nominees outpolled the anti-O'Neill Unionists by two to one, but it was not enough. As ever, the hard right was not a majority, but was still formidable enough to frustrate reform. In his own constituency the overall result was reflected in microcosm. O'Neill was elected, but did not secure a majority of the votes cast; his margin over Paisley was less than 1,500 votes out of a poll of over 16,000. It was a humiliating victory.

On the other side of the electoral divide, the civil rights activists had done well. The eclipse of the old Nationalist Party, the last remaining political link with the Ireland of Parnell, was symbolised by the defeat of its leader, Eddie McAteer, by John Hume, the vice-chairman of the Derry Citizens' Action Committee.

Terence O'Neill's political position was fatally weakened by the general election of February 1969. Nominally there were forty Unionists in the House of Commons, whose total membership was fifty-two. However, the Prime Minister could only rely on the personal support of twenty-seven of them, and three of these were independent Unionists not subject to the party whip. He nevertheless determined to push through the one measure which, more than any other, symbolised reform in Catholic eyes: one man one vote. The announcement was made in late April. Promptly his amiable cousin, James Chichester-Clark, the Minister of Agriculture, resigned because he feared that the concession in the violent circumstances then prevailing would enflame Unionist opinion; he had, however, acquiesced in the measure when it was discussed in the cabinet.

The Prime Minister was on the way out. He was given the final push by a team of bombers who blew up a number of water pipe-lines in the Belfast region, badly affecting the city's water supply. It was assumed at the time that this was the IRA, and the Prime Minister naturally felt the wrath of the law-and-order lobby from the extreme right, who insisted on saying that they had told him so. In fact the explosions were the work of Protestant extremists, anxious to push O'Neill into resignation. They succeeded: he quit on 28 April.

Terence O'Neill was not a politician of the first rank, but he was a decent man with decent instincts. He tried at least to create an atmosphere in which ordinary life could be lived without the poison of sectarian hatred seeping in

Derry, August 1969.

everywhere. In the context of Ireland in the 1960s, he was a moderniser in the sense of wishing to import the standards of other places and cultures and displace native habits which were backward and wasteful. It is worth recording that, until the civil disturbances began, the overwhelming weight of opinion both for and against him believed that he was succeeding in his attempts to liberalise conditions in Northern Ireland: the sheer venom and intensity of Paisley's campaign against him is eloquent testimony to this. It was O'Neill's misfortune to have had to operate in the most primitive political environment in the developed world, where even his brand of cautious Tory paternalism was regarded as radical. The soul of his party was in hock to the ultras. He needed a lot of time and a degree of nerve and skill verging on the Napoleonic to achieve his ends. It is all too easy to enumerate his failures, but it should be recalled that, in a mere six years as leader of the Unionist Party, he had made a sufficient impression on Protestant opinion to secure two-thirds of the Unionist vote in a general election held in the most enflamed conditions. Clearly he had brought Protestant opinion a long way from where it had been in Brookeborough's day, even when one makes due allowance for the fact that some of the pro-O'Neill support came to him because of his position rather than his opinions. The failure of O'Neill was the failure of the state, or at least of the regime. If Unionism could not take O'Neill, it could take nothing meaningful in the way of reform.

The new Prime Minister was Major James Chichester-Clark, who beat Brian Faulkner by one vote. By a delicious irony, the single vote that beat Faulkner was Terence O'Neill's, who thus deprived his arch-rival of the prize he so obviously coveted.* Chichester-Clark managed to reconcile the two wings of Unionism for a while: he brought Faulkner back into the cabinet while pressing ahead with the reform programme. He got the party to agree to admit the principle of 'one man one vote' for future local elections and announced an amnesty for all prisoners who had been convicted for 'political' offences arising out of the troubles.

Spring ripened into summer and the marching season approached. There was trouble following the Twelfth of July marches in a number of centres, notably in Derry, where rioting lasted for three days. At the beginning of August a Protestant mob tried to storm Unity Flats, a Catholic enclave in West Belfast. One man died in police custody. By now few Northern Catholics had a shred of trust in the RUC, and as the police became more and more stretched by the escalating disturbances, the B Specials, who were ostensibly a police reserve but were in reality an armed but totally untrained and poorly disciplined Protestant militia, were increasingly deployed. The

---

*The wits observed that it was 'one man one vote' that had done it!

222

fear and hatred of Catholics for the B Specials was intense beyond description. The scene was set for the climacteric of mid-August.

The annual parade of the Apprentice Boys of Derry takes place on 12 August, and in 1969 it was allowed to go ahead as usual despite ample evidence that Derry was a tinder-box. The Apprentice Boys are an Orange fraternity who traditionally marched around the city walls, marking out their territory for the benefit of the Catholics below in the Bogside. It was the custom for some in their number to show their contempt for the poverty of the Bogside by flicking down pennies to the resentful spectators. It was not the kind of demonstration that any responsible government should have allowed to proceed in the circumstances of a place like Derry on 12 August 1969.

The Apprentice Boys began their proceedings, as usual, with a service in St Columb's Cathedral, where the sermon was delivered by the Rev. Canon William Kerr, the rector of Moy, Co. Tyrone. His theme was peace:

Let us therefore make up our minds today to press on, having this end in view, to do good to all men, come what may. Asking for no greater reward than to be known, wherever we live, as lovers of humanity and fellow-workers in God.

And with this flapdoodle ringing in their ears, the Apprentice Boys sallied forth.

The Bogside was prepared for trouble. It was determined that there would be no repetition of the police invasion of early January. Barricades were in position, supplies were laid in, and petrol for molotov cocktails was freely available.

When the Apprentice Boys reached the edge of the Bogside, missiles were thrown at them. Stewards in the Bogside tried to restrain the stone-throwers, and when they failed the RUC got involved. Slowly but inexorably, the tension mounted until, just after 7 p.m., the police tried to force their way into the Bogside, but failed. Petrol bombs rained down on them from the roofs of Rossville Flats, and these, together with the barricades, held the line against the RUC's armoured cars and CS gas.

The siege lasted for fifty hours. In effect, the Bogside seceded from the United Kingdom — to the extent that it had ever been in it in the first place. The defence of the area passed from the hands of the middle-class civil rights activists to those of the radical left and the republicans, a peculiar coalition of the two extremes by no means unique to Derry in the late sixties. The most prominent of the defenders was a twenty-two-year-old girl from Cookstown, Co. Tyrone, Bernadette Devlin, MP for Mid-Ulster since April.

She had been selected as a Unity candidate for a by-election in Mid-Ulster, where there was a natural Catholic majority. In the past this had frequently split between an abstentionist republican and a Nationalist, allowing the Unionist in to take the seat. Not this time. Bernadette Devlin, a final-year psychology student at Queen's and a founder member of the People's Democracy, was acceptable to all shades of Catholic opinion. She was elected and made an electrifying maiden speech in the House of Commons on the day she took her seat. For a brief few weeks she was an honoured celebrity in London political society.

By August she had put all that behind her. Now she was playing a role to which her politics seemed best suited: not a cautious, prevaricating parliamentarian, but *La Passionaria*, the very spirit of a people in revolt.

That is precisely what the Catholics of Derry were. It was, in a sense, the ultimate sectarian battle, between Catholics who had for years been discriminated against and demeaned in a city where they were a clear numerical majority, and the Protestant police force and armed militia, the RUC and the B Specials. The Catholics, anxious to have the pressure taken off them, called for diversions elsewhere in the province to stretch the resources of the police. The call was answered, especially in Belfast.

The insurrection by the majority population in the second city of Northern Ireland had transformed the situation. In the South Jack Lynch made a bellicose speech to the nation on television, which was really aimed at the Fianna Fáil hard right, but which, in the enflamed atmosphere of Northern Ireland, had a galvanising effect on both sides: the belief was widespread that the Republic was going to take an active hand in the situation. Of course, it did not and could not have done. There was only one force which could separate the two sides, and that was the British army. It moved into Derry on the evening of 14 August; the RUC and the Specials withdrew from the edge of the Bogside, and the siege was raised.

The jubiliation of 'Free Derry' was soon overshadowed by the appalling events that now occurred in Belfast. There Catholics were in a minority, and nearly all Catholic areas were close to, or even surrounded by, large areas of Protestant population. On the evening of the 14th, loyalist mobs, incensed at the Catholic victory in Derry and provoked by the irresponsible hooliganism of some Catholic youths, launched a wholesale assault on Catholic areas; in their midst were B Specials, toting their legally held firearms. The RUC, having first engaged the Catholic youths, were in effect drawn into the disturbances on the Protestant side, and their behaviour over the next two days was shamefully — and in many cases enthusiastically — partisan. By the time the British army moved into Belfast on the 16th over 150 Catholic houses had been burnt out and six people were dead, including one nine-year-old boy, killed in his bedroom by a discharge from an RUC armoured car. There was a flight from mixed areas as Catholics hastily made for the safety

The 1960s ended with what had seemed the unthinkable coming to pass: British troops back on Irish streets. This photograph was taken on the Falls Road, Belfast, on 16 August 1969.

of their ghettoes, and barricades were erected as a defence against further Protestant incursions.

The events of August 1969 torpedoed the slender hopes of the reconcilers and the liberals in Northern Ireland. Their flame, which had guttered fitfully throughout the decade, was finally extinguished. The ancient, insoluble hatred of Protestant and Catholic re-established itself as the prime reality of Ulster life. Catholics, in particular, learned this lesson. In their supreme hour of need, with their houses being burnt over their heads, their traditional defenders, the IRA, were nowhere to be seen. The new, left-wing leadership of the movement had starved Belfast of arms, having taken the view that that sort of thing was hopelessly anachronistic. They, like many others in time, were to discover that in Northern Ireland nothing is ever anachronistic for long.

On the Protestant side, the insurrection in Derry supplied all the evidence needed in support of the views of the ultras. Just as August 1969 vindicated the opinions of the traditional republicans and led ineluctably to the formation of the Provisional IRA, so, on the other side of the sectarian divide, it vindicated their mirror-image, Paisley and the anti-O'Neill Unionists.

As the year drew to a close the British army became more and more entrenched in the North, and the Westminster government became more exigent in its demands for reform. The Cameron Report amply documented the long-standing denial of civil rights. A few weeks later the Hunt Report recommended the disarming and reform of the RUC and the disbandment of the B Specials. In the South shadowy events were gestating which were to lead, a few months later, to the trauma of the Arms Trial and an open split in the hitherto infrangible Fianna Fáil party.

The Northern explosion had changed everything and changed nothing. From the moment that the lorries bearing the men of the 1st Battalion, Prince of Wales's Own Regiment, drove across Craigavon Bridge and into Derry on 14 August, Stormont was doomed. But the underlying reality which Stormont represented — the adamantine determination of Ulster Protestants not to be absorbed by Irish Catholic nationalism — remained. After 1969 the irreconcilable quarrel simply moved onto new ground, and in so doing it cast its shadow over the whole island. The 1960s, overwhelmingly a time of hope and faith in the future, ended with the eyes of Irish people, North and South, turned nervously to the past.

Chapter Twelve

CONCLUSION

A *question of identity*

Since it has pleased God to endow us with some capacity for reason, so that we may not be, like the beasts, slavishly subject to the general laws, but may adapt ourselves to them by judgment and free will, we ought indeed to yield a little to the simple authority of nature, but not to let ourselves be tyrannically carried away by her. Reason alone should guide us in our inclinations.   MONTAIGNE

What might have been is an abstraction
Remaining a perpetual possibility
Only in a world of speculation.
What might have been and what has been
Point to one end, which is always present.
Footfalls echo in the memory
Down the passage which we did not take
Towards the door we never opened
Into the rose-garden.   T. S. ELIOT

FOR forty years until the early 1960s Ireland North and South had turned away from the gaze of the wider world beyond her own shores. In the North the Protestant state had gone quietly about its business, observing the formalities of democracy and representative government the better to camouflage its real intentions. It was no wonder that the Unionist Party resented and feared the prospect of television, or Labour politicians from Westminster, or any other nosey-parker outsiders who would judge their little bit of heaven by the ordinary standards of the modern developed world. In the South the generation that inherited the newly independent state attempted a cultural revolution. The country was to be Gaelicised; it was to turn inward to its own historical resources, to draw on that indigenous culture which had been all but swamped by the presence of the erstwhile imperial power. The South of Ireland resolved to renounce the world and all its works. But after the 1960s it was no longer possible to believe in the Gaelic myth.

Irish nationalism, which had flourished in its modern form since the 1820s (or, if you prefer a republican view of things, the 1790s), antedated all theories of cultural separatism. Nationalism was, despite the adherence of small numbers of unrepresentative Protestants over the years, basically a movement of Irish Catholics to secure control of their own internal affairs. Ideas of Gaelic revival were grafted on by cultural theorists, first in the 1840s and more decisively from the 1890s onwards. Neither Daniel O'Connell nor Charles Stewart Parnell, the most successful nationalist leaders of the nineteenth century, took seriously the view that what distinguished the Irish from the English — or, more precisely, what prevented the Irish from feeling British — was a cultural difference rooted in language. It was not that language could be totally ignored in calculating the Anglo-Irish equation, although O'Connell — a native speaker — came very close to doing precisely that; it was rather that history had submerged Gaelic culture to the point where its relevance was marginal and vestigial. All through the nineteenth century the great bonding force for the mass of Irish nationalists was not Gaelic culture, but Catholicism. It was through their common Catholicism that the historical memory of expropriation, persecution and exclusion was reflected. When nationalism succeeded in mobilising the Irish people in overwhelming numbers, it did so either with the direct assistance of Church structures or through a compact with the hierarchy: hence O'Connell's Catholic Association, and the Irish Parliamentary Party's undertaking to represent the educational interests of the Church at Westminster in return for organisational support at home. Insurrectionaries, on the other hand, could afford the luxury of anticlericalism.

The Gaelic revival of the 1890s raised the nationalist struggle to a new plane and gave it a sense of historical and cultural dignity which was understandably flattering to the Irish people. It was heady stuff. In the atmosphere of cynical failure following the fall of Parnell, it gave a fresh lustre to the struggle for Irish freedom. It did so, however, at the price of describing the Irish people to themselves in terms which were palpably false. It identified as the quintessentially Irish characteristics precisely those features of social and cultural life which were in the most rapid decline. It characterised as un-Irish and anti-national those features which, under the influence of rapid anglicisation in the second half of the nineteenth century, were waxing strongest. Once the English language had supplanted Irish as the common vernacular of Irishmen, all appeals to radical cultural separatism rang false. It is a supreme irony that such theories were only formulated after the living realities of Irish life made them untenable in practice.

Nevertheless, it was a form of nationalism profoundly influenced by the cultural theorists which eventually triumphed in the South of Ireland. With its instinctive anglophobia, it was inclined to associate modern industrial development with the imperial enemy, and it placed a premium on backwardness and quaintness generally. It is little wonder that the Irish political revolution failed to produce a parallel social and economic revolution. It encouraged the quixotic cult of the West. It attempted, vainly, to restore the Irish language, and for forty years it hectored the Irish people to the effect that the language was the true soul of the nation.

The great achievement of Irish life in the 1960s was to close the gap which had opened up between theory and reality. Officially we had been describing ourselves to ourselves in terms which we knew in our hearts to be false. We were not a Gaelic nation, either in fancy or in fact. We were not unlike another country at the periphery of Europe, Russia, pulled in two directions at once by history. We were partly modernised, and this process had entailed a wholesale borrowing of ideas and skills from abroad, which in our case usually meant Britain. What else could one expect in a small, underdeveloped island lying in the shadow of one of the most powerful and influential nations in the world? But we were not English — or even British — and our nationalism made us face the other way: inwards, away from the greater world — just as Russian nationalism did and does.

By the 1960s Irish people had wearied of the backwardness and failure associated with the Sinn Féin ideal. Its abandonment in economics led to that doubling of the nation's wealth in a decade which prompted the country to reorientate its gaze outward. What made the process so tumultuous was the coincidence of a number of mainly external factors: the development of television; the more or less simultaneous arrival of the transistor radio and rock 'n' roll; the earthquake in the Catholic Church caused by ecumenism and *aggiornamento*; the development of short-haul jet aircraft and roll-on roll-off car ferries which facilitated the rapid spread of the foreign holiday. The physical means to maintain the old cultural *cordon sanitaire* were simply no longer to hand. The Irish nation began to behave in a fashion that approximated more and more to the broader Anglo-American and Western European culture which was characteristic of the developed capitalist world. Ireland abandoned an officially prescribed make-believe culture in favour of the noisy, vulgar, but real charms of a freely available alternative. The new order was reflected in the structure of the Irish economy and industry; in the movement of the Irish population towards towns and cities; in its leisure activities and interests which, particularly for the urban young, became almost indistinguishable from those of their contemporaries abroad; in its new openness to and interest in foreign ideas and standards; in the country's abandonment of the coarser forms of provincialism and petty-mindedness.

This transformation undid the work of the Gaelic myth-makers. Irish people now acknowledged openly what they had previously acknowledged quietly by their refusal to learn Irish: that it was not necessary for Gaelic culture to be revived in order to provide a bonding agent for the Irish nation.

229

The traditionalists who feared that the further erosion of the Gaelic revival by the forces of the new cosmopolitanism would lead to a selling of the nation's soul were labouring under a misapprehension. The soul of modern Ireland was not a Gaelic soul. Gaelic culture was not a bonding agent for ordinary, living, breathing Irish people.

What was? The answer that most readily suggests itself, in the 1960s as for 150 years or more, is Catholicism. Of all the forces that have contributed to the making of nationalist Ireland, none has been more powerful or pervasive in its relentless daily effect upon the lives of ordinary Irish people. Superficially the 1960s does not seem to have been a decade in which the Irish Catholic identity was strengthened, at least in a strictly religious sense. Old modes of expression and familiar habits of authority were no longer possible for the Catholic Church. But religious denomination in Ireland has an ethnic as well as a theological dimension. Although, looked at in the very long term, the 1960s began a process of social transformation which if pursued to its logical conclusion would create the conditions for a non-confessional nationality in which Protestant, Catholic and Dissenter could truly unite in the common name of Irishman, its immediate consequences tended to reinforce the bond between Catholicism and nationalism.

There were two reasons for this. One, already dealt with, derived from the stripping away of the Gaelic myth. Once this mask had been removed, it was possible to acknowledge what was underneath. There was a certain natural reluctance to do this, for to admit the reality of the Catholic/nationalist nexus was to come close to allowing that the Republic was but the mirror-image — in conception if not in its daily practices — of the Northern Protestant state. Moreover, a generational change in the South, allied to the more relaxed and self-confident atmosphere bred by ecumenism and prosperity, was eliminating many of the traditional Catholic suspicions about the equivocal loyalty of Protestants in the Republic. There was no more hopeful omen in Ireland in the 1960s than this, but it was over-shadowed at the end of the decade by the second development which emphasised the closeness of the connection between Catholicism and nationalism: the Northern explosion, inevitably. In no time at all this led to appeals in the South for assistance for 'our people' over the border, in terms which left nobody in any doubt as to who 'our people' were, or what was their distinguishing characteristic. In the mouths of the right-wing republicans, the union between 'Irish' and 'Catholic' was complete. The same people, of course, were never done quoting Wolfe Tone.

The remarkable thing was the passivity with which the generality of Southern Catholics listened to the appeals to help 'our people'. Of course, the Republic did not wholly stand aside from the Northern troubles: the murky deals that set up the Provisional IRA were done in Dublin. But there was no mass involvement. From the beginning the overriding anxiety in the Republic was to stop the Northern troubles from spilling over the border; only the atavistic spasms induced by Bloody Sunday in 1972 and the H-Block hunger-strikes ten years later have disturbed the studied apathy induced by this fear.

There is a nice irony in all this. The Northern crisis had catapulted the past into the present. Why did Southern Catholics choose to ignore their co-religionists and fellow-nationals in their hour of trial? If Catholicism really was the bonding agent in Irish nationalism, why was there no pan-Catholic solidarity when the old bugles sounded again? What had changed?

Catholic nationalism, having established its own state and grown comfortable in it, was increasingly inclined to discount those Catholics caught on the wrong side of the border. This partitionist mentality was born out of the homogeneity of the Republic. Irish unity would threaten that homogeneity, for it could only be achieved at the price of absorbing a million Protestants who, both by definition and declaration, were non-nationals, and ruggedly hostile non-nationals at that. The 1960s reinforced this view, for not only did the sudden new prosperity of the Republic give its citizens an unwonted stake in the *status quo*, it also gave them, for the first time, a real feeling of Southern superiority. The Republic seemed to be marching towards the future while the North was stuck in the past.

What had emerged in the South was a sophisticated, camouflaged version of traditional Catholic tribalism. National feeling was focused on the maximum area within which Catholic hegemony was unchallenged; any extension of the national territory would involve a degree of political com-promise wholly foreign to the Irish tradition. Within the boundaries of the Catholic state, however, the spirit of the age could be safely let loose. The cautious liberalism of the sixties and seventies was an earnest of the Republic's desire to modernise and reach out to a wider world, but with the state's flank well covered. It is no surprise that Irish liberals have been over-whelmingly anti-republican since the sixties, for republicanism is not only the call of the past, but the call to a civil disorder which would threaten the material ground gained when times were good. Irish unity might offer the prospect of a theoretical liberal pluralism, but partition, allied to Southern prosperity, offered the certainty of at least some progress, however halting, in that direction.

In the 1960s Southern Catholics fixed the boundary to the march of their nation, and fixed it firmly where the Boundary Commissioners had left it in 1925. *Klein Irland* ensured its own stability by eschewing *Gross Irland*, although continuing to pay lip-service to it. The nature of political

Catholicism in Ireland was tribally exclusive: the circumstances of its historical formation had precluded the development of a pluralistic, accommodating spirit. It could only flourish where its tribal assumptions were unchallenged. The losers in all this were the members of the tribe caught on the wrong side of the border, for their continued exclusion from the Catholic state became the price of that state's survival. When the Northern troubles erupted in 1969, Southern Catholics — who liked to blather about unity when there was no danger of it happening — were invited to put up or shut up. As in all such matters, self-interest ruled: they shut up.

The new Southern liberalism rested on the rock of partition. After forty years of independence, and with the confidence born of having money in the bank, the Republic was anxious to take its place among the nations. It shed the Gaelic myth, borrowed new standards of behaviour from abroad, and even put away some of the outer trappings of its traditional Catholic ethos. In deference to ecumenism, and anxious to avoid the charge of sectarianism, it hastened the final integration of its tiny Protestant minority. But Catholicism, albeit more muted and less demonstrative than before, remained its salient feature. Whether or not the Republic could transcend its historic Catholic legacy and focus its nationality on some other, more secular, principle was a question for the future.

The Republic of Ireland experienced a revolution from the top down in the 1960s. The original impetus for change, which led to the development of the First Programme for Economic Expansion, came from the highest echelons of the civil service. The most enthusiastic Europeans and free traders tended to be university-educated professionals. The new corporate planning structures were established largely on the initiative of a few leading political figures, of whom Seán Lemass was the most prominent; the general run of TDs, even in the Fianna Fáil party, were for a long time indifferent to these pillars of the new economic order.

Lemass liked to observe that a rising tide lifts all boats. This was manifestly untrue. If you were a western smallholder in the 1960s, for instance, you were beached above the tideline with no hope of your boat going anywhere. Just as the ideas for the new society proceeded from the top down, so did its rewards. Ireland in the 1960s was good to its middle class: the population drift to the towns and the growth of industrial and commercial employment ensured that the Irish middle class expanded in numbers and in regional distribution. It was a process not completed until the seventies, but one of the very first importance. The prevailing ethos in Ireland ceased to be that of the strong farmer, with his intensely localised view of the world.

Henceforth it was to be formed more and more by the suburban bourgeois, with links through his employment to a wider world of business and industry. The increasing concentration of the Irish middle class in the eastern half of the country brought them into multi-channel land, thus reinforcing this cultural transfusion from overseas.

The rising tide may have lifted the boat of organised labour, but only at the top of the trade union structure was there any enthusiasm for the disciplines of economic planning. The corporatism of the National Industrial and Economic Council found little support among ordinary working-class people, who were among the most conservative groups in Irish society. This was not surprising, for the rewards of the new prosperity reached them last and in most diluted form. Moreover, traditions of working-class solidarity and the persistence of extended family structures increased the pressures towards social conformity and discouraged innovation.

Some small but vital working-class groups learned the less savoury ways of a more open, acquisitive society, and learned them well. The maintenance men were, of course, the great exemplars in this area. Their strike earned them the same degree of public odium as property speculators and other insensitive self-servers. There was indeed clear evidence in the second half of the decade that what had developed in Ireland was a kind of frontier society, in which standards of behaviour, especially in the public domain, were provisional and arbitrary. Irish Catholicism, with its overwhelming emphasis on private piety and its failure to convey a sense of moral outrage in any area other than the sexual, undoubtedly contributed to the frequently observed absence of a sense of civic morality in the new Ireland. The partial cultural vacuum created by the abandonment of the Gaelic fortress also facilitated this unhappy process, for the Gaelic myth at least had the virtue of coherence and unity; the halting secular capitalism which sought to replace it failed to establish itself universally. In this sense, the new Ireland believed in nothing profound and was a fair field for opportunists and cynics of all kinds.

But at least they represented a spirit of energy and purpose, however unattractive. If Ireland remembers the sixties with affection, it is for that characteristic above all others. After the inertia of the fifties, here at last was life, in all its variegated forms. It was too much to hope that Irish society could be thrown open to wealth and material success without some rotten apples appearing. What was more worrying was that there was no sign of a new, integrating principle of Irish culture. Between the high-mindedness of the economic planner and the opportunism of the parvenu lay the field on which the moral battle would be fought, with disturbing evidence to hand, as the decade closed, that the initial advantage lay with the latter.

The most visible manifestation of the decline in public standards was the growing cynicism of the Fianna Fáil party. Overwhelmingly it represented the new establishment, and yet it was set in an old mould. Alone of all the major public institutions of Irish life, the political system suffered hardly any structural change. The frequent predictions that the old party system, based on cross-class alliances between groups whose original quarrel lay in the Civil War, must yield like everything else to the temper of the times proved hopelessly optimistic. In particular, the expectation of the left that class politics must inevitably follow modernisation and industrialisation was disappointed.

Political party alignments in all countries are surprisingly durable and appear to be heavily conditioned by the timing of universal suffrage. In most countries this is the moment when the entire nation is finally mobilised into the political process. In Ireland the arrival of universal suffrage and the foundation of the state itself were separated by only a few years. So, if the premise is correct, it is not to be wondered at that the party alignments which emerged from the Civil War have proved as permanent as they have. Nor is Ireland by any means unique in having a party system divided primarily along lines other than class: one only has to think of the United States, for instance.

Ireland has, in fact, developed a lop-sided version of the conventional Anglo-American two-party system. There was no threat to this 'Fianna Fáil *versus* the Rest' system in the 1960s because there was no fault-line in the system itself which might have undermined it. In electoral terms, the Rest kept dropping the ball by their unwillingness to coalesce, thus flying in the face of the system's internal logic. All three principal parties underwent a generational renewal — Fianna Fáil most successfully, Fine Gael least so — but that was the extent of change demanded by the circumstances of the time.

All three parties were coalitions of different interests, notably Fianna Fáil. And just as the logic of the system pulled disparate interests together in this way, so it tended to do with all those who were generally 'anti-system'. Thus, for example, the dissident RTE producers of 1969 found themselves in total agreement with Conradh na Gaeilge's accusation that RTE had been responsible for the Anglo-Americanisation of the Irish mind. The Conradh was as conservative in its cultural politics as the producers were radical in theirs. But both groups were outside the mainstream political consensus; this common exclusion tended to throw them together. On a more general canvas, it explains the persistent attraction which socialists and republicans have for one another, and the convoluted dialectics that are required in order to furnish a fig-leaf of intellectual respectability for this peculiar attraction of opposites. Such temporary coalitions of 'out groups' were a feature of the late 1960s, particularly at the student teach-ins which proliferated at the time: socialists, 'Save the West' men, Irish-Irelanders, small farmers and anyone else who had a grievance raised their voices in common denunciation of the new consensus, which they held to be spiritually and morally bankrupt.

In part, this was rather typical of the 1960s, with its intellectual effervescence. But it bespoke a deeper restlessness. Ireland had learned a lot about itself in ten years. It had emerged from the secure childhood of the Gaelic myth into the noisy adult world of cosmopolitan consumer capitalism. Although a Catholic country, the traditional modes for the public expression of Catholicism seemed as embarrassingly *passé* as the ideals of Irish-Ireland. It was a country in search of its own soul, and partly afraid of what it might find. For in a sense, we were rediscovering our English past. That process of anglicisation, which it had been the original aim of the Gaelic League to undo, had been slowed for forty years but not stopped. In the sixties it accelerated again, for the cosmopolitan delights upon which we fell so eagerly were by then largely Anglo-American in character, and anyway the outside world habitually reached us through the filter of the English language.

It was a conclusion we were anxious to avoid drawing, but the insistence with which it kept presenting itself to us troubled us then and troubles us still. For if culture is to be defined by the daily lives of ordinary people, then we were all West Britons of one sort or another. The kids who abandoned Drumcondra for Manchester United, or who went into a frenzy over the Beatles or the Rolling Stones; the families who holidayed in Lloret de Mar; the old ladies who played bingo and watched 'Coronation Street'; the bourgeois who discovered continental food; the intellectuals who made 'socialism' a respectable word; the advertisers who made us lust after Mammon; the capitalists who lured us into cities and towns: all conspired to push us to a point where we lived, in large part, like provincial Britons.

The 1960s was a time when the world was made small by technology. Absolute cultural independence was no longer possible, even for the larger nations. For Ireland, the arrival of the decade coincided happily with the moment when we were ready to shed the mantle of national innocence. If, in so doing, we seemed to ourselves to have shed our distinguishing characteristics, perhaps we can console ourselves with the thought that it seldom seems thus to foreigners. We may occasionally have trouble in recognising ourselves; others rarely have any.

References

Chapter 1 (Introduction) pp. 1-8
1. Quoted in K. Neill, *The Irish People: An Illustrated History*, Dublin 1979, 209.
2. Moynihan, ed., *Speeches and Statements by Eamon de Valera*, 466.
3. Brendan Walsh, 'Economic Growth and Development, 1945-70' in Lee, ed., *Ireland, 1945-70*, 32.
4. Lyons, *Ireland since the Famine*, 628.

Chapter 2 (1960) pp. 9-32
1. Quoted in Bew and Patterson, *Seán Lemass and the Making of Modern Ireland*, 122.
2. Carty, *Electoral Politics in Ireland*, 106.

Chapter 3 (1961) pp. 33-54
1. Garret FitzGerald, 'The Census Figures', *Irish Times*, 30 Aug. 1961.

Chapter 4 (1962) pp. 55-73
1. Bell, *The IRA*, 337-8.

Chapter 5 (1963) pp. 74-94
1. McCarthy, *Decade of Upheaval*, 74.
2. The employment statistics in this section were supplied by the Northern Ireland Department of Economic Development.
3. The numbers of members elected for each party in Stormont general elections from 1921 to 1969 are given in Harkness, *Northern Ireland since 1920*, 184.
4. Farrell, *Northern Ireland: the Orange State*, 228. Farrell actually gives the date as 23 March, but this is incorrect.
5. Bleakley, *Faulkner*, 64-6. Bleakley gives his source for this, rather enigmatically, as 'personal information', but the context suggests that the source was Morris May himself.
6. Moynihan, ed., *Speeches and Statements by Eamon de Valera*, 476: 'Could he not find in his heart', etc.

Chapter 6 (1964) pp. 95-116
1. FitzGerald, *Planning in Ireland*, chapter 4.
2. For the circumstances of the ban see Hugh Hunt, *Seán O'Casey* (Gill's Irish Lives), Dublin 1980, 130-1.
3. Brody, *Inishkillane*, 88. This is not the real name of the parish in question. The research for the book was done in the second half of the 1960s.
4. Ibid., 98.

5. McDyer, *Father McDyer of Glencolumbkille*, 85.
6. Much of the account of Glencolumbkille which follows is based on two articles by Michael Viney in the *Irish Times*: 'The Miracle of Glencolumbkille' (24 Jan. 1963) and 'The Fighting Valleys' (22 Jan. 1964).
7. Andrews, *Man of No Property*, 246.
8. This figure was given in the Dáil by Childers in May 1963.
9. McCarthy, *Decade of Upheaval*, 59-60.

Chapter 7 (1965) pp. 117-137
1. James Meenan, 'The Evolution of the Modern Bank' in Lyons, ed., *Bank of Ireland*, 185.
2. McDonagh, *Ireland*, 139.
3. Faulkner, *Memoirs*, 40.
4. Andrews, *Man of No Property*, 250-1.

Chapter 8 (1966) pp. 138-157
1. Byrne, *To Whom It Concerns*, 75. Much of this passage about 'The Late Late Show' is based on Byrne's account.
2. Garret FitzGerald, 'The Population Increase', *Irish Times*, 7 Sept. 1966.

Chapter 9 (1967) pp. 158-179
1. See, for example, his comments on the attraction of foreign capital in *Up Dev*, 117.
2. Adams, *Censorship*, 199.
3. John Sheahan, 'Education and Society in Ireland' in Lee, ed., *Ireland, 1945-70*, 62; original emphasis.
4. See Whyte, *Church and State*, 340-1, for more details on this point, for which his source is none other than Cardinal Conway himself.
5. Farrell, *Lemass*, 107.
6. Whyte, *op. cit.*, 338-9.

Chapter 10 (1968) pp. 180-205
1. Murray Kempton, quoted in Joe McGinniss, *The Selling of the President*, London 1970, 147.
2. Andrews, *Man of No Property*, 277, 278.
3. Ibid., 275.

Chapter 11 (1969) pp. 206-226
1. A. J. P. Taylor, *English History, 1914-1945*, Harmondsworth 1970, 213.
2. The account of the maintenance men's strike which follows is based largely on chapter 5 of McCarthy, *Decade of Upheaval*.
3. Ibid., 220.
4. Conor Cruise O'Brien, 'The Embers of Easter' in Dudley Edwards and Pyle, ed., *1916: The Easter Rising*, 235. Originally published in the *Irish Times Review of the Easter Rising*, 8, 11 (supplement to *Irish Times*, 7 Apr. 1966).

Select bibliography

THIS is intended as a guide to further reading rather than as an exhaustive list of every secondary work consulted in the course of the research for this book. It is confined mainly to works which concern themselves with events, movements, and developments which, directly or indirectly, had a bearing on the evolution of Irish society in the 1960s, or which reflect the changes that occurred in the decade.

It will be clear to the reader that the substance of the research for this book has been a thorough reading of contemporary newspapers. The three Dublin-based national dailies, the *Irish Independent*, the *Irish Press*, and the *Irish Times*, together with the *Cork Examiner* and the *Belfast Telegraph*, were the newspapers principally employed in this regard. In addition, a number of other periodicals were consulted, although in a less systematic way, and references to material taken from such papers is given at the appropriate points in the text. It is important to remember the valuable contribution made to the revitalisation of Irish intellectual life by specialist journals of a scholarly or intellectual nature. In this connection, the Jesuit quarterly *Studies* deserves particular mention as do two journals which were in the vanguard of the revolution in Catholic life and thought, *Doctrine and Life* and *The Furrow*.

It is worth making a few brief observations about some of the titles listed below. **C. S. Andrews** is unusual among figures in Irish public life in having written a robust autobiography: it is a lucid exposition of the opinions, preferences, and prejudices of at least one member of the Irish establishment, and its value is in direct proportion to its uniqueness. **Bew** and **Patterson** have written the only systematic academic study of the development of Lemass's thinking from protection to free trade; although not always an easy read, it rewards any effort taken over it, but it should be borne in mind that T. K. Whitaker has written dismissively of its revisionist conclusions regarding his relationship with Lemass. **Hugh Brody**'s study of West of Ireland life in the 1960s is now established as a minor classic: its sympathetic but relentless delineation of the bleak choices facing the West is a useful corrective to the colourful conspiracy theories that are occasionally advanced in support of the view that the West is a victim of eastern neglect. **Terence Brown**'s cultural history is simply unique: nobody else has even attempted a work of such scope and Brown's book is absolutely essential reading for anybody interested in modern Ireland. It is never less than interesting, and in places is positively brilliant. By contrast **Corkery**'s work is pleasantly bland, but is of interest as the contemporary view of a sympathetic outsider. **Humphreys** is worth reading for his observations on the development of suburban Dublin, probably the most important sociological feature of Ireland in the 1960s. The volume of Thomas Davis lectures edited by **J. J. Lee** deals with Ireland in the quarter century following the end of World War Two, but inevitably concentrates much of its attention on the 1960s. Like all such books the quality of the individual essays is uneven, but most major subjects are examined in an accessible style, and Lee's own two contributions are written with typical flair and brilliance. **Lyons**'s *Ireland Since the Famine* remains the great modern work of synthesis on Irish history. Both as background reading and for its account of the events of the 1960s, it is indispensable. The untimely death of its author in 1983 was a sad blow to Irish scholarship and letters. **McCarthy**'s account of Irish trade unions is the only book in this bibliography which deals exclusively with the 1960s: it is scholarly, eloquent, and considering the rather tortuous nature of its subject, remarkably lucid and accessible. Finally **Whyte**'s splendid survey of Church/State relations has long since established itself as the definitive work in this crucial area.

Adams, Michael, *Censorship: the Irish experience*, Dublin 1968

Akenson, Donald H., *A Mirror to Kathleen's Face: education in independent Ireland*, Montreal 1975

Andrews, C. S., *Man of No Property*, Cork 1982

Bell, Geoffrey, *The Protestants of Ulster*, London 1976

Bell, J. Bowyer, *The Secret Army: a history of the IRA 1916-70*, London 1970

Bew, Paul and Henry Patterson, *Seán Lemass and the Making of Modern Ireland 1945-66*, Dublin 1982

Bleakley, David, *Faulkner*, London 1974

Boland, Kevin, *The Rise and Decline of Fianna Fáil*, Cork 1982

Boland, Kevin, *Up Dev!*, n.p., n.d.

Boulton, David, *The UVF: an anatomy of loyalist rebellion*, Dublin 1973

Boylan, Henry, *A Dictionary of Irish Biography*, Dublin 1978

Brody, Hugh, *Inishkillane: change and decay in the West of Ireland*, London 1973

Brown, Terence, *Ireland: a social and cultural history, 1922-79*, London 1981

Buckland, Patrick, *A History of Northern Ireland*, Dublin 1981

Byrne, Gay, *To Whom It Concerns: ten years of the Late Late Show*, Dublin 1972

Carty, R. K. , *Electoral Politics in Ireland: party and parish pump*, Dingle 1983

Chubb, Basil, *The Government and Politics of Ireland*, 2nd ed., London 1982

Coogan, T. P., *The IRA*, London 1970

Corkery, Donald S., *The Irish*, London 1968

Darby, John, ed., *Northern Ireland: the background to the conflict*, Belfast 1983
    de Paor, Liam, *Divided Ulster*, London 1970

Doolan, Lelia, Jack Dowling and Bob Quinn, *Sit Down and Be Counted*, Dublin 1969

Edwards, Owen Dudley and Fergus Pyle, eds, *1916: The Easter Rising*, London 1968

Fanning, Ronan, *Independent Ireland*, Dublin 1983

Farrell, Brian, *Seán Lemass*, Dublin 1983

Farrell, Michael, *Northern Ireland: the Orange State*, London 1976

Faulkner, Brian, *Memoirs of a Statesman*, London 1978

Fennell, Desmond, *The Changing Face of Catholic Ireland*, London 1968

Fennell, Desmond, *The State of the Nation*, Dublin 1983

Fisher, Desmond, *Broadcasting in Ireland*, London 1978

FitzGerald, Garret, *Planning in Ireland*, Dublin 1968

Gallagher, Michael, *The Irish Labour Party in Transition 1957-82*, Dublin 1982

Garvin, Tom, *The Evolution of Irish Nationalist Politics*, Dublin 1981

Harkness, David, *Northern Ireland since 1920*, Dublin 1983

Healy, John, *The Death of an Irish Town*, Cork 1968

Hickey, D. J. and J. E. Doherty, *A Dictionary of Irish History since 1800*, Dublin 1980

Hultman, Charles, *Ireland in World Commerce*, Cork 1969

Humphreys, Alexander J., *New Dubliners*, London 1966

Lee, J. J., ed., *Ireland 1945-70*, Dublin 1979

Lyons, F. S. L., *Ireland Since the Famine*, London 1971

Lyons, F. S. L., ed., *Bank of Ireland 1783-1983: bicentenary essays*, Dublin 1983

McCann, Eamonn, *War and an Irish Town*, Harmondsworth 1974

McCarthy, Charles, *The Decade of Upheaval: Irish trade unions in the 1960s*, Dublin 1973

McClean, Raymond, *The Road to Bloody Sunday*, Dublin 1983

MacDonagh, Oliver, *Ireland*, New Jersey 1968

MacDonagh, Oliver, *States of Mind: a study of Anglo-Irish conflict 1780-1980*, London 1983

McDyer, James, *Father McDyer of Glencolumbkille: an autobiography*, Dingle 1982

McElligott, T. J., *Education in Ireland*, Dublin 1966

Manning, Maurice, *Irish Political Parties*, Dublin 1972

Meenan, James, *The Irish Economy Since 1922*, Liverpool 1970

Moynihan, M., ed., *Speeches and Statements by Eamon de Valera*, Dublin 1980

Murphy, John A., *Ireland in the Twentieth Century*, Dublin 1975

Nevin, D., ed., *Trade Unions and Change in Irish Society*, Cork 1980

O'Brien, Conor Cruise, *States of Ireland*, London 1972

O'Leary, Cornelius, *Irish Elections 1918-79*, Dublin 1979

O'Mahony, David, *The Irish Economy: an introductory description*, Cork 1967

O'Neill, Terence, *The Autobiography of Terence O'Neill*, London 1972

Peillon, Michel, *Contemporary Irish Society*, Dublin 1982

Rumpf, E. and A. C. Hepburn, *Nationalism and Socialism in Twentieth-Century Ireland*, Liverpool 1977

Shearman, Hugh, *Northern Ireland 1921-1971*, Belfast 1971

Sheehy, Michael, *Is Ireland Dying?*, London 1968

Sunday Times 'Insight' Team, *Ulster*, Harmondsworth 1972

Whitaker, T. K., *Interests*, Dublin 1983

Whyte, J. H., *Church and State in Modern Ireland 1923-79*, 2nd ed., Dublin 1980

Index